£11.95

Measurement and Assessment
in Education and Psychology

Measurement and Assessment in Education and Psychology

Robert Wood

Collected Papers 1967–87

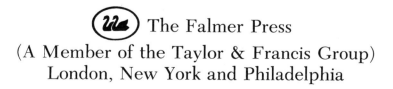 The Falmer Press
(A Member of the Taylor & Francis Group)
London, New York and Philadelphia

UK   The Falmer Press, Falmer House, Barcombe, Lewes, East Sussex, BN8 5DL

USA   The Falmer Press, Taylor & Francis Inc., 242 Cherry Street, Philadelphia, PA 19106-1906

First published in 1987

Library of Congress Cataloging-in-Publication Data

Wood, Robert, 1941–
   Measurement and assessment in education and psychology.

   Includes bibliographies.
   1. Educational tests and measurements.   2. Psychological tests. I. Title.
   LB1131.W596 1987   371.2'6   87–545

   ISBN 1–85000–161–8
   ISBN 1–85000–162–6 (pbk.)

Jacket design by Caroline Archer

Typeset in 10/12 Caledonia
Imago Publishing Ltd., Thame, Oxon.

Printed in Great Britain by
Redwood Burn Limited, Trowbridge, Wiltshire
and bound by Pegasus Bookbinding, Melksham, Wiltshire

Contents

Contents

List of Papers and Acknowledgements

Paper 1:   Wood, R. (1967) 'More on assessment', *Forum*, 10, pp. 22–3.

Paper 2:   Wood, R. and Napthali, W.A. (1975) 'Assessment in the class-room: What do teachers look for?', *Educational Studies*, 1, pp. 151–61, reprinted by kind permission of Carfax Publishing Company.

Paper 3:   Wood, R. (1976) 'Halo and other effects in teacher assessments', *Durham Research Review*, 7,pp. 1120–6, reprinted by kind permission of the Durham and Newcastle Research Review.

Paper 4:   Wood, R., 'Your Chemistry equals my French', *Times Educational Supplement*, 30 July 1976 and 20 May 1977, reprinted by kind permission of Times Newspapers Ltd.

Paper 5:   Wood, R. (1977) Introduction and chapter 1 of 'Multiple choice: A state of the art report', *Evaluation in Education: International Progress*, 1, 3, pp. 191–280, reprinted by kind permission of Pergamon Books Ltd., copyright © 1977.

Paper 6:   Wood, R. (1976) 'Inhibiting blind guessing: The effect of instructions', *Journal of Educational Measurement*, 13, pp. 297–307, reprinted by kind permission of the National Council on Measurement in Education.

Paper 7:   Wood, R. (1976) 'Trait measurement and item banks', in de Gruitjer, D.N.M. and Th. van der Kamp, L.J. (Eds) *Advances in Psychological and Educational Measurement*, London, John Wiley and Sons Ltd., reproduced by permission of John Wiley and Sons Ltd.

Paper 8:   Wood, R. (1978) 'Fitting the Rasch model — a heady tale', *British Journal of Mathematical and Statistical Psychology*, 31, pp. 27–32, reprinted by kind permission of the British Psychological Society.

Paper 9:   Wood, R. (1982) 'The Rasch model and modelling', unpublished.

Paper 10:   Wood, R. (1986) 'D.N. Lawley and the convergence of factor analysis and latent trait theory', unpublished.

Paper 11: Wood, R. (1985) 'Testing', unit 21 of Course E206, Open University, reprinted by kind permission of the Open University. Acknowledgement is made to Peter Barnes for editorial assistance and to Desmond Nuttall for planning the contents of the unit.

Paper 12: Wood, R. (1984) 'Sex-linked discrimination in educational selection', unpublished.

Paper 13: Wood, R. (1984) 'Observations on criterion-referenced assessment', prepared for the Senior Secondary Assessment Board of South Australia, Adelaide, August.

Paper 14: Wood, R. (1984) 'Verbal test D — a review' in Levy, P and Goldstein, H. (Eds) *Tests in Education*, London, Academic Press, reprinted by kind permission of Academic Press Inc. (Harcourt, Brace Jovanovich, Inc. © 1984).

Paper 15: Wood, R. (1986) 'Belated homage to Cronbach and Gleser', *Guidance and Assessment Review*, 2, pp. 2–3, reprinted by kind permission of the British Psychological Society.

Paper 16: Wood, R. (1985) 'Achievement tests' in Postlethwaite, T.N. and Husén, T. (Eds) *International Encyclopedia of Education: Research and Studies*, Oxford, Pergamon Press, pp. 31–55, reprinted by kind permission of Pergamon Books Ltd © 1985.

Paper 17: Wood, R. (1984) 'Doubts about "under-achievement", particularly as operationalised by Yule, Lansdown and Urbanowicz', *British Journal of Clinical Psychology*, 23, pp. 231–2, reprinted by kind permission of the British Psychological Society.

Paper 18: Wood, R. (1986) 'As long as it gets me from A to B: psychologists and statistics', unpublished.

Paper 19: Wood, R. (1986) 'Aptitude testing is not an engine for equalising educational opportunity', *British Journal of Educational Studies*, 44, pp. 26–37, reprinted by kind permission of Basil Blackwell Publisher Ltd © 1986.

Paper 20: Wood, R. and Power, C. (1984) 'Have national assessments made us any wiser about "standards"?', *Comparative Education*, 20, pp. 307–21, reprinted by kind permission of Carfax Publishing Company.

Paper 21: Wood, R. (1986) 'The agenda for educational measurement' in Nuttall, D.L. (Ed.) *Assessing Educational Achievement*, Lewes, Falmer Press, reprinted by kind permission © 1986.

Paper 22: Wood, R. and Power, C. (in press) 'Aspects of the competence-performance distinction: Educational, psychological and measurement issues', *Journal of Curriculum Studies*, reprinted by kind permission.

I would like to thank Colin Power for allowing me to reproduce our joint papers. If he sees this, I hope Warwick Napthali will not mind my using our paper.

Autobiographical Note

I joined the National Foundation for Educational Research in England and Wales in October 1964 at the age of 23, having 'got' education. That was the year the Conservative government was thrown out and idealism was rife. I was put to work on the Block and Day Release project which was supposed to determine which of these off-job educational regimens would benefit apprentices most. Twenty-three years later and I am back in the same milieu, directing a project for the Manpower Services Commission which is evaluating work-based assessment. Only now we don't talk of apprentices, just trainees.

I spent fourteen months on that project before falling out with the project leader. I thought he was incompetent and took my case to the Director, Dr. W.D. Wall. Naturally, I lost and had to tender my resignation. As it happened, this did me no harm. Douglas Pidgeon, the Deputy Director, had been present at the showdown and must have thought that there was something to me. At any rate, he was looking for someone to work on what became the Item Bank project and asked me if I was interested. The resignation was rescinded and I joined Larry Skurnik in the Examinations and Test Research Unit in March 1966. I have a lot to thank Douglas Pidgeon for, and Bill Wall too, for although I never knew what part he played, if any, in my recall, in later years he became a good friend and mentor.

One thing I did get out of my time on the Block and Day Release project was a taste for psychometrics. I think it was reading papers on item analysis by Vernon and Gourlay in the old *British Journal of Psychology* (*Statistical Section*) which got me going. There can't be any standard way of getting into psychometrics and for me it was that. From then on I read the journals and started to educate myself.

The Item Banking project was a pioneering effort, and I was lucky there. Looking at the Report now (Wood and Skurnik, 1969), it is obviously a 'prentice' work and, although I thought about it, I could not bring myself to reproduce any part of it here. I wrote it very quickly and because I was so green I had no idea you weren't supposed to write as fast as that. Nobody told me. I knew I was leaving the country in September 1968 to go to the University of

Chicago, and I didn't want to have to finish it there. Why was I leaving the country? Because the Schools Council refused to give an extension to the project, a project which, I think I can say, received rather more favourable attention, and was rather more influential, than many another Schools Council project. But then the Schools Council is dead (Plaskow, 1985) and I am still around.

I had decided to get some training in psychometrics and there were no possibilities in this country. Having made contact with Ben Wright and Ben Bloom at the University of Chicago, and encouraged by Bruce Choppin who had finished at Chicago a year earlier, I applied for and was awarded a fellowship to study for a PhD. Once in Chicago I was assigned to the great man himself — Bloom, not Wright (Wright had only just made a splash, see paper 9). He — not unnaturally — had tired of behavioural objectives (the Taxonomy having appeared in 1956) and his great enthusiasm when I got there was *mastery learning*, to which I was expected to apply myself. Ben would get me in his office, stand in front of the board, often puffing a cigar, and draw graphs which invariably looked like this ⌒. He was telling me that if only students were allowed enough time, they would master instruction. After a time, I decided that, for Ben, the wish was father to the deed. That can be seen in the title of a paper he wrote about that time 'Individual differences in school achievement: A vanishing point?' (Bloom, 1971). He didn't need the data, he had the vision. And that's what he was — and is — a visionary. But we didn't get on terribly well. I guess my scepticism showed. He was used to having as students pliable young Americans, aged say 21–23, eager to grab the main chance, or else older students from countries like Korea and India who had been sent to Chicago expressly to work with the great man and who would certainly not make waves. I was 27 and — I have to admit — a natural member of the awkward squad. I got on the wrong side of Ben Wright for the same reason — refusal to become a 'true believer'. Anyway, a showdown with Ben Bloom was averted when he went off to the think-tank in Stanford for the year 1969–70 and I had to find a new supervisor. Darrell Bock agreed to take me on and I don't suppose we have had a cross word since. I switched to latent trait theory and finished up doing a thesis called 'Computerized adaptive sequential testing'. It was one of the first, if not the first, practical implementations in the field (using a portable terminal) of tailored testing.

Came the summer of 1971 and I returned to England, to a job with the University of London University Entrance and School Examinations Council (the London GCE Board) — almost certainly a career mistake. But jobs in the States had dried up, and my family wanted to return. Besides I had received a letter from the local draft board just three weeks before I left, and Vietnam did not feature in my plans. Having got trained up in educational measurement and psychometrics, there seemed an opportunity to make a contribution. At least, an examination board had plenty of measurement problems to which I might apply myself.

How right I was. When I came on the scene the 16+ feasibility studies were just getting under way (no, I don't suppose any of us thought it would be

1988 before GCSE came to pass but, as someone once remarked, the speed of exam reform in Britain is glacial — too fast, I would say). Foremost among the raft of problems thrown up by 16+ was *teacher or school assessment*, (of which more later). I think the same could be said of GCSE, so nothing much has changed. The other focal point for us researchers was *comparability*, a can of worms if ever there was one. More on that in the introduction to Section III.

I spent far too long at the London Board. Maybe I should have taken the offer in July 1974 of a lectureship in the Department of Psychology at the University of Birmingham. At any rate, I was more than ready in January 1980 to join Harvey Goldstein and Tessa Blackstone on the Evaluation of Testing in Schools Project. But I think that staying too long in the other job had a knock-on effect. I was too restless. When the possibility of a Chair in the School of Education in the University of the West Indies in Jamaica came up, I went for it and got it. So in September 1981 we emigrated to Jamaica.

I expect, in my eagerness for change, I misread the prospects for Jamaica. The promised new era under Seaga was certainly short-lived. By October 1983 I had decided there was no future at UWI or if there was, it was not worth putting up with the local aggravations. I would like to have done more work grounded in local problems but I did manage to do one thing of which I am proud; a study of cross-age tutoring in five Jamaican schools (Wood with Stodolsky, 1986).

A fellowship at Flinders University in South Australia followed and Colin Power and I worked on the competence-performance distinction (see the final paper in this collection). In September 1984, I was appointed Director of the New Zealand Council for Educational Research, but withdrew in March 1985 without taking up appointment. One of these days I will tell the story of this debâcle; a shabby tale of chauvinism, is how a colleague described it.

Now I earn my living as a psychologist, although in 1987 I will get out my educational hat again when I become Visiting Professor at the University of London Institute of Education. When Steve Blinkhorn set up Psychometric Research and Development Ltd. in St. Albans he invited me to join him, for which I remain grateful. One of the things we do is computerized testing, so another wheel has come full circle from the time in Chicago in 1970 when a small firm, Computer Horizons Inc. took me on to help build up that side of their operations. It folded then; will it now? I think not.

Reference

BLOOM, B.S. (1971) 'Individual differences in school achievement: a vanishing point?', *Phi Delta Kappan Monograph*, Bloomington, Indiana.

PLASKOW, M. (Ed.) (1985) *Life and Death of the Schools Council*, Lewes, Falmer Press.

WOOD, R. and SKURNIK, L.S. (1969) *Item Banking*, Windsor, National Foundation for Educational Research in England and Wales.

WOOD, R. with STODOLSKY, S.S. (1986) Donald and the Crocodile: An Account of Crossage Tutoring in Jamaica, *International Review of Education* (to appear).

Introduction

This book comprises a selection of my writings over the past twenty years although, in fact, it is heavily weighted towards the present; two-thirds of the papers were written after March 1982. Why this format? Some write books, some write papers. I feel that I have been saying what I wanted to say through my papers and that collecting together a selection of them between two covers will be as effective as attempting a straight textbook which would inevitably entail reprocessing and repackaging the contents of those papers. And because so much is recent, I find I can leave the best part of it intact.

Effective for what? It seems to me that someone teaching a course in this area could use the papers to raise discussion and, through the many references, enable students to get to other people's work. Courses on educational and psychological measurement are never easy to teach, at any level, and I found this method worked when I was at the University of the West Indies. Other than that, the book is a source of ideas for browsing through.

I would accept that the style is often polemical, certainly argumentative, but I believe that it will lend itself to the thrashing-out of issues. Take the issue of guessing on multiple-choice items (overdone in my opinion). I think I have provided enough material in the two papers and letters and the references and the commentary to enable an informed discussion of this issue to take place. More generally, most of the issues which have exercised workers in educational and psychological measurement during the past twenty years are to be found somewhere in the book.

Evidently, this is not a nuts-and-bolts book, a how-to-do-it manual. David Satterly's *Assessment in School* is not all nuts and bolts either (Satterly, 1981) but there are enough to make his a good companion book. I would also recommend, for more advanced study, Thorndike's *Applied Psychometrics* (Thorndike, 1982). The texts you sometimes see recommended for British consumption — Lewis (1974), Deale (1975) and Shipman (1983) — are not what is wanted, to my mind.

There is some brand new material to be found in the linking commentaries and in this Introduction. I have edited down the Australian paper (13) to remove some local references and lightly edited some of the others but only to get rid of extraneous or thoroughly dated material. I have not rewritten anything in order to make myself appear in a better light.

The title of the book is chosen deliberately to bring out the four operational categories. There has been much confusion of these categories, some of it wanton, and I would like to take this opportunity to nail down what I think is intended in each category. In a previous attempt (Wood, 1984), I noted that assessment has too many meanings and this, indeed, is at the root of the problem.

Confusion starts.whenever assessment is used as a stylistic alternative to measurement, as it often is, perhaps by people who cannot bring themselves to say measurement because they find what they see as the pretensions to exactitude oppressive or indefensible. I have always regarded measurement as contained within assessment, as contributing to it. Harris (1970) was very clear about this:

> I would define both evaluation and assessment as enterprises in which a number of technical measurement problems are embedded; and I would not set the three on the same level and compare them. I would deal with measurement only within these two ... I would like measurement to mean some very specific sets of technical problems associated with our concepts of reliability, validity and so forth. Measurement problems are embedded in assessment; they are embedded in evaluation; they are embedded in research.

In this view, assessment is regarded as providing a comprehensive account of an individual's functioning in the widest sense — drawing on a variety of evidence, qualitative as well as quantitative, and therefore going beyond the testing of cognitive skills by pencil-and-paper techniques which, for many people, is measurement (or assessment, as some would have it). The analogue is the physician who makes a number of tests on the individual and blends the results with the history and with personal observations to arrive at an overall judgment (assessment) of the individual's condition. Scarr (1981), for instance, calls for children's motivational history and their present self-esteem and adjustment to be taken into account explicitly when assessing their achievement. Raven's (1982) proposals are in the same spirit, although more radical. Some will think this not very different from the practice of enlightened clinical and educational psychologists when carrying out what used to be called (and perhaps still are) psychometric assessments.

So we have meanings for educational and psychological assessment; the distinction resting on whether the assessment is made by the teacher or the psychologist. I put the distinction in these terms because it is not always easy to distinguish 'educational' and 'psychological,' given that matters psychological are often investigated in educational settings. What is significant is that psychological assessment is thought to be for the abnormal only. Why, asks

Scarr, should we not have an educational assessment which is to do with all children?

Broadening the range of measurements to enrich assessments will generally throw up more measurement problems, and this follows from Harris's formulation. Trying to measure something like 'interpersonal impact' is not a routine matter. Harris was pushed to make a forthright statement because he was reacting to Ben Bloom who was arguing that measurement, assessment *and* evaluation ought to be subsumed within a theory of *testing*! Bloom himself was using assessment in a particular sense which still surfaces from time to time, for example, Trickett *et al* (1982). This is assessment as assessment of the environment, a usage very much associated with the name of George Stern and one I became very familiar with during 1968–69 when I attended Bloom's lectures at the University of Chicago. Is the environmental *press* nourishing or hostile, is the sort of question we had to deal with.

I would like to suggest that this version of assessment be firmly set aside. These days there is another meaning for assessment which is liable to crop up more often and which cuts straight across the meaning I associated with Scarr's ideas. It is the assessment in National Assessment or in Assessment of Performance Unit. It is a usage more common in the US than in the UK. Whereas individual achievement testing seeks to estimate and report individual scores, assessment ignores individual scores and reports on the state of a system, which might be school-wide, country-wide, state-wide, etc. Obviously different testing methodologies are required and these are discussed, for instance by Bock and Mislevy (1986), who actually have proposals for coping with both demands simultaneously. Just to complicate matters further, they refer to achievement testing and assessment as two types of educational measurement!

So we come full circle; some want to embed measurement within assessment, others want to embed assessment within measurement. It is not that there is anything wrong with the latest usage of assessment — we need a name for it. (Systemic measurement would have done.) If you would like to go on calling it assessment, I can't stop you, but remember the clash with the other usage which I, for one, intend to go on favouring. Remember too, that it will make no sense to talk of psychological assessment.

It remains to make a distinction between educational and psychological measurement. As I argue elsewhere in the book (paper 21), educational measurement meant, for a long time, psychological measurement in educational settings. Examples are school examinations and Richmond test batteries. The similarities with IQ tests — genuine psychological measurement — are much greater than the differences. All have the function of differentiating people, of inducing variance. As Jim Popham has remarked, educational measurement experts became after-the-fact diversity-detectors (Popham, 1980). Putting the education into educational measurement means connecting testing to learning (and, of course, teaching) on an intra-individual basis. The seminal paper in this respect is Carver (1974). Yes, 'edumetrics' is an ugly word so let's try to breathe new meaning into educational measurement, which was my purpose in papers 21 and 22.

I had thought to draw a little 2 × 2 diagram with label pairs EP and MA and fill the boxes with examples, but I see no need. EM is represented by a graded test (see paper 11), EA by an elaborated school report, PM by a word association test and PA by a diagnosis of autism. If I am pessimistic, I would say that examples of authentic EM and EA are still rare, nor am I sure where the motor is for change. My inclination is to pursue more vigorously the measurement of growth and learning.

References

BLOOM, B.S. (1970) 'Towards a theory of testing which includes measurement-evaluation-assessment' in WITTROCK M.C. and WILEY D.E. (Eds.), *The Evaluation of Instruction*, New York, Holt, Rinehart and Winston.

BOCK, R.D. and MISLEVY, R.J. (1986) 'Comprehensive educational assessment: The duplex design', University of Chicago, unpublished.

CARVER, R.C. (1974) 'Two dimensions of tests: Psychometric and edumetric', *American Psychologist*, 29, pp. 512–8.

DEALE, R.N. (1975) *Assessment and Testing in the Secondary School*, London, Evans/Methuen.

HARRIS, C.W. (1970) 'Comments', in WITTROCK M.C. and WILEY D.E. (Eds.), *The Evaluation of Instruction*, New York, Holt, Rinehart and Winston.

LEWIS, D.G. (1974) *Assessment in Education*, London, University of London Press.

POPHAM, W.J. (1980) 'Educational measurement for the improvement of instruction', *Phi Delta Kappan*, April, pp. 531–4.

RAVEN, J. (1982) 'Broadening the base for educational assessment: Some reasons, some problems and some suggestions', *Bulletin of the British Psychological Society*, 35, pp. 342–4.

SATTERLY, D. (1981) *Assessment in Schools*, Oxford, Basil Blackwell.

SCARR, S. (1981) 'Testing *for* children: assessment and the many determinants of intellectual competence', *American Psychologist*, 36, pp. 1159–66.

SHIPMAN, M. (1983) *Assessment in Primary and Middle Schools*, Beckenham, Croom Helm.

THORNDIKE, R.L. (1982) *Applied Psychometrics*, Boston, MA, Houghton Mifflin Inc.

TRICKETT, E.J. *et al* (1982) 'The independent school experience: Aspects of the normative environments of single-sex and co-ed secondary schools', *Journal of Educational Psychology*, 74, pp. 374–81.

WOOD, R. (1984) 'Assessment has too many meanings and the one I think we want isn't clear enough yet', *Educational Measurement: Issues and Practices*, 3, pp. 5–7.

I   Opening Statement

Comments

The first piece I wrote for public consumption was actually a long letter — to *Forum* — and I have reproduced it here as down memory lane indulgence. I must have thought it such inflammatory stuff that I gave my home address! After that I got cracking on *Objectives in the teaching of mathematics*, which I have to say I based on a paper by D.G. Lewis with science in the title. This paper achieved some recognition and was reprinted in a couple of American textbooks, although I never saw any royalties. Just the other day I was told that students are still using it. Eighteen years on, this is worrying, to say the least. But you can't make papers self-destruct, whatever half-life you put on them.

I wish I could claim some prescience in this piece. I suppose you can say it is ideologically sound for the time, priggish even; a typical Young Turk effort. I am surprised there is no mention of criterion-referenced testing, but it was only just coming in. 1967 was the year when Jim Popham first came to our attention.

Perhaps all you can say about this piece is that it shows a willingness to take up cudgels, amply confirmed later on.

Paper 1: More on Assessment*

As someone who is working with new methods of assessment, may I be permitted to answer some of the points Mr. Bryan Chapman raised in connection with Mr. Eggleston's article (*Forum*, 9, 3)?

1 All assessments, whether of achievement or aptitude, are used to make predictions. As Anastasi says in *Psychological Testing* (page 455), 'It should be obvious that all psychological tests measure the individual's current behaviour, which inevitably reflects the influence of prior learning. The fact that every test score has a "past" does not however preclude its having a "future". While revealing the effects of past learning, test scores may, under certain conditions, serve as predictors of future learning.' No assessment procedure should be used to compare teachers, and as far as I know none is, except possibly by teachers. Assessment procedures should be designed, not so much to influence teaching, not so much to influence teaching methods, but to give the teacher freedom to teach his own syllabus. With some reservations, CSE Mode 3 is a good example of this.

2 Curriculum objectives only achieve that status when they can be expressed as assessable student behaviours. Objectives are implicit in all courses; they are not white rabbits which appear mysteriously from nowhere.

3 Most teachers are already heavily involved in a fairly complex assessment procedure. The weekly mark book bears witness to a history of observations which teachers habitually make. Schemes of assessment like the one Mr. Eggleston outlined in his article will seek to refine and systematize this periodic stock-taking. Because it draws on a variety of expressions of behaviour, solitary oral evidence, communal discussion, project work, as well as pencil-and-paper tests,

*Reprinted from *Forum*, 1967, 10, pp. 22–3.

continuous assessment can probably be more thoroughly assimilated into the day to day teaching programme than the usual system of periodic tests and homework. Assessment will become less obtrusive, and the teacher should benefit from a looser identity with it.

4   The only way to avoid the assumption that the strength of a behaviour, or any mental variable for that matter, can be precisely measured is by remembering that every score consists of two components. One is the true state of what you are measuring, and the other is error, your error in making the measurement. If every score were to be accompanied by its standard error, then the possibility of drawing false conclusions about its accuracy should be removed.

5   Having made the attempt to isolate and quantify different behaviours, the last thing one wants to do is to lose this information by re-combining sub-scores into a single global score. There is no reason why differential performance cannot be represented as a profile of behaviours.

Any examination benefits from some reflection about its objectives. If you are not clear what you are trying to measure, how can you hope to measure? I do not think a glamorous examination is a substitute for this process. If an examination is 'imaginative' it is because it has been carefully designed to test whether objectives have been attained.

Mr. Chapman wants affirmation of some guiding principles. I will readily agree that the student rather than the system is the first concern of any assessment procedure. The development of new methods of assessment, with their emphasis on revealing the whole array of a student's abilities, is evidence of this. It is the present system which can be harmful to students. Because consumers of certificates are told nothing about a person's cognitive abilities, they have to fall back on crude conventions, such as that of demanding four or five 'O' levels as a minimum qualification for a post. Whereas a person's profile of abilities might fit the job requirements (assuming these are known) he is screened out because his profile of certificates does not.

Mr. Chapman is worried that the predictive validity of new methods of assessment will become so good that people will be allocated to jobs, once and for all. This is most unlikely. The notion that for every individual there is one 'perfect' occupation or vocation, for which his abilities and aptitudes fit him uniquely, is no longer held. What matters first is the pattern of cognitive abilities. These will indicate to the psychologist a group of many occupations which are 'possible'. The choice between these will depend mainly upon interest and motivation.

I think Mr. Chapman is failing to distinguish between an efficient and a coercive system. What is sinister about an assessment procedure which is instrumental in introducing a person to the 'right' group of occupations? What surely matters is that, in those cases where vocational guidance breaks down, there should be enough flexibility in the employment system for a person to have a second chance without having to go back to square one.

Mr. Chapman's third principle is of course quite perverse. No test constructor could tolerate low reliability; much less emphasize it.

If you want to jettison tests then you lose a good opportunity of improving labour placement. It seems a dubious service to individual freedom to ask adolescents to continue hawking themselves round employers until they find something. Will not the disappointment which many will later experience from settling prematurely for the wrong job outweigh the possible benefits of dispensing with guidance?

Throughout his piece, Mr. Chapman seems to be bridling against an analytic approach to testing. This is a curious position for someone who claims to be in sympathy with the improvement of assessment procedures. Talk of testing something 'broader and less definable' takes us right back to the kind of romantic impressionism which Galton set out to dispel. His melodramatic warnings about the possible abuse of tests are noted, but it seems to me that if we are ever in the position where people are forced to take a job and remain in it, then it will be due to a perverted political idea, not an educational one.

II   Teacher Assessment

Comments

When I went to the London GCE Board in 1971, the 16+ feasibility studies, so-called, were just getting under way, and near the top of the research agenda was *teacher assessment*. Since it struck me then as a meaty topic — still does — I was quite prepared to get stuck in. In the five or six years I worked on the topic, I tried to study it in a variety of ways — anecdotal, substantive, analytical, procedural. Teacher assessment is now fully established in the GCSE but the problems raised ten-fifteen years ago are still there. That is why I feel able, in what follows, to draw on a talk I gave in 1974 (Wood, 1974).

Discussion of teacher assessment tends to suffer from confusion about what the measurement function of teacher assessment should be. One thing it is not, or should not be, is a prediction of what pupils will do in an examination. Although the result may be the same this is not, as some people, seem to think, the same as assessing a pupil's achievement in a subject over a period of time. Rather it is a travesty of teacher assessment as it is meant to be because it concentrates on the examination as a single event. The fact that teachers are able to predict examination performance perfectly well, is, from the point of view of the proper function of teacher assessment, neither here nor there. In the first part of his study, Murphy (1979) mounted a typical prediction exercise and found a reasonably high level of agreement; in the second part, when he asked teachers to use their own criteria, considerable disparities were revealed between the two sets of rank orders. Murphy was inclined to think that the more teachers' assessments are taken out of the context of external examinations, the more they will tend to differ from the results of external examinations.

J.A. Petch, the old Secretary of the Joint Matriculation Board, wrote as incisively as anyone about the relationship between external examinations and teacher assessments:

> The qualities tested in the examination room may not be identical with the qualities which may emerge during the course of preparation. The pupil who assiduously, slowly and perhaps diffusely plods through his

preparation may lack the quicker appreciation and applied concentration which are helpful for, if not essential to, being tested within the limiting conditions of the examination room. But if the two orders of merit show no agreement whatsoever it would seem reasonable to conclude either that the preparation has been unwise, even ill-advised, or that the examining has been incompetent or unfair or at least that preparation and examining were out of joint. If on the other hand the two orders of merit were always found to be in complete agreement, it could be argued that there was a redundancy somewhere. (Petch, 1964, p. 6)

Notice that Petch mentions certain qualities which are not — cannot be — measured directly by examinations. Assiduity, perseverance, conscientiousness are some of these qualities. It has seemed to some quite the best defence of teacher assessment that it should supply what the external examination cannot, that it should be supplementary as well as complementary. The trouble is that there is far from unanimity on what, of those evidences examination cannot supply, should be required of teacher assessment. One school of thought is adamant that the 'grafting' qualities should not be omitted. One CSE board warned that 'the teacher may be influenced too much by his attitude to the child, for example, the pupil's characteristics such as effort, industry and perseverance may be rewarded too generously'. Note the implicit acceptance that a dispassionate appraisal of these qualities is not possible. The same document continues, 'In the CSE these qualities should be rewarded only insofar as they.affect attainment'. Which you might think rather cancels out the effect of the previous warning since it is hard to imagine how industry and attainment can be separated.

Integrating attitudinal and intellectual data is, of course, the hallmark of authentic educational assessment (harking back to the Introduction), so teacher assessment, done properly, very much belongs to that category. That teachers will be influenced by all sorts of considerations (tastes, preferences, prejudices, etc) is brought out by the first paper in this Section. As we say there, the starting point for the research was an apprehension that attempts to standardize assessments through the use of apparently specific schemes purporting to describe achievement, constitute both a recognition and a concealment of the possibility that teachers vary both in what they regard as achievement, and in their capacity to pick out defined attributes or behaviours, that is, to use such schemes. Other research since has come up with similar findings. An Irish study (Pedulla, Airasian and Madaus, 1980) found that students with high ratings for politeness tended to get high ratings in mathematics and English. More generally, academic ratings were somewhat correlated with behavioural/social ratings. In contrast, standardized test results bore virtually no relationship to the behavioural/social ratings. Interestingly, given teacher assessment's rise to respectability in the U.K., the Irish used these results to support the introduction of standardized testing into the schools and, therefore, to downgrade the contribution of teacher assessment. They didn't trust it on its own. Which brings me to moderation.

Here is J.A. Petch again:

Being examined externally might be dispensed with if the world outside would accept without question the assessment of every pupil by his school only — and if every pupil (and his parents too) would accept without question that assessment. (Petch, *Ibid*)

Petch might have added teachers to the doubting Thomases. That there is cause for concern is undeniable. The individual teacher must grade in isolation and cannot be expected necessarily to have a firm grip on absolute standards. I have always seen the problem as one of distinguishing between the making of what are very proper corrections to counter grade inflation and the making of unjustified over-corrections downwards when in truth there are good and sufficient reasons why a teacher should offer assessments which, according to examination results, are too generous. Suppose a teacher sets out to bring most of her students to a high level of achievement, ie, employs a mastery learning strategy. Suppose also that she succeeded, but that her efforts do not show through in the external examination to the same degree (perhaps because of the very factors inherent in examinations which pull down some students' perform-ances). The act of statistical moderation would be to deprive some of these students of grades they may well have earned.

I do not think this particular nettle has ever been grasped, and I am not at all sure that inspection of work by visiting moderators necessarily produces a just solution. When you actually look at raw teacher assessment data (Wood, 1977) the interesting thing is that it tends to be both generous *and* bunched together; in other words, the typical distribution is negatively skewed com-pared to that for external assessments in the same group. This is precisely what you would expect if teachers were implementing mastery learning strategies successfully. In any case, as Heyns (1980, pp. 28–9) has argued persuasively, there are theoretical reasons for expecting that the distribution of 'true' achievement is skewed. Numerous experimental studies of learning imply that the rate of skill acquisition is not linear with respect to time; and that individual growth is proportional to the prior level of skill. Put the two together and one would expect a skewed skill distribution that would become more skewed over time. I do not say that these findings apply faithfully to achievement test scores, and I accept that if they did we would not find bunching of teacher assessments, on the contrary some students would get well ahead of the rest. I merely suggest that here are important issues to do with measurement *metrics* which we have hardly noticed. We are too habituated to bell-shaped distribu-tions. It would be good to see some attempts at modelling teacher assessments.

Investigating the measurement characteristics of teacher assessments, although not the metric as such, is something I took up in the other paper reproduced here (see also Wood and Ferguson, 1975). I suppose I am quite fond of it, because I was able to apply a newish methodology (generalizability theory) to a worthwhile problem, and produce some results which, if modest, were indicative and could have formed the basis for further work. Now I have the opportunity to use the methodology again, this time to ascertain the sources of variability affecting assessments of competence in the work place (Wood, 1986). The necessity for multiple assessments over time to counter premature attribution competence will be a feature of the project. As far as I can tell, little work has been done on the growth problem; the paper by Bryk, Strenio and Weisberg (1980), does not take the matter very far. Those seeking a more recent application of generalizability theory in the context of a British study might turn up the paper by Johnson and Bell (1985).

Among the things teacher assessment is not about is how teachers use (or don't use) tests in the classroom. From its portentous title 'The ecology of classroom assessment' you might think the article by Stiggins and Bridgeford (1985) was about teacher assessment, as I have been treating it here, but this turns out not to be the case. Instead it is another paper on how teachers need help with assessment tests — from a US-centric point of view. During the eighteen months I directed the project reported in Gipps *et al* (1983), I became rather familiar with the British teacher's attitude to standardized tests — one of considerable ambivalence but with a determination to keep the tests nicely at arms' length. I say a little more about this in paper 21.

References

BRYK, A.S., STRENIO, J.F. and WEISBERG, H.I. (1980) 'A method for estimating treatment effects when individuals are growing', *Journal of Educational Statistics*, 5, pp. 5–34.

GIPPS, C.V. *et al* (1983) *Testing Children: Standardized Testing in Local Authorities*, London, Heinemann Educational Books.

HEYNS, B. (1980) 'Models and measurement for the study of growth,' in DREEBEN R. and THOMAS J.A. (Eds.) *The Analysis of Educational Productivity*, Vol. I., Cambridge, MA, Ballinger Publishing Co.

JOHNSON, S. and BELL, J.F. (1985) 'Evaluating and predicting survey efficiency using generalizability theory,' *Journal of Educational Measurement*, 22, pp. 107–19.

MURPHY, R.J.L. (1979) 'Teachers' assessments and GCE results compared,' *Educational Research*, 22, pp. 54–9.

PEDULLA, J.J., AIRASIAN, P. and MADAUS, G. (1980) 'Do teacher ratings and standardized tests of students yield the same information?', *American Educational Research Journal*, 17, pp. 303–7.

PETCH, J.A. (1974) *School Estimates and Examination Results*. Manchester, Joint Matriculation Board.

STIGGINS, R.J. and BRIDGEFORD, N.J. (1985) 'The ecology of classroom assessment', *Journal of Educational Measurement*, 22, pp. 271–86.

WOOD, R. (1974) 'Teacher assessment is about people', *Conference Report*, No. 14, London, University of London University Entrance and School Examinations Council.

WOOD, R. (1977) 'A commentary on selected aspects of the Dunning Report,' Report to the Scottish Education Department, unpublished.

Wood, R. (1986). 'Developing technically sound and credible methods of work-based assessment: A proposal to the Manpower Services Commission', St. Albans, Psychometric Research & Development Ltd.

Wood, R. and Ferguson, C.M. (1975). 'Teacher assessment of practical skills in "A" level chemistry', *School Science Review*, 57, pp. 605–8.

Paper 2: Assessment in the Classroom: What Do Teachers Look For?*

Introduction

When not indulging in partisan rhetoric, discussions of teacher assessment of classroom achievement have tended to be about matters like reliability, moderation, agreement or lack of it with examination results. Relatively little attention has been given to the validity of these assessments, at any rate when they are used as part of an external examination system. It seems reasonable to suppose that teachers are liable to pick out different aspects of achievement, their perceptual field being governed by a complex of personal characteristics, modified by experience. It also seems likely that what they choose to notice depends on the children they are assessing. Hoste and Bloomfield (1975) review some of the literature in this area. It is the possible effects of individual teacher variability which commentators are likely to have in mind when they refer, approvingly, to the impartiality of external examinations (Christopher, 1972). The fact that examination results are influenced for good or ill by teachers but in a different, less obvious way, is rarely remarked upon.

It seems to us that attempts to standardize assessments through the use of apparently specific schemes purporting to describe achievement constitute both a recognition and a concealment of the possibility that teachers have different views of what constitutes achievement and different capacities to pick out defined attributes. Most of these schemes rely heavily on Bloom's Taxonomy and there seems to be an assumption that a request to teachers to rate pupils on 'analysis' or 'application' or some such will be received and acted upon more or less identically throughout all institutions. Nothing is likely to be further from the truth. Whatever value the Taxonomy has in concentrating the mind it has failed to secure anything like a universally agreed interpretation. Reports of confusion between categories are the rule rather than the exception (see, for instance, Poole, 1972; Fairbrother, 1975). At best teachers may

---

*Reprinted from *Educational Studies*, (1975), 1, 3, October, pp. 151–61.

manage to fit their own differentiated schema of attributes into the categories they are given; at worst, these categories are liable to be greeted with blank incomprehension and quickly discarded in favour of a 'seat of the pants' approach. Either way, there is no guarantee whatsoever of uniformity of practice. One man's 'interest' is another man's 'sycophancy'.

But even if the attribute names commonly in use were to be more carefully defined and validated, some teachers would still experience problems. If it were not already apparent, we know from the psychological literature that there are individual differences in the ability to differentiate people on a number of dimensions, whether aesthetic, affective or intellectual in character. Some people are incapable of operating in more than one dimension. The more complex the intelligence, the more dimensions the individual can work with although, in general, increasing the number of dimensions decreases the information extracted from each (Johnson, 1972, pp. 378–80).

Just as their differing backgrounds, personalities and competencies may cause teachers to interpret rating instructions differently, so they are prone to showing what would generally be called bias. The literature contains reports of different behaviour towards high and low achievers (Pidgeon, 1970), boys and girls (Carter, 1952) and good looking and plain children (Dion, 1974). Nash (1973b) has described how teachers' subjective ideas of social class distort assessment and Simon (1970), in a polemical article, has related how pupils secure favourable treatment by giving the teacher what they think he wants — 'look, the guy likes Buber, so I give him Buberisms'.

Nor is this all. Differences may vary according to the sex of the teacher. For instance, Dion maintains that women teachers are likely to be much more lenient towards an attactive boy than they are to an unattractive boy or an attractive girl.

The theme running through these findings is the interplay between teachers' expectation and pupils' performance, a subject which, of course, has received great attention in the last few years (Rosenthal and Jacobson, 1968; Pidgeon, 1970; Nash, 1973a and 1973b). It seems to us that our study belongs to this line of research. It also fits into another closely related line of work — interpersonal perception (Cook, 1971).

The purpose of the study is to investigate the attributes of achievement which teachers actually assess as opposed to those they are supposed to assess. For our investigative tool we have borrowed what has become a favourite instrument of those engaged in the lines of research just mentioned, the repertory grid. This is a technique for eliciting what lies behind people's judgments. Rather than supply teachers with lists of attributes to assess — originality, dexterity, independence etc. — they should be asked what aspects of achievement are important to them. The results should give some idea of the variety of ways teacher assessment schemes are received and acted upon.

Collecting the Data

A modified form of the repertory grid procedure was administered to sixteen secondary teachers (twelve male, four female) at a mixed comprehensive school in an outer suburb of London. Ten of the teachers were involved in the teaching of mathematics and the other six were concerned with the teaching of geography. Data were gathered from these teachers for third form ($n = 179$) and fifth form ($n = 176$) pupils.

A maximum of twelve bi-polar constructs were elicited from each teacher by the triadic method (Bannister and Mair, 1968), this number being the most which could reasonably be asked for in the circumstances. Each teacher then ranked his constructs in accordance with the direction, 'If you were taking over a new class which pieces of information about pupils contained in these constructs would you find the most useful?' By asking the question 'In general, are children towards this end or that end of the construct most likely to succeed at school?' teachers' pole preferences were established.

The eight most highly ranked constructs were taken to constitute the core of each teacher's judgmental repertoire. For each class taught by a particular teacher pupils were scored on each of these eight constructs using a five point scale of the following type:

1 very poor worker
2 poor worker
3 average worker
4 good worker
5 very good worker

The ratings were entered on a grid and the totals for each pupil summed.

Thirty completed repertory grids were obtained from the teachers. Each third form class supplied two complete grids, one from a mathematics teacher and one from a geography teacher. Fifth form subject sets supplied one grid from each teacher. There were eight third form class sets, nine fifth form mathematics sets and six fifth form geography sets. One fifth form teacher did not complete a grid.

Analysis

The thrust of the analysis is to determine the number of constructs or ways of classifying pupils each teacher uses, as well as their relative importance to him. These can then be compared. Cook (1971, p. 45) maintains that the number of independent constructs is often surprisingly small, for people tend to use the same classification very widely, but give it different names, so that everyone they class as 'likeable' is also classed as 'good looking', 'intelligent' and 'friendly'. He also claims that most grids have a prominent evaluation construct that accounts for much of the person's classification of others, what would ordinarily be called a 'halo effect'.

It remains to be seen how far our results tally with Cook's observations. The following steps were taken:

1 Produce correlations between constructs for each teacher (Spearman's *r* was used).
2 Subject these to factor analysis, teacher by teacher.
3 Compare the incidence of constructs in terms of dominant factor loadings.
4 Group the constructs according to perceived affinity.
5 Classify these broader constructs into three categories, 'cognitive', 'affective' and 'motivational'.

Results

1. Correlations

Of the thirty correlation matrices, two are selected for illustrative purposes. Table 1 shows the construct names, the correlations and identifies the source of the data.

Table 1   Correlations between constructs for a particular teacher and class

Construct names:		Teacher G6: Geography Class: Third form (N = 25) 1. Behaviour 5. Conscientiousness 2. Class participation 6. Intelligence 3. Work output 7. Presentation of work 4. Diligence 8. Quietness						
Constructs	2	3	4	5	6	6	8
1	0.53	0.80	0.84	0.85	*0.15*	0.70	0.87
2		0.74	0.67	0.55	0.58	0.54	*0.19*
3			0.93	0.81	0.54	0.77	0.57
4				0.79	*0.42*	0.74	0.60
5					*0.19*	0.68	0.72
6						0.51	*−0.03*
7							0.54

This teacher used only one patently cognitive construct to rate her pupils, viz. 'intelligence', construct 6. The ratings on this construct show little association with the 'behaviour' and 'quietness' constructs.

'Presentation of work' appears to play a central part in this teacher's judgment since it relates highly to all the other constructs.

The second set of data shown in Table 2 is remarkable for the idiosyncratic constructs chosen by the teacher concerned. 'Mathematics ability' is the only cognitive construct elicited from this teacher. Correlations between this construct and the affective constructs of 'precocity' and 'aggression' are low. 'Precocity' and 'maturity' are perhaps different ways of expressing the same idea with the poles reversed. The first four constructs seem to go together as might be expected and a good deal of semantic overlap is suspected.

Table 2   Correlations between constructs for another teacher and class

Construct names:		Teacher M1: Mathematics Class: Fifth form ($N = 27$) 1. Motivation 2. Work output 3. Mathematics ability 4. Reliability		5. Precocity 6. Maturity 7. Tidiness 8. Aggression			
Constructs	2	3	4	5	6	7	8
1	0.94	0.62	0.93	−0.46	0.47	0.54	−0.54
2		0.64	0.98	−0.56	0.48	0.59	−0.57
3			0.66	*0.01*	0.52	0.51	−0.05
4				−0.57	0.53	0.66	−0.61
5					−0.25	−0.45	−0.81
6						0.53	−0.17
7							−0.35

In general, the highest correlations in the matrices were between cognitive constructs. On some occasions, a high correlation was obtained between a clearly cognitive construct and a construct like 'confidence in dealing with the subject', which might just be a surrogate for 'ability in the subject'. In no case was a construct that was apparently unrelated to performance in a subject found to be more highly correlated with a cognitive construct than cognitive constructs were between themselves. Thus constructs such as 'quietness', 'friendliness', 'grooming' and so on showed low or relatively low correlations with cognitive constructs. As one would hope, a teacher's assessment of the intellectual ability of a pupil is less affected by his appraisal of the pupil's affective makeup than it is by his assessment of the pupil on a range of cerebral activities.

2. Factor Analysis

With so many correlations to sift through, some reduction was called for if sense was to be made of the data. Factor analysis exists for this purpose. Using the

SPSS routine, a principal components factor analysis was carried out for each correlation matrix. Those factors with eigenvalues greater than one were rotated, according to the varimax criterion, so resolving the correlations into a simpler pattern. In the end, twenty three correlation matrices produced two factors, three produced three factors and from the remaining four only one factor was extracted.

Table 3 shows the result of a typical factor analysis. For factor I, consistently high loadings are observed on the constructs 'subject understanding', 'conceptual ability' and 'geography ability', identifying this *prime assessment factor* as being concerned solely with cognitive features of performance. Factor II appears to relate more closely to what we have termed 'motivational' constructs, in this case 'motivation', 'interest' and 'diligence', and is the *secondary assessment factor* for this teacher. This pattern was repeated in most cases where two or more factors were extracted, with the first factor loading more heavily on cognitive constructs — Cook's evaluation construct — and the other factor relating more to qualities such as 'industry' and 'application'.

Table 3   Loadings from a typical factor analysis

	Teacher G3: Geography Class: Third form (N = 22)	
	Varimax rotated factors	
Constructs	Factor I loadings	Factor II loadings
1. Subject understanding	0.988	0.124
2. Conceptual ability	0.988	0.124
3. Motivation	0.173	0.192
4. Interest	0.269	0.904
5. Diligence	0.080	0.866
6. Performance	0.611	0.667
7. Geography ability	0.932	0.129
8. Quietness	−0.003	−0.571
Estimated common variance	69.1%	30.9%

3. Comparison of Constructs

We are now in a position to appraise the variety of constructs elicited from the teacher. Table 4 lists fifty-six distinctively worded constructs. Because different teachers used different numbers of classes, the number of occasions each construct was used varies, the number being recorded in column B, along with the number of occasions each construct achieved a loading of 0.7 or more on a factor. The range of constructs used is self evident. It is possible to learn much from this table alone. The constructs most frequently used were 'interest' (used by eight teachers out of sixteen), 'class participation' (six teachers), 'mathematics ability' (six teachers out of ten), 'quietness' (six teachers), 'confidence' (six teachers) and 'tidiness' and 'behaviour' (five teachers each).

There are, of course, many constructs used uniquely by individual teachers and the idiosyncratic wording of the rarer constructs makes comparison difficult. Suspecting overlap or even equivalence between construct names, the step was taken of assigning common names to constructs which were believed to be concerned essentially with the same trait but which differed semantically. The results of this exercise appear in table 5. Next the twenty-two new composite constructs were treated as in table 4 with results which can be seen in table 6. Column A indicates the number of occasions a derived construct was used to rate pupils in one of its various forms and column B indicates the number of occasions the construct achieved a factor loading of 0.7 or more. It is

Table 4   Constructs elicited from teachers — alphabetically listed

Column A   Number of teachers who used this construct.
Column B   Number of occasions this construct was used to rate pupils.
Column C   Number of occasions this construct achieved a loading of 0.7 or more on factors produced by a varimax rotation of the initial factor matrix.

Construct	A	B	C	Construct	A	B	C
Aggressiveness	2	4	2	Indolence	1	2	1
Activeness	1	1		Industry	1	1	
Amount of work	1	2	2	Intelligence	2	3	2
Analytical outlook	1	2	1	Interest	8	15	11
Application to work	3	6	6	Keenness	1	2	2
Attendance	3	5	1	Likeability	1	2	1
Attitude to work	4	8	8	Map understanding	1	3	2
Attractive personality	1	1	1	Mathematics ability	6	10	9
Behaviour	5	9	4	Maturity	4	7	1
Class participation	6	10	7	Motivation	2	7	5
Class questioning	1	1	1	Natural ability	4	7	7
Concentration	2	4	4	Oral participation	1	2	1
Confident approach	6	10	7	Perception of subject	2	4	3
Concept acquisition	1	2	2	Performance in subject	2	5	2
Concept ability	2	7	7	Perseverance	1	2	1
Cooperation	3	4	4	Precocity	1	3	2
Conscientiousness	1	1	1	Presentation of work	3	5	2
Diligence	4	8	7	Purposefulness	1	1	
Enthusiasm	1	2	2	Quietness	6	10	3
Extraversion	4	6	3	Reliability	1	3	3
Factual recall	1	2	2	Self-discipline	1	3	3
Friendliness	1	1	1	Seriousness	1	1	1
Geography ability	2	7	7	Tidiness	5	10	6
Good worker	1	1		Tries	1	1	1
Grooming	1	1		Understanding subject	1	4	4
Honesty	1	2	1	Willingness to work	1	1	1
Homework regularity	3	5	5	Written expression	2	5	4
Independence	3	4	3	Work output	2	5	5

Total number of construct ratings = sum of column B = 240

apparent from table 6 that the dominant constructs by which teachers differentiate between pupils are broadly those that signify active participation

Table 5 Construct derivation and renaming

Derived construct	Grouping of old constructs	Derived construct	Grouping of old constructs
1 Pupil involvement	Application to work, attitude to work, amount of work, diligence, conscientiousness, good worker, homework regularity, motivation, willingness to work, work output, tries, purposefulness, enthusiasm, industry, keenness, seriousness, indolence, perseverance, cooperativeness.	12 Analytical outlook	Analytical outlook
2 Natural ability	Intelligence, natural ability, concept ability, concept acquisition	13 Concentration	Concentration
3 Class participation	class participation, class questioning, oral participation, activeness in class	14 Factual recall	Factual recall
4 Likeability	Attractive personality, friendliness, likeability	15 Interest	Interest
5 Subject ability	Mathematics ability, geography ability, map understanding	16 Performance in subject	Performance in subject
6 Perception of subject	Perception of subject, understanding of subject	17 Extraversion	Extraversion
7 Reliability	Reliability, self discipline	18 Grooming	Grooming
8 Behaviour	Behaviour, quietness	19 Honesty	Honesty
9 Aggressiveness	Aggressiveness	20 Written expression	Written expression
10 Maturity	Maturity	21 Confident approach	Confident approach
11 Presentation of work	Presentation of work, tidiness	22 Attendance	Attendance

in the learning process. On 60 occasions out of a possible 240, a construct within this category was used to rate pupils. More importantly, on fifty-two of these occasions the construct received a loading of 0.7 or more on a general factor. Given the satisfaction which is gained from arousing interest in a subject, it is perhaps not surprising that half of the teachers used 'interest' as a construct in assessing pupils or that on eleven of the fifteen occasions it was so used, it achieved a loading of 0.7 or more on one of the factors. The results for 'class participation' tell the same story. Table 6 also leaves no doubt that 'subject ability', 'natural ability' and 'behaviour' are constructs that are frequently used by teachers in assessing pupils. Interestingly, Nash in his study of primary school children and their teachers reported that the two most common constructs used by teachers were 'well-behaved — poorly behaved' and 'high ability — low ability' (Nash, 1973b).

4. Classification of the Constructs

In discussions of achievement it is often convenient to speak of two classes of constructs — cognitive and affective. From this study there is evidence of a third class which, for want of a better term, has been called 'motivational'. Distinguishing attributes like 'application to work', 'class participation', and 'perseverance' from affective qualities has its problems but these attributes seem to exert a separate influence. Specifically, positive endorsement invariably leads to higher ratings on cognitive constructs, what might be expressed in simple-minded terms as ability + application = achievement. The threefold classification of the derived constructs is set out in table 7. Using material in tables 1 and 7 it is possible to express more succinctly the relative significance

Table 6   Classification of derived constructs in terms of (a) use and (b) factor loadings

Column A   Number of occasions a construct within this class of constructs was used to rate pupils.

Column B   Number of occasions a construct within this class of constructs achieved a factor loading of 0.7 or more.

Derived construct	A	B	Derived construct	A	B
Pupil involvement	60	52	Reliability	6	6
Subject ability	20	18	Extraversion	6	3
Natural ability	19	18	Performance	5	2
Behaviour	19	7	Written expression	5	4
Presentation of work	15	8	Attendance	5	1
Interest	15	11	Likeability	5	3
Class participation	14	9	Concentration	4	4
Maturity	11	4	Factual recall	2	2
Confident approach	10	7	Honesty	2	1
Perception of subject	8	7	Analytical outlook	2	1
Aggression	7	4	Grooming	1	0

of the loadings attached to cognitive, motivational and affective constructs. The result is shown in table 8. It may be seen that on over 90 per cent of the occasions on which cognitive constructs were used to rate pupils, a factor loading of 0.7 or more was achieved. As would be expected, cognitive constructs play a central although not overwhelming part in the assessment of achievement.

Table 7   Classification of derived constructs in terms of psychological categories

Cognitive (N = 4)	Affective (N = 10)	Motivational (N = 8)
Subject ability	Behaviour	Pupil involvement
Natural ability	Interest	Presentation of work
Factual recall	Maturity	Class participation
Analytical outlook	Aggression	Confident approach
	Reliability	Perception of subject
	Extraversion	Performance in subject
	Attendance	Written expression
	Likeability	Concentration
	Honesty	
	Grooming	

Table 8   Comparison of the three classes of constructs in terms of factor loadings

Column A   Number of occasions constructs from this class were used to rate pupils.
Column B   Number of occasions a construct from this class achieved a loading of 0.7 or more on a factor
Column C   Percentage column B is of column A.

Construct class	A	B	C
Cognitive	43	39	92.3%
Motivational	121	93	76.8%
Affective	76	40	52.6%

Discussion

From this study it seems that when assessing achievement teachers are likely to differentiate between pupils on the basis of all or some of six derived constructs, presented in no particular order of importance.

(a)   The involvement of the pupil in the learning situation.
(b)   The ability the pupil has in the subject.
(c)   The overall ability of the pupil.
(d)   The behaviour of the pupil.
(e)   The quality and tidiness of work presented.
(f)   The interest displayed by the pupil in the subject.

Although consideration of intellectual or cognitive qualities bulks large, teachers are influenced by other factors; in particular, the extent of pupil commitment and interest in the subject appears to be significant. This raises the question as to whether the influence of motivational factors alongside cognitive factors means that there is more likelihood that unconforming, difficult pupils may deserve higher ratings than they get. Allen (1972) asks, 'Do we really want a system that prevents the scruffy, lazy uncooperative urchin with ability coming out on top?' Although the contrast is exaggerated, the point is taken. The tendency for girls to be rated more highly than boys has already been noted. If, for whatever reason, girls do perform better than boys then the chips must fall where they may but the worry is that mediocre but compliant girls may attract better ratings than more talented but difficult boys.

The plethora of constructs revealed (see table 4) is circumstantial evidence that teachers do vary considerably in what they look for. It would be odd if it were otherwise; there seems to be a connection between what people consider to be important and their own personalities and competencies (Smith, 1966). Supposing, for the sake of argument, that the simple-minded model, ability + application = achievement, has some validity, then each teacher will mix the ingredients in a personal way and will differ over the weights they give to each. Some teachers will attempt to exclude non-cognitive considerations, others will give them increasing emphasis. In practice, of course, it must be very difficult to unscramble application and ability, as the following remarks from one of the teachers quoted by Hoste and Bloomfield (1975) make clear.

> We make no formal attempt to assess non-cognitive qualities but let me say in qualification of that, that all the points are inherent in the assessment because it's so subjective. You cannot assess a child whom you have taught for five terms and not have in your assessment some recognition of these qualities. It's impossible.

Just what qualities the teacher sees and how he values them is, of course, the nub of the whole issue.

It remains to study systematically the variables that may condition teachers' judgments. Constructs such as 'behaviour', 'quietness', 'class participation' etc. may be used more often by younger, less experienced teachers. In this particular study the constructs 'grooming' and 'quietness' were used by a part-time teacher who admitted having a discipline problem. It was also the case that words associated with classroom behaviour were more likely to be used by teachers working with less able classes.

What effect the issuing of more carefully worded rating instructions might have on the variability of perception is not known. Too much advice might be as bad as too little. It would certainly be possible to structure assessments more tightly by specifying precisely how ability and application measures should be combined but that in itself would not remove individual differences in the capacity to distinguish between the two or indeed different notions about what the terms mean in the first place.

One improvement might be to develop behaviourally-anchored scales based on a consensus view of what most teachers consider achievement to consist of. In a behaviourally-anchored scale each point on the scale is associated with a more or less explicit description of the behaviour or performance which qualifies for the mark or grade in question. An example is given by Duffey (1972). To gain a grade A on this interest scale a pupil needs to be: 'Eager and curious, lively in discussion, quick to see connections, often asks questions, needs only a hint to get started, makes suggestions which show links with other fields of knowledge, shows occasional originality or ingenuity.' At the other end of the scale, Duffey suggests for the E category; 'Not in the least interested, quite incurious and insensitive, utterly passive in his responses, takes little or no voluntary part in class discussions.'

Now while it is true that these descriptions offer teachers more trait names to differ about, they do seem to us to be first approximations to thumbnail sketches from which pupils might be recognized. In order to tie down the best part of achievement a number of scales may be needed (for methods of constructing them, see Taylor, 1968). If it is objected that in championing scales we are reverting to the situation criticized earlier, of imposing alien concepts on teachers, we would argue that the situation is improved in two respects. First, the scales will be based on what most teachers think, which has not always been the case and second, more strenuous attempts will be made to provide descriptions of attainment which will ring bells in teachers' minds and so facilitate assessment and lead to greater fairness.

Summary

The idea that teachers look for different behaviours to reward when making assessments of students' achievement is explored. Using a repertory grid technique, teachers of geography and mathematics were asked to name the attributes they look for and to rank them in order of importance. Cognitive attributes were generally predominant but there was a class of attributes, termed 'motivational', which appear to exert considerable moderating effects. It is in their response to sets of behaviours like 'industry' and 'perseverance' that teachers may show greatest individual differences in rating performance. Suggestions are made for bringing greater systematization into assessments although it is recognized that there is likely to be a limit to what it is possible to do.

Note

Dr. Napthali carried out the work reported in this article while in receipt of a Research Studentship from the University of London University Entrance and School Examinations Council (for more details, see Napthali, 1975). The views expressed do not necessarily reflect those of the Council.

References

ALLEN, A. (1972), 'Judgement days,' *New School Master*, October, pp. 224–5.

BANNISTER, D. and MAIR, J.M.M. (1968), *The Evaluation of Personal Constructs*, London, Academic Press.

CARTER, R.S. (1952), 'How invalid are marks assigned by teachers?', *Journal of Educational Psychology*, 43, pp. 218–28.

CHRISTOPHER, R. (1972), 'The prospect of examinations,' *Dialogue*, 10, pp. 3–5.

COOK, M. (1971), *Interpersonal Perception*, Harmondsworth, Penguin Books.

DION, K.K. (1974), 'Children's physical attractiveness and sex as determiners of adult punitiveness', *Developmental Psychology*, 10, 5, pp. 772–8.

DUFFEY, J. (1972), 'The assessment of progress in science', *School Science Review*, 54, 86, pp. 13–25.

FAIRBROTHER, R. (1975), 'The reliability of teachers' judgements of the abilities being tested by multiple-choice items', *Educational Research*, 17, 3 pp. 202–10.

HOSTE, R. and BLOOMFIELD, B. (1975), 'Continuous assessment in the C.S.E.: Opinion and practice', *Schools Council Examinations Bulletin*, 31. London, Evans/Methuen Educational.

JOHNSON, D.M. (1972), *A Systematic Introduction to the Psychology of Thinking*. New York, Harper & Row.

NAPTHALI, W.A. (1975), 'Achievement at 16 plus: A study of the personal constructs used by teachers in assessing both pupils and the achievements of pupils in mathematics and geography', unpublished doctoral dissertation. University of London Institute of Education.

NASH, R. (1973a), *Classrooms Observed*, London, Routledge and Kegan Paul.

NASH, R. (1973b), 'Keeping in with teacher', *New Society*, 14 December.

PIDGEON, D.A. (1970), *Expectation and Pupil Performance*, Windsor, NFER Publishing Co.

POOLE, R.E. (1972), 'Characteristics of the taxonomy of educational objectives: Cognitive domain — a replication', *Psychology in the Schools*, 9, pp. 83–8.

ROSENTHAL, R. and JACOBSON, J. (1968), *Pygmalion in the Classroom*, New York, Holt, Rinehart & Winston.

SIMON, S.B. (1970), 'Grades must go', *School Review*, 78, pp. 397–402.

SMITH, H.C. (1966), *Sensitivity to People*, New York, McGraw-Hill.

TAYLOR, J.B. (1968), 'Rating scales as measures of clinical judgement: A method for increasing scale reliability and sensitivity', *Educational and Psychological Measurement*, 28, pp. 747–66.

Paper 3: Halo and Other Effects in Teacher Assessments*

Introduction

With teacher assessments of students' competence playing a greater part in achievement testing, there has naturally been speculation as to what measurement characteristics such ratings might have. Very little hard evidence is currently available. The purpose of this paper is to present a systematic method for investigating and describing the several sources of variability which might enter into teacher assessments. The treatment — a variance components analysis — is in the spirit of Cronbach, et al[1].

To be able to discuss variability at all, it is necessary to have repeated measurements or assessments. Single terminal assessments are no good. Thus we deal in this paper with situations where a *teacher* rates his *students* over a number of *experiments* on one or more *attributes*. In set-ups of this kind, the object is to isolate the several sources of variability and to estimate their magnitudes. Since coefficients of reliability are ratio measures of 'true' variability to error there can be as many coefficients of reliability as there are sources of variability. The one habitually referred to as *the* reliability, the variability of persons' scores relative to error, is only one index, although admittedly an important one. Others estimate the efficiency with which teachers are able to discriminate between attributes, the inverse of the so-called 'halo' effect, and whether this capacity varies from experiment to experiment and so forth. The power of a variance components analysis is that it enables each of these effects to be quantified and compared for size (for an educational illustration, see McGaw, B, Wardrop, J.L. and Bunda, MA[2]).

Data

For two years, many of the teachers following the University of London 'A' level chemistry syllabus B have been making assessments of their students'

*Reprinted from *Durham Research Review* (1976) 36, pp. 1120–6.

practical laboratory work as part of a non-operational trial scheme. During and after a series of nominated experiments, teachers are asked to rate their students' performance on four attributes, manipulative skills, observational skills, interpretive skill, and planning skills, using a labelled scale from 1 to 5. The likelihood that not every experiment will lend itself to the rating of all four attributes is pointed out to teachers, and in fact, the data are characteristically incomplete, having something like the following structure for teacher j assessing n_j students.

		Experiment							
		1				2			
	Attribute	A	B	C	D	A	B	C	D
1			x		x		x	x	x
			x		x		x	x	x
Students			•		•		•	•	•
			•		•		•	•	•
	n^j		x		x		x	x	x

The fact that the data are typically incomplete is somewhat inconvenient from the point of view of analysis, since the estimation equations are considerably more complicated than where there is complete data. It is always possible, of course, to make incomplete data complete by collapsing sufficient numbers of consecutive experiments to produce a reduced number of 'occasions' but we prefer to use all the information, if we can. A straightforward analysis, with complete data, will be treated first. The perspective will be univariate, treating each observation in isolation. Further data will then be used to illustrate the incomplete analysis.

Analysis

Variance components are measures of the true variability of sources of variation referred to defined populations. They are calculated by solving equations generated from an analysis of variance model. For these particular data, the analysis has certain features which make it not quite routine. In a so-called fully-crossed, random effects model, where the students, experiments and attributes can be said to be randomly sampled from appropriate but infinite populations, the analysis is straightforward and well-charted and the expected mean squares, from which variance components can be determined, are readily available[3]. If, however, as in this case, some effects are fixed — the number of students within a teaching set and the number of traits is in each case *the* population — or are randomly sampled, but from a *finite* population, for example the experiments, then modifications are necessary. The modifications are not especially complicated. Cronbach *et al* indicate what has to be done, and Searle and Fawcett[4] give rules for converting expected mean squares in the fully-crossed, random effects case. The general effect is to multiply certain components by a factor of $\left(1 - \dfrac{n}{N}\right)$, where n is the number of elements sampled from a population of size N. If $n = N$, the effect is fixed and the multiplier vanishes, while if N is very large relative to n, as it often will be, the multiplier is, to all intents and purposes, equal to 1. Only if $\dfrac{n}{N}$ is a substantial fraction does the multiplier exert an effect.

In the set up we are dealing with it is not quite clear what will happen. The number of experiments assessed is a sample of all the experiments that are or might have been given in the course of a year, the number of which is certainly finite; one per week seems a reasonable estimate of the population size, in other words, 30–40. If 8 is the most common number of experiments assessed, the multiplier $\left(1 - \dfrac{n}{N}\right)$ is about .75, perhaps not likely to make a great deal of difference. However, we have varied the experiment population size, from 20 through 30 to 50, to see what effect, if any, this has on the estimates.

As for the other dimension, the students within a teaching set are completely enumerated and so can be said to be fixed. It might be argued, with a stretch of the imagination, that the four attributes are a sample of all the various attributes or attribute names which could have been presented to the teachers. Thus, if we wished, we could extend the analysis by varying the attribute population size and investigating the effects on the variance component estimates. But this seems somewhat contrived and the attribute dimension will be treated as fixed.

Results

To calculate estimates of the variance components we use a program called CRONB[5], modified to accommodate designs with finite populations. Table 1 gives estimates for the five complete data sets of varying dimensions, the number of observations per attribute ranging from 65 to 225. It will be noted how small the numbers of students are; this is characteristic of Advanced level teaching sets. Fortunately, there is some evidence from simulation work[6] that reliability estimates are quite robust against non-normality as long as the number of replications or experiments is fairly large, which means 8 or thereabouts. As the median number of experiments assessed by teachers over the two years of the scheme happens to be exactly that figure, the reliability estimates are probably trustworthy.

Evidently, the experiment population size makes little odds to the interpretation of the results. The student-attribute interaction is most affected by the size of the sample/population proportion; this is obviously a function of the degree of generalizability called for.

Among the results for individual teachers, those for teacher 1 are the most

Table 1 Estimates of variance components, multiplied by 1,000, for five teachers presenting complete data

Source of Variation	Experiment Population Size	Teacher (Students × Experiments)				
		1 (17 × 7)	2 (34 × 3)	3 (15 × 15)	4 (11 × 6)	5 (13 × 5)
Students	20	92	208	61	150	281
	30	90	208	61	150	281
	50	89	208	61	149	281
Experiments	20	45	2	0	12	0
	30					
	50					
Attributes	20	55	0	3	34	46
	30	55	0	3	34	46
	50	54	0	3	33	46
Students × Experiments	20	126	0	0	48	0
	30					
	50					
Students × Attributes	20	19	15	31	23	19
	30	15	12	26	20	16
	50	11	9	22	17	14
Experiments × Attributes	20	34	0	4	20	2
	30					
	50					
Residual	20	283	203	297	226	158
	30					
	50					

striking. Not only is the variability spread across all sources but the largest variance component (excepting error) is not associated with students, as would be expected and is the case elsewhere, but with the student x experiment interaction. This means that students are being assessed differently from experiment to experiment (there were seven of them) and in orderings which are sufficiently uncorrelated to cause an overall lack of differentiation between the students. The experiments chosen for assessment must have been quite diverse, as compared with other teachers.

With teacher 2 the pattern of results is very different. Here the student variance component is dominant. It would appear that this teacher has assessed his students in more or less the same way on each experiment, and that his assessments were based on a generalized view of practical skills. We can tell this from the fact that the experiment variance component is negligible and the student x attribute component is very small. Only if the value of this last component is reasonably large can it be claimed that a teacher has been successful in distinguishing between attributes in his rating behaviour. Otherwise it is conventional to say that 'halo' effect has been operating.

Various kinds of halo can be defined. There is *absolute* halo which is confounded with true individual variance. There is what Guilford[7] has called *relative* halo or the tendency for different raters to rate individuals differently. What we customarily think of as a halo effect is something else; the trait-individuals interaction, or the tendency for all raters to fail to differentiate between traits when rating, in accord with Thorndike's original definition[8]. This effect is obviously connected with the average inter-trait correlation and, in fact, Willingham and Jones[9] showed that the trait-subject interaction can be expressed as one minus the average inter-trait correlation, assuming all trait measures standardized to unit variance. These writers argued that the use of separate trait scores as distinct criteria cannot be justified unless the trait-subject interaction is significant, in the formal statistical sense. F tests of the student-attribute interactions for the five teachers indicate that only for teacher 3 can this interaction be considered significant.

Teacher 3 shows much the same pattern as teacher 2 except that the student variance component is so much smaller relative to the error component, which means that his assessments were less reliable, in the customary use of the term. However, he does seem to have been more able than the other teachers to distinguish between the four attributes.

Teacher 4 resembles teacher 1 more than any other; in both cases the variation is spread over the several sources. Again this seems to be a case where quite different experiments were chosen for assessment, with a suggestion that the teacher's notion of what he was assessing may have varied according to the experiment.

Teacher 5's assessments were more reliable than anyone else's, reliability being calculated as a ratio of true variability, σ^2_{stud}, to true variability plus residual variability σ^2_e, or observed variability.

$$= \frac{\sigma^2_{stud}}{\sigma^2_{stud} + \sigma^2_e} = \frac{281}{281 + 158} = 0.64$$

compared to a value of $\frac{61}{61 + 297}$ or 0.17 for teacher 3.

This is especially interesting because teacher 5 made the fewest observations and teacher 3 the most. In fact, the greater the number of experiments assessed, the lower is the reliability of assessment. This must be because the assumption of unidimensionality — experiments measure the same qualities — which is reflected in uniform correlation between experiments, is violated; in other words, there is a significant student-experiment interaction. It might be thought that this interaction would be likely to increase with the number of experiments, yet for teacher 3, with 15 experiments, the variance component is non-existent.

Some student-experiment interaction is, of course, to be expected. On certain experiments, students will perform markedly better or worse than their general level of performance. Where this occurs, the conventional estimate of reliability, which is predicated on the absence of such interaction, becomes misleadingly low as we have seen and other ways of summarizing assessment behaviour have to be found. This is what we are engaged upon.

It is reasonable to suppose that assessments improve in accuracy and differentiation as time goes on. It might be wondered, therefore, whether the assessments from the first experiment a teacher assesses are responsible for an undue amount of 'noise'. We have not found this to be the case; excluding the first series of assessments does not alter the substance of the outcome for any of the five data sets analyzed.

A more pressing question concerns the capacity of teachers to differentiate between attributes when they themselves nominate the attributes, experiment by experiment. Such is the unusual state of affairs in this assessment scheme, resulting in the incomplete data sets referred to earlier. In these circumstances, improved differentiation seems likely to occur. We now see whether there was any evidence of this.

When data are incomplete, much depends on the sparseness and distribution of the observations; with too few observations awkwardly distributed there are insufficient degrees of freedom to estimate all the interactions. Fortunately, the effect we are most interested in, the student-attribute interaction, is usually estimable by virtue of the fact that all attributes are adequately measured over the period of a course.

The estimation model for the so-called unbalanced case is based on Searle's work[10]. Incomplete data from four centres, varying in degree of incompleteness, serve to illustrate the analysis. The dimensions were $13 \times 12 \times 4$, $13 \times 11 \times 4$, $17 \times 13 \times 4$, $12 \times 6 \times 4$, representing 512/624, 216/572, 234/884 and 221/288 observations respectively. Estimates of variance components are presented in table 2. The figures in brackets indicate the degrees of freedom available for estimating components of variance. Evidently some are rather low.

The negative values in table 2 require some explanation; variance components, like variances, ought not to be negative. In fact, negative estimates will occur occasionally because of restricted degrees of freedom and excessive within-group variation; this is especially likely to happen in unbalanced designs. How to interpret negative values is a matter of controversy among statisticians; a conventional solution, and the one we will adopt, is to treat them as non-existent.

With this point established, it will be seen that the message of table 2 is not dissimilar to that of table 1. Again the student × attribute interactions are very small, further evidence of strong halo effects. What is more, they are relatively smaller in the incomplete case; maybe choosing the attributes to

Table 2   Estimates of variance components, multiplied by 1,000, for four teachers presenting incomplete data (degrees of freedom are given in brackets after each estimate)

Source of Variation	Teacher							
	I		II		III		IV	
Students	104	(12)	221	(12)	109	(16)	204	(11)
Experiments	237	(11)	−22	(10)	−90	(12)	−25	(5)
Attributes	193	(3)	19	(3)	45	(3)	232	(3)
Students × Experiments	374	(126)	53	(93)	382	(107)	116	(50)
Students × Attributes	0	(36)	7	(36)	25	(46)	35	(33)
Experiments × Attributes	20	(27)	72	(11)	169	(9)	94	(11)
Residual	367	(297)	188	(50)	597	(40)	249	(108)

assess does not lead to greater differentiation between attributes.

Differences in the capacity of teachers to differentiate between students is again noticeable. Teacher II shows greatest reliability in this sense but he, like teacher 2 in table 1, seems to have set similar experiments and to have rated students' competence in a generalized way. Teachers I and III show lowest reliability but the strong student × experiment interactions indicate that students are not performing uniformly across experiments with the consequence that overall orders of merit are not clear-cut.

Discussion

The results of work to date have confirmed that variance components analysis offers a powerful method of investigating the variability of the sort of assessments of achievement teachers are increasingly being called upon to provide. An analysis of a number of teachers' assessments has revealed real differences in rating behaviour. This is hardly surprising but it does underline the difficulty of bringing teachers' rating standards into line as opposed to statistical moderation which may only give an appearance of congruence.

It would not be surprising if teachers, being relatively untrained in the job of making complex judgments, find it difficult to distinguish between what are often poorly defined and inter-related attributes, and the results we have obtained do nothing to invalidate this view. Of course, halo effect is endemic in any multiple-rating procedure: perhaps what Sommer[11] has to say about the Hawthorne effect is true also of the halo effect. Far from being a trappable source of error, he says, it is ubiquitous and of the greatest interest, representing 'our major *raison d'être* as psychologists'. A similar view is put by Hastorf, Richardson and Dornbusch[12] who argue that halo effect is not necessarily a nuisance or an error, but can have functional value as when trait intercorrelations permit prediction of others' behaviour on the basis of partial information.

At the same time some differentiation ought to be possible, otherwise multiple rating is a waste of time. If, as appears to be the case with this particular scheme, differentiation is very limited then remedial action needs to be taken. First, it must be established whether differentiation is to be expected and how much. There may be little intra-individual variation in the skills concerned, in which case differentiation may have to be built into the assessment scheme. This might mean amplifying the definitions of the attributes, providing more guidance and training through the provision of exemplary material, refining the labelling of points on the rating scale, or even abandoning the constructs and finding out from the teachers themselves what ·are the salient aspects of behaviour they look for. Most studies use traits selected by investigators with little concern for the relevance of these traits for the individual[13]. The increasing use of repertory grid techniques to make personal constructs explicit signals a change of outlook in this respect (see, for instance, Wood and Napthali[14]).

Where one of the dimensions is a time scale there is the possibility that the observations alter systematically over time. Students might improve their ratings the more experiments they do; in a way it would be disturbing if they did not. Regular trends in performance violate a major assumption, underpinning the variance components model, which is that the expected score under any condition is the same, no matter where in the series of observations within a time span that condition or experiment is located. As Cronbach *et al* point out[15] this is a limitation common to all reliability theory, although attempts have been made in the past to deal with trends and order effects (see Alexander,[16]; Hoffman,[17]).

For these data the test for trend over experiments on all traits turned out to be negative in all cases. If this is worrying in the light of previous remarks, it should be borne in mind that teachers are unlikely to apply the same absolute scale from experiment to experiment, which is not to say that growth does not occur. Moreover, a five-point rating scale hardly allows room to express growth, especially as no instructions were given to teachers to gauge their standards from the beginning so as to be able to capture growth. Were such instructions to be given, and growth registered, the analysis would have to be modified to take account of this fact. More work is needed on this problem.

Acknowledgement

I thank my colleague, Douglas Wilson, for programming the modifications to CRONB and for producing the estimates.

References

1 CRONBACH, L.J., GLESER, G.C., NANDA, H. and RAJARATNAM, N. (1972). *The Dependability of Behavioural Measurements*, New York, John Wiley & Sons, Inc.
2 McGAW, B., WARDROP, J.L. and BUNDA, M.A. (1972). 'Classroom observation schemes: Where are the errors?' *American Educational Research Journal*, 9, 1, pp. 13–27.
3 CRONBACH, L.J., GLESER, G.C., NANDA, H. and RANJARATNAM, N. (1972) *op. cit.*, p. 43.
4 SEARLE, S.R., and FAWCETT, R.F. (1970). 'Expected mean squares in variance components having finite populations', *Biometrics*, 26, 2, pp. 243–54.
5 CORNELIUS, E.T., WOODWARD, J.A., and DEMAREE, R.G. (1972) 'CRONB: A Fortran IV program to compute variance components for various experimental designs', Texas, Texas Christian University Institute of Behavioural Research.
6 BAY, K.S. (1973) 'The effect of non-normality on the sampling distribution and standard error of reliability coefficient estimates under an analysis of variance model', *Brit. Jour. Math. Stat. Psychol.*, 26, 1, pp. 45–57.
7 GUILFORD, J.P. (1954). *Psychometric Methods*, New York, McGraw-Hill.
8 THORNDIKE, E.L. (1920). 'A constant error in psychological rating'. *Journal of Applied Psychology*, 4, pp. 25–9.
9 WILLINGHAM, W.W., and JONES, M.B. (1958). 'On the identification of halo through analysis of variance'. *Educ. Psychol. Measmt.*, 18, pp. 403–7.
10 SEARLE, S.R. and FAWCETT, R.F. (1970) *op. cit.*
11 SOMMER, R. (1968). 'Hawthorne dogma', *Psychol. Bull.*, 70, 6, pp. 592–5.
12 HASTORF, A.H. RICHARDSON, S.A. and DORNBUSCH, S.M. (1958). 'The problem of relevance in the study of person perception', in TAGIURI, R. and PETRILLO, L. (Eds.) *Person Perception and Interpersonal Behaviour*. Stanford, CA, Stanford University Press.
13 KOLTUV, B.B. (1962). 'Some characteristics of intrajudge trait intercorrelations', *Psychol. Mongr.*, 76, 552.
14 WOOD, R. and NAPTHALI, W.A. (1975). 'Assessment in the classroom: What do teachers look for?' *Educational Studies*, 1, 3, pp. 151–61' (and in this volume).
15 CRONBACH, L.J., GLESER, G.C., NANDA, H. and RAJARATNAM, N. (1972) *op. cit.*, pp. 363–4.
16 ALEXANDER, H.W. (1947). 'The estimation of reliability when several trials are available', *Psychometrika*, 12, pp. 79–99.
17 HOFFMAN, P.J. (1963). 'Test reliability and practice effects', *Psychometrika*, 28, pp. 273–88.

III   Examinations Research

Comments

Somebody once defined research as *research* — looking for something you didn't find the first time round. That sums up pretty well what we research officers in the GCE boards thought about *comparability*. The trouble was, you kept on looking and found nothing. Some thought they had the answer (subject pairs, the use of an aptitude test as a control) and stopped looking; the more fastidious among us simply thought the problem insoluble. There were always far too many reasons why results which purported to show comparability, or lack of it, might be invalid. Yet we were obliged to plug away. For our masters, the Board secretaries, comparability was such a sensitive nerve that the merest touch would set the minions running. Never mind that the secretaries themselves might not believe in the possibility of comparability; they had to be seen to be taking action. Towards the end, my ambitions were no higher than looking for signs of a kind of 'relaxed' comparability ie, nothing grotesquely out of true. As I read the reports now (Hecker and Wood, 1979; Garrett and Wood, 1980) I see how painstakingly we built proviso upon proviso, caveat upon caveat, usually starting with how little time was available for the exercise. I suppose there was some grim intellectual pleasure in it.

I rather suspect that the comparability problem will be legislated out of GCSE, to avoid the agonizing of the 1970s. The rationalization of the boards into consortia may be thought to have reduced the problem to the point where it can be ignored.

In the summer of 1976 I was totally fed up with comparability and the publication of the so-called Willmott Report simply blew the lid off. I decided to include as paper 4 the piece I wrote for the *Times Educational Supplement* and the companion letter I wrote a few months later, just in case any future historian of comparability wants to know what all the fuss was about.

Working in examinations research was to make your own job. At any rate, that's how it was for me. Once you had attended to comparability and to a lesser extent, teacher assessment, you had to decide how to fill in the rest of your time. Rather like a man marooned on a desert island who, to stave off terminal boredom, interests himself in the stars and the weather and plants and ants, I, at the London GCE board, tried to get lines of research going. Sometimes I used 'found' data, of which, of course, there was masses; at other times I induced data by getting 'experiments' going.

So, in a small way, I got involved in, among other things, some on-going controversies of the 1970s ((ii), (iii), (v) and (vi)).

(i)   Sex differences in achievement in mathematics and English (Wood and Brown, 1976; Wood, 1976; Wood, 1978).

(ii) Mixed vs single sex schooling and how the sexes might benefit from each (Wood and Ferguson, 1974).

(iii) Comprehensive vs. grammar school results via the ILEA (Wood and Ferguson, 1976).

(iv) How written instructions (examination rubrics and the questions themselves) affect answers.

(v)   Does schooling make a difference? (Brimer *et al*, 1978).

(vi) The acceptability of multiple-choice testing (see next Section).

The sex difference stuff was fun to do. It is a bit finicky to reproduce here. It was the material I did not publish which, through others, made the headlines. This indicated that the introduction of multiple-choice into a subject would, in the generality, affect girls' chances adversely. As far as I know, the issue has gone dead. My feeling was that the imbalance was likely to be self-adjusting and even tip the other way. Imagined girls coming to terms with multiple-choice, that is with the format and the nature of the task itself, and then, with their known superiority in essay work (which the boys would have done nothing to redress), actually gain advantage. It would be interesting to know whether this has come about.

The question-answer project (iv) was meant to be quite ambitious but produced much less than I hoped. In the end there was only the *Times Educational Supplement* article (Wood, 1976) and an unpublished paper (Wood, 1974) to show. The inspiration was a mixture of Peter Wason with his idea that you learn what you want to say as you write (Wason, 1970) and Pat Wright of the Applied Psychology Unit, Cambridge, who was working on how to get information across. I wanted to make people in the Board aware that the wording of questions and rubrics was crucial in determining choice of questions and responses. (In fact, a committee was formed to tidy up rubrics.) I remember we took some 'O' level politics questions and varied them, putting in more or less structure and information, and administered the variants in a research design. What happened after that I am not sure; it seems to me we couldn't handle the scoring, or perhaps we failed to produce any daylight between the variants. At any rate, it fizzled out. I worked with Wright on the effect of varying the rubric for the multiple-choice item type called multiple-completion, although I was not best pleased when she published a paper (Wright, 1975) which omitted any mention of our work and the data I supplied.

I noticed the other day a study which investigated what happens when the rubric is omitted altogether by asking the student to judge each statement separately, making the item indistinguishable from the multiple true/false type. It appears that this arrangement was preferred by the majority of students (Harasym, Morris and Lorscheider, 1980). Certainly, we found that the rubric (mark A if I, II and IV are correct etc) favoured the more capable students (Wood, 1974).

References

BRIMER, M.A., MADAUS, G.F. CHAPMAN, B.L.M., KELLAGHAN T. and WOOD, R. (1978) *Sources of Differences in School Achievement*, Windsor, National Foundation for Educational Research in England & Wales.

GARRETT, S.K. and WOOD, R. (1980) 'Report of a GCE interboard cross-validation exercise in history at Ordinary level: 1978', University of London School Examinations Department.

HARASYM, P.H., MORRIS, D.A. and LORSCHEIDER, F.L. (1980) 'Evaluating student multiple-choice responses: Effects of coded and free formats', *Evaluation and the Health Professions*, 3, pp. 63–84.

HECKER, P.C. and WOOD, R. (1979). 'Report of a cross-moderation study in physics at Advanced level: 1977', University of London School Examinations Department.

WASON, P.C. (1970) 'On writing scientific papers', *Physics Bulletin*, 21, pp. 407–8.

WOOD, R. (1974) 'Multiple-completion items: Effects of a restricted response structure on success rates', University of London School Examinations Department, unpublished.

WOOD, R. (1976a) 'Barking up the wrong tree? What examiners say about those they examine', *Times Educational Supplement*, 18 June.

WOOD, R. (1976b) 'Sex differences in mathematics attainment at GCE ordinary level', *Educational Studies*, 2, pp. 141–60.

WOOD, R. (1978) 'Sex differences in answers to English language comprehension items', *Educational Studies*, 4, pp. 157–65.

WOOD, R. and BROWN, M. (1976) 'Mastery of simple probability ideas among GCE Ordinary level mathematics candidates', *International Journal of Mathematical Education in Science and Technology*, 7, pp. 297–306.

WOOD, R. and FERGUSON, C.M. (1974) 'Unproved case for co-education', *Times Educational Supplement*, 4 October.

WOOD, R. and FERGUSON, C.M. (1976) ' "A" level results in the ILEA', *Times Educational Supplement*, 1 October.

WRIGHT, P. (1975) 'Presenting people with choices: The effect of format on the comprehension of examination rubrics', *Progress in Learning and Educational Technology*, 12, pp. 109–14.

Paper 4: Your Chemistry equals my French*

In his excellent article last week Leslie Cohen rightly remarked that complex issues are raised by any discussion of exam standards. These arise because there is a permanent tension between achieving comparability or uniformity of grading standards and providing diversity of choice in curricula and examinations. Boards cannot be expected to be different yet the same and the more they differ the less chance there is that they will award comparable grades.

Admittedly the choice is sometimes more apparent than real. GCE boards have their preserves and centres have their allegiances which may owe little to their teachers' tastes. Some would also say that the boards tend to imitate rather than innovate and the gradual introduction of common papers certainly indicates some growing together. All the same, different outlooks and practices persist and are generally welcomed.

I think 'A' level biology is fairly typical in this respect. *A Survey of Biology Syllabuses and Examinations at Advanced Level* issued by the Biological Education Committee of the Royal Society in 1974 drew attention to the remarkable diversity available in the approach to modern biology in schools and the remarkable variety of examining methods between the different boards.

In 1973 the survey notes that one board set three theory papers lasting eight hours. They consisted of in paper one thirty compulsory short answer questions, in paper two six compulsory structured questions and in paper three a choice of three from five traditional essay questions. By contrast another board set two theory papers, both like the paper three of the other board, but lasting only five hours in total, the other three hours being allotted to a practical exam, not set at all by the first board.

Being regionally based so that schools must take their local board, CSE boards rely on Mode 3 to generate diversity of choice. With 11,837 schemes examined by CSE boards in 1974 — 2143 in one board alone — comparability could hardly be more difficult. An example taken from the recent published Schools Council Mode 3 survey (Examinations Bulletin 34) gives an indication of the magnitude of the problem.

Reprinted from *Times Educational Supplement*, 30 July 1976.

On pages 47 and 48 two history assessment schemes are discussed. School eight teaches a world history syllabus. There are two written papers, each worth 50 marks, plus a project and an essay on the project, also worth 50 marks. The candidate's two best marks are used to form the aggregate mark. School nine uses a Mode 1 British history since 1700 syllabus, but as it prefers to use assessment techniques which avoid 'sudden death' judgments, awards marks as follows — intermittent tests plus one two-hour test plus four essays, 20 per cent; project, 20 per cent; a biography, 5 per cent; a survey of reference history, 5 per cent; report of field work visits, 20 per cent; course work, 20 per cent; oral, 10 per cent.

History is in any case a notorious subject for producing comparability difficulties, but when the assessment schemes are as different as this it is hard to know where to start. Yet boards are obliged to swear that the grades awarded are comparable even though the material evidence suggests otherwise. Perhaps, like Lewis Carroll's Bellman, some believe that if they say it three times it must be true.

The premise behind any claim concerning comparability is that with proper preparation individuals of ability X, 'ability' conceived in some Platonic sense, can attempt different types of exam and obtain the same grades. This may or may not be a useful model.

What is undeniable is that it requires different talents to achieve the same grade in exams as disparate as those just described. Those talents might be highly correlated within individuals, in which case comparability starts to mean something, but we do not know this and are unlikely to be able to find out. Consequently claims concerning comparability can never be verified satisfactorily.

These last observations apply equally well to the issue of comparability of standards across the years and, even more forcibly, to comparability of standards across subjects. In 1968, the base year for the calculations made by Alan Willmott in his unpublished survey, the London 'O' level chemistry exam consisted of one three-hour written paper with question choice and the description of the syllabus in the regulations covered two pages. In 1976, and 1973 for that matter, the same exam (from a certification point of view) consisted of a multiple-choice paper lasting one-and-a-quarter hours and a two-hour paper comprising, in one section, six compulsory structured questions and in the other four essay questions from which candidates had to answer two. The syllabus now occupies twelve pages in the regulations, including a book-list where there was none before.

It seems to me quite likely that in 1968, with the dependence on one examining technique only, the exam failed to assess adequately what many candidates had learned, whereas now, with the inclusion of more techniques, there is more opportunity for candidates to reveal what they know. Alternatively one could argue that both exams were appropriate to their syllabuses but that the versions of chemistry learned and examined were not the same. Either way, comparability of grades between the two years means little.

41

With such vexatious problems surrounding comparability in the same subject, even within the same board, one might be forgiven for raising one's eyebrows at the suggestion that standards in different subjects ought also to be comparable. Just the thought of French and chemistry examiners sitting at the same table to discuss standards is enough to dispose of this lunatic idea.

The only way standards might be equated is through some external statistical intervention except that there is no statistical adjustment which can equate simultaneously correlations between subjects for all boards so that grade comparisons can be put on the same footing. In any case, I cannot see examiners, candidates or the public tolerating fudging of grades to make them conform to a statistical model dreamed up by researchers from the National Foundation for Educational Research.

A candidate who studied especially hard for a subject and did well in the exam only to have his grade pegged back because the subject is considered 'easy' would rightly feel aggrieved. The idea is about as feasible as making sure that everyone gets up at the same time every morning.

It is the syllabus and exam which must be looked at to see whether , given realistic estimates of teaching competence and time available for the subject, too much is being asked. Altering the statistics and not the subject leads nowhere.

If I seem to be advocating a laissez-faire attitude towards the fixing and maintenance of standards this is not so, but like Leslie Cohen I believe there is a limit to what can be done. In recent years the exam boards have decided that cross-moderation exercises in which examiners in a particular subject gather together to discuss their syllabuses and exams and to scrutinize scripts from each others' candidates are likely to be as productive as the external statistical methods used by the NFER, if only because they bring together those who made the grading decisions.

The fundamental difficulty of comparing performances on different mixtures of papers attracting varying weights remains. In a recent 'O' level English language exercise the percentage weights attached to comprehension and composition respectively by the four participating boards were 36:64, 50:50, 50:50 and 75:25 — but at least the reasons for adopting such different weights can be aired. There is no right way of examining a subject let alone defining it. If examiners are willing to re-examine their own beliefs and to tolerate criticism of their marking and grading practices, cross-moderation exercises will have served their purposes.

Over the next five years, the GCE boards will be carrying out a programme of cross-moderation exercises in the major subjects, at 'O' and 'A' levels. During that time we are promised more reports from the examinations and tests research unit of the NFER, who for ten years now, under the sponsorship of the Schools Council, have been trying to pin down comparability using statistical techniques of analysis.

Leslie Cohen has made many of the important points about Willmott's report, especially about the muddle over sex differences. He did not, however, draw attention to the 'results at all costs' mentality which pervades the report. Seldom have I seen an analysis driven through in such flagrant disregard of what the data are saying.

Dr. Willmott believes that it is better to produce results which may give rise to useful discussions of the assumptions, methodology and indeed the results themselves, than to consider that the problem is too diffuse for study. But you can have discussions about methodology without publishing results. As Dr. Willmott knows, we have talked about comparability methodology for years without apparently influencing his thinking. Besides, results are either reliable, in which case there is no need to apologize for them, or they are not, in which case they should be played down.

You cannot do as Willmott has done and toss in results on a take-it-or-leave-it basis, much less over-interpret them. It is as if the Wright brothers had said 'Our aeroplane doesn't fly yet but here is a pair of wings which you can use until it does'.

Comparability is a complicated business and no interests are served by trying to make it less so. It could well be that to accommodate board-subject peculiarities a statistical model would have to contain so many parameters that all the advantages of parsimony and tractability in the analysis would be lost. For ten years the NFER has been using what amounts to the same methodology and assumptions. It is in a statistical cul-de-sac and shows no sign of getting out.

Looking ahead to the 16+ whatever the final examining arrangements turn out to be, comparability problems are not going to go away. With the multiplying of assessment techniques and the establishment of the new systems orthodoxy, which presents its own technical difficulties, they may get worse. (Question: 'How is a system where some candidates (the sheep) are entered for harder papers and the rest (the goats) are put in for easier papers any different from GCE and CSE?')

Middle courses do not necessarily work, but if one is to be steered an obvious move would be to reduce the number of boards and to place restrictions on the number of Mode 3 schemes. At the same time, for the sake of maintaining some choice, all centres and teachers should be allowed to shop around.

A complement of, say, five boards ought to be enough to satisfy the examining needs of this country at 16 and 18+. With this number it would be easier to organize regular meetings of examiners in the large entry subjects and to coordinate standards. Users of certificates could benefit, too, in that they would be able to form a clearer idea of what each board is offering and so be in a better position to interpret grades, of which there would be fewer varieties.

Comparability is a problem to the extent that there are different views concerning what should be taught and how it should be examined. The biology and English language examples mentioned earlier are proof of that. No doubt the Department of Education and Science could appoint committees to lay down approved methods, after which it could introduce a centrally dictated curriculum, French-style, and a national examining board. Comparability of standards (at least within subjects) would then be guaranteed, or as near as it can be. This is a scenario which has strong appeal these days and those who resist it are going to be under pressure to justify why choice of curricula and examinations is important.

Letter Written by Robert Wood and Published in *The Times Educational Supplement*, 20 May 1977

Having had my say last summer about Alan Willmott's methods and comparability problems in general (Your Chemistry equals my French, *TES*, 30 July 1976) I was content to let matters rest but I see that the public is still being left with the notion that GCE grading standards fell between 1968 and 1973 (with the implication that they have fallen farther since). I refer to your headline (April 29, 1977), 'Dr. Willmott says it again: "O" level standards dropped'.

Let us be clear. Here is a report which contains two pages of caveats (110–112), any one of which, if true, would invalidate the results obtained. We are told that the sampling was suspect ('*Undoubtedly the major shadow* which is cast over the interpretation of the results must be the fact that although it is known that schools differ markedly among themselves, they were used as the sampling unit'), that Test 100 was far from ideal, that the statistical model was not quite suitable for the data (in fact the model did not fit the data), and that GCE standards were studied only incidentally (see page 12).

In spite of all this, Willmott wants us to believe that a difference of but one-third of a grade (a figure which, I repeat, was calculated only by ignoring aspects of the data which were inconvenient for the model) should be taken seriously. There may be arguments about the interpretation of the differences found. Did the boards fall down? Did teaching improve? But the differences themselves are sound.

Well, I do not think the results are sound at all — we have no idea what the 'true' difference was, if any, and we never will have. No amount of huffing and puffing can conceal the fact that with as many reservations as this, none of the figures which have been produced can be trusted.

Willmott's method is best appreciated on page 112 where he admits that the right way of sampling was too difficult to bring off so he had to do the next best thing. Like the boatman who says, 'I cannot take you across the river but I can row you two-thirds of the way', it does not seem to occur to him that the result of doing 'the next best thing' is not necessarily worth anything.

Instead, he indulges in rhetoric about his work being essentially investigative, about the need to discuss problems openly, etc, etc, but as I said in my article you do not need to publish suspect results (much less over-interpret them) in order to discuss methodology, just as you do not need to row two-thirds of the way to find out that that is as far as you can go.

IV Multiple Choice Tests

Comments

I have included as paper 5, the Introduction and Chapter 1 from the monograph I wrote at Bruce Choppin's instigation. Just two months before his tragic death in Chile in July 1983, Bruce had agreed to work with me on the revision of the monograph.

The material here seems to me the freshest. It features strongly what I have been at pains to say about multiple choice; that it is a technique which does a particular job and no more; that it should not be judged against criteria which would not be applied to other techniques; and that the job it does — making students read and think (hopefully) but *not* write — is worth doing.

I have always thought that there was too much fuss about guessing, which is why I have included the other paper and some correspondence which goes with it. It has been a pleasure to make the acquaintance again of those charming Dickensian correspondents, Miss Siggers and Mrs. Sneezum.

Recent papers I have seen on multiple choice by British workers do not seem to me to have advanced the arguments very far; Akeroyd (1982) has most substance. American papers take multiple choice so much for granted that we can't expect any root-and-branch reappraisal from there. However, I did think there was something in Gulliksen's idea (see Wainer, 1983) of defeating guessing by supplying, at the beginning of the test, all the options for the subsequent items.

Akeroyd wants to argue that there is widespread dissatisfaction with assessment procedures and that some of it arises from the absence of any systematic body of explanatory theory underpinning the choice of particular assessment methods. Decisions concerning testing procedure derive mainly from experience rather than being based on research into carefully worked out theories of assessment practice.

I would not dissent in the main from those sentiments, although I believe that the cupboard is not entirely bare. The case for multiple choice I mentioned earlier — read, think but not write — is, I think, a valid precept. Granted, it does not tell you how much multiple choice to have. I think, also, that in the final paper in this collection, Power and I manage to derive reasons why multiple choice would not be suitable for measuring competence as we conceptualize it.

One outstanding problem which we could certainly move to resolve — it is the multiple choice scoring problem writ large — is how to combine marks or scores according to some defensible principle of reward. Here is a problem which has hardly been noticed. I touched on it in Wood and Wilson (1980). Briefly, the simple linear combination of marks ($\Sigma \alpha^m$ where $m = 1$) rests on the principle of compensation or, as it is commonly called, roundabouts and swings. And it is the only objective which is necessarily achieved by combination. Compensation is not the only principle which might be observed. The marks need not be added at all and could be left as a profile. That would be observing the principle of *differentiation*. Or else marks could be combined so as to reward *steadiness* or else *variability*. In the combination formula steadiness could be rewarded by setting $m < 1$, and variability by setting $m > 1$.

Thus there are choices available when combining marks. The 'best' formula cannot be discovered empirically; rather it is a matter of deciding on a principle of reward and acting accordingly.

To return to Akeroyd, rather than take on the theory building task, for which I do not blame him, he confines himself to the guessing problem. What he has to say impacts directly on to my paper. Possibly the most efficient scoring system to date, he argues, is what he calls the Dual Response system (which only he seems to have trialled). Scoring is as follows:

1 mark for indicating the correct answer
$\frac{1}{2}$ mark for indicating TWO answers, ONE of which is CORRECT
$\frac{1}{4}$ mark for an omission
0 marks for an incorrect answer OR combination of answers
For 5 choice items the omission award becomes $\frac{1}{5}$

Various advantages for this system are adduced and readers can work these out for themselves. Perhaps the most significant is that if he can eliminate two distractors the student has 100 per cent chance of $\frac{1}{2}$ mark not 50 per cent chance of 1 mark. I accept that the method I investigated (Bonus Award) does not correct for the informed guess which can cause fluctuations of student scores.

It would be good to see Akeroyd's system given a good trial. He maintains that when systematic research has indicated the 'best' system for correcting for guesses which have a probability of success in the 20–50 per cent range we can then start investigation of systems which allow for a 'best guess' and a 'fallback' second choice. Such systems, he argues, are currently too complicated for the present generation of examinees. Perhaps. What is the best scoring system if tests are computerized? 'Answer-until-correct' appeals immediately but we know little about its properties. It does not obviously solve the problem of how to correct for the informed guess. We need to know what it means at the margin to use one scoring system over another. I used to argue that by the time you had applied a percentage weighting of, say, 30 per cent to a multiple choice score, any differences attributable to choice of scoring system would be negligible. Up the weighting to 50 per cent, and it could matter to some candidates. This is the sort of information we do not have at our fingertips. Neither does the Orang-outang, but then we don't have the problem of combining his multiple choice and essay scores. Perhaps we ought to concentrate on making it more difficult for him to win a bit of banana, by using Gulliksen's idea, or, generally striving to reduce the probabilities of guessing, informed or otherwise.

References

AKEROYD, F.M. (1982) 'Progress in multiple choice scoring methods, 1977/81', *Journal of Further and Higher Education*, 6, pp. 87–90.

WAINER, H. (1983) 'Are we correcting for guessing in the wrong direction?', in WEISS, D.J. (Ed.) *New Horizons in Testing: Latent Trait Test Theory and Computerized Adaptive Testing*, New York, Academic Press.

WOOD, R. and WILSON, D.T. (1980). 'Determining a rank order when not all individuals are assessed on the same basis'. in Th. van der KAMP, L.J., LANGERAK, W.F. and de GRUITJER, D.N.M. (Eds.) *Psychometrics for Educational Debates*, London, John Wiley & Sons Ltd.

Paper 5: Introduction and Chapter 1 of 'Multiple Choice: A State of the Art Report'*

Introduction

Potential readers of this book will want to know where it stands relative to predecessors like Vernon (1964), Brown (1966) and Macintosh and Morrison (1969). The answer is that it is meant to be a successor to Vernon's monograph which, first class though it still is, was thought to be in need of updating and expanding. It is therefore not a practical handbook like the other two books. Although I often give my opinion on what is good practice, the book concentrates on marshalling and evaluating the literature on multiple choice testing, the aim being to clarify what is known about this testing technique: in short, what is intended is a state of the art report.

Multiple choice is but one of a number of testing techniques. Anyone who wonders why it seems to dwarf the others in the attention it receives and the controversy it arouses might choose among the following reasons:

1 The technique originated in the USA and attracts irrational hostility on that account.
2 Choosing one out of a number of alternative answers is thought by some to be a trivial mental exercise.
3 The answer deemed to be correct can be obtained by blind guessing.
4 The format raises a number of methodological problems, real and imagined — setting, scoring, etc.
5 The data multiple choice tests produce lend themselves to elaborate statistical analysis and to the shaping of theories about response behaviour. Without multiple choice, modern test theory would not have come into existence (which would have been a blessing some might think).
6 Because of a widespread belief that multiple choice tests are easily

*Reprinted from *Evaluation in Education: International Progress* (1977), 1, 3, pp. 193–280.

prepared for, there has come into being what amounts to an industry consisting of writers turning out books of multiple choice items usually directed at specific examinations. Often the content of these collections is shoddy and untested but their continual publication and reviewing keeps multiple choice before the public eye and affords hostile critics the opportunity to lambast the technique.

7   The opportunities for research investigations offered by 3, 4 and 5 above have sustained many American academics in their careers and their offerings have filled and continue to fill the pages of several journals, notably *Educational and Psychological Measurement* and the *Journal of Educational Measurement*. The absence of such specialized journals in Britain has meant less of an outpouring, although in recent years most subject-based educational journals, particularly those connected with the sciences, have carried at least one article concerned with 're-inventing the wheel', in apparent ignorance, wilful or otherwise, of developments elsewhere.

It is with multiple choice in the context of educational achievement testing that I am mainly concerned in this book. This concentration stems from my own background and current employment although I also believe that it is with achievement tests that multiple choice finds its most important application. I work for the University of London School Examinations Department which is one of the bodies in England charged with conducting GCE (General Certificate of Education) examinations at Ordinary and Advanced levels. Ordinary or 'O' level is usually taken by students at the age of 16 and Advanced or 'A' level at age 18. I hope this explanation will enable readers to understand the odd references in the text to GCE or to 'O' and 'A' level or to the London GCE Board. In the one place where CSE is mentioned this refers to the Certificate of Secondary Education taken by less able students, also around the age of 16. (From 1986 the two examinations are to be merged into the GCSE.)

When referencing I have not attempted to be exhaustive although neither have I been too selective. I hope I have mentioned most work of the last ten years; older work can be traced through the references I have cited. Where I think there is a good bibliography on a topic I have said so.

The weighing up of research evidence is a difficult business and I do not pretend to have any easy solutions. The fact that numerous studies have used American college students, often those studying psychology — 'Are they people?' someone once asked — throws doubt on some of the literature but I take the view that it is possible to perceive tendencies, to see where something definitely did not work and to judge where promise lies. Often the accounts of experiments are less interesting than the speculative writing of the investigators. Sometimes there are no experiments at all but just polemical writing, nearly always hostile to multiple choice. It is with these polemics that I start.

Polemics

> The Orang-outang score is that score on a standardized reading test that can be obtained by a well-trained Orang-outang under these special conditions. A slightly hungry Orang-outang is placed in a small cage that has an oblong window and four buttons. The Orang-outang has been trained that every time the reading teacher places a neatly typed multiple choice item from a reading test in the oblong window, all that he (the Orang-outang) has to do to get a bit of banana is to press a button, any of the buttons, which, incidentally, are labelled A, B, C and D. (Fry, 1971)

Although the quotation above is acid enough, no one has savaged the multiple choice test quite like Banesh Hoffman and Jacques Barzun. Both are American academics, both regard multiple choice as the enemy of intellectual standards and creative expression. In their different ways they have made out a case against multiple choice which must be taken seriously even if Hoffman's diatribes have a superior, fanatical tone which soon grates.

In his various onslaughts, Hoffman (1962, 1967(a) and 1967(b)) has insisted that multiple choice 'favours the picker of choices rather than the doer', and that students he variously calls 'gifted', 'profound', 'deep', 'subtle' and 'first rate' are liable to see more in a question than the questioner intended, a habit which, he claims, does not work to their advantage.

In favouring the 'doer', Hoffman is expressing a preference which he is entitled to do but he produces no evidence for supposing there are distinct breeds of 'pickers' and 'doers', just as he is unable to demonstrate that 'picking' is necessarily either a passive or a trivial activity. To choose an answer to a question is to take a decision, even if it is a small one. In any case, this is not the point; as I shall argue presently, why should not students 'pick' and 'do'? The fact is that much of the distaste for multiple choice expressed by American critics like Hoffman and Barzun arises from fears about the effects of using multiple choice tests exclusively in American school testing programmes and the consequent lack of any opportunity for the student to compose his own answers to questions. Reports from the USA, which have linked what is seen as the growing inability of even university students to write competent English with the absence of essay tests, would seem to justify such fears although no convincing analysis substantiating the link has yet been offered and other factors in American society, such as the low value placed on writing outside school, may well be implicated. As far as the British situation is concerned, examining boards are agreed that multiple choice should be only one element of an examination, and often a minor element at that; many examinations do not contain a multiple choice element at all or are even likely to. In practice, the highest weight multiple choice will attract is 50 per cent and then only rarely; generally it is in the region of 30–40 per cent.

The case for using multiple choice rests in large part on the belief that there is room for an exercise in which candidates concentrate on giving answers to questions free of the obligation to write up — some would say dress up — their answers in extended form, a point made by Nuttall (1974, p. 35) and by Pearce (1974, p. 52). Instead of asking candidates to do a little reading and a lot of writing with (hopefully) some thinking interspersed — what, I suppose, Hoffman would call 'doing' — they are asked to read and think or listen and think before 'picking'. I see nothing wrong in this. By and large there has been an over-emphasis on writing skills in our examinations — unlike the USA — and the different approach to assessment represented by multiple choice serves as a corrective. I would accept that a concentration on reading and thinking is to some extent arbitrary in terms of priorities. After all, a strong case could be made out on behalf of oral skills yet how little these feature in external examinations, leaving aside language subjects. That they have been so neglected is, of course, directly indicative of the over-emphasis that has been placed on written work, which in turn can be traced to the conservatism of examiners and teachers and to the difficulties of organizing oral assessments.

If the quality of written work produced by the average candidate in the examination room was better than it is, one might be more impressed by the arguments of those who insist on written answers or 'doing' in all circumstances. But, as anybody knows, examination writing is far from being the highest form of the art; how could it be when nervous individuals have to write against the clock without a real opportunity to draft and work over their ideas, a practice intrinsic to writing? As Wason (1970) has observed, one learns what one wants to write as one goes along. Small wonder, then, that the typical examination answer is an unsightly mess of half-baked ideas flung down on the paper in the hope that some, at least, will induce a reward from the examiner.

No doubt the fault lies in the kind of examination that is set or in setting examinations at all. Certainly examinations have been roundly condemned for stultifying writing in the schools by placing too much emphasis on one kind of writing only, namely the impersonal and transactional, at the expense of the personal and expressive (Britton *et al.*, 1975). Yet it sometimes seems that whatever attempts are made to liberalize examinations, the response in the schools is inexorably towards training pupils in the new ways so that these soon become as routinized as the bad old ways. Elsewhere (Wood, 1976) I have written of the deadlock which exists between examiners, teachers and students and the solution is not at all clear. At least with multiple choice all parties understand what is required of them.

That some individuals will rise above the restrictive circumstances of a written paper and demonstrate organization, originality and so forth is not in dispute. What they must be aware of is being thought too clever or of producing answers which are regarded as interesting but irrelevant. The people who frame multiple choice questions are, by and large, the same people who frame and mark essay questions. Most will have graduated from one to the other. If their thinking is 'convergent' it will show in both cases. Vernon (1964, p. 7) may have had this in mind when he remarked that it is by no means certain that conventional examinations are capable of eliciting what are often called the higher qualities. He observed, quite correctly, that the typical examination answer, at least at 15–16 years, tends to be marked more for accuracy and number of facts than for organization, originality etc., not least because this ensures an acceptable level of reliability. This being so, it seems to me that what Hoffman claims is true of teachers of 'gifted' students — 'that such teachers often feel it necessary to warn their intellectually liveliest students not to think too precisely or deeply when taking mechanized tests.' (Hoffman, 1967(a), p. 383) — might equally well be applied to essay tests. If this reads like a 'plague on both your houses', that is not my intention. The point is that multiple choice is not alone in having deficiencies — they can be found in all the techniques used in public examinations. As long as it serves a useful assessment function — and I have tried to establish that it does — the weaknesses, which are technical or procedural, can be attended to. In this respect I wish that the essay test had received even half the attention bestowed on multiple choice.

If Hoffman's first charge is seen to be shallow, what of his second — that the gifted, creative, non-conformist mind is apt to see more in multiple choice questions than was intended, the consequence of which is to induce uncertainty, perplexity and ultimately incorrect answers? All the examples Hoffman produces are designed to show that to the 'gifted' the question is not meaningful, or contains more than one answer or else does not contain the answer at all. 'Only exceptional students are apt to see the deeper defects of test items' (Hoffman, 1967(a), p. 383) he remarks at one point, but is not a student exceptional precisely because he can see the deeper effects? What Hoffman, who naturally includes himself among the 'gifted', and other critics forget, is that the items they take apart are meant for average 16 or 18-year-olds who do not possess their superior intellects. In these circumstances it is hardly surprising that hard scrutiny of questions will reveal 'ambiguities', unseen by the average eye. Whether or not 'gifted' persons find these ambiguities in the examination room and how they react to them, having found them, is very much open to question. Too little work has been done on this subject but the best study to date (Alker, Carlson and Hermann, 1969) concluded that 'first-rate' students were not, in general, upset and penalized by multiple choice questions. They found that characteristics of both superficial and deep thinking were associated with doing well on multiple choice questions. There the matter rests until more evidence comes along. A further study along the lines of the one just discussed would be worth doing.

Whenever we refer to 'ambiguities' we must bear in mind that knowledge is always provisional and relative in character; most of us are given, and then settle for, convenient approximations to 'true' knowledge. Writing about science, Ravetz (1971, chapter 6) has remarked on the tendency of teachers, aided and abetted by textbook writers, to rely on standardization of scientific material and for this purpose to introduce successive degrees of banality as the teaching becomes further displaced from contact with research and high class scientific debate. The end product is what he calls *vulgarized* knowledge or what Kuhn (1962), more kindly, calls *normal* science.

Ravetz's analysis is hard to fault but the solution is not easy to see. Driver (1975) is surely right that 'there are not "right answers" in technology', yet when she writes 'instead of accepting the teacher's authority as the ultimate judge, the pupils can be encouraged to develop their own criteria for success; to consider their own value systems and to make judgments on them' one recoils, not because of the radical nature of the sentiment but because the teaching programme implied seems too ambitious for the majority of 15 and 16-year-olds, at any rate. Can you teach children to be sceptical about ideas before they know anything to be sceptical about? Perhaps it can be done but it needs a particular teaching flair to be able to present knowledge with the right degree of uncertainty. In general it seems inevitable that most children will be acquainted only with received knowledge and ideas which contribute to an outdated view of the physical world. Whether they are willing or able to update this view later will depend on training, temperament and opportunity.

The relevance of all this for multiple choice is obvious. For Hoffman and other critics, multiple choice embodies vulgarized knowledge in its most blatant form; it deals, in Barzun's (1959, p. 139) term, with the 'thought-cliché'. Through the items they set, examiners make public their versions of knowledge and through the medium they foster the impression that every problem has a right answer. The sceptical mind is given no opportunity to function — a choice must be made. Worse, the format may reinforce misconceptions. Finally, not only does multiple choice reflect the transmission of standardized knowledge, through so-called 'backwash' effects, it encourages it. That, at any rate, is what the critics say. Myself, I see no point in denying that multiple choice embodies standardized knowledge. If that is what is taught, then all examining techniques will reflect the fact. More than anything else, examinations serve to codify what at any time passes as 'approved' knowledge, ideas and constructions. Those who find the spectacle distasteful attack multiple choice because it is such a convenient target but what could be more standardized than the official answer to a question like 'It is often said that Britain has an unwritten constitution. Discuss.'

One place where the arguments about multiple choice as a representation of objective knowledge have come to a head is over the English Language comprehension exercise set at Ordinary level by the London GCE Board and similar tests set by other examining boards. Basically there is a conflict between those who insist that judgment about meaning is always subjective and who deny that there are any 'correct' interpretations (for example, Honeyford, 1973) and those (for example, Davidson, 1974) who see multiple choice as a formalization of a public discussion about meaning. It seems to me that the resolution of this conflict depends, once again, on who and what is being tested. Were the subject at issue Advanced level English Literature, where one must expect candidates to come forward with different interpretations of texts, I would want to give Honeyford's argument a lot of weight, even if marking raises severe problems. For if, as he maintains, comprehension is an essentially private experience it is logical nonsense to attempt to standardize examiners' opinions. One of the severest critics in print on multiple choice found himself caught in just this dilemma when championing essay tests, 'If you standardize essay tests, they become as superficial as multiple choice; if you do not standardize them, they measure not the abilities of the examinee but function rather as projective tests of the graders' personalities' (La Fave, 1966). Presumbably, the proper approach to marking in these circumstances is to allow different interpretations, providing they can be supported convincingly. This presupposes a broadmindedness on the part of examiners which may not exist, but I see no other solution. With Ordinary level English Language comprehension, on the other hand, the latitude for varying inerpretations of meaning is not so great. The candidates are younger and the material is simpler. Sometimes it appears at first glance debatable whether a word or phrase conveys a meaning best but on close analysis it usually turns out that the examiners have gone for finer distinctions in order to test the understanding of the more competent candidates. In doing so, however, they run the risk of provoking controversy; it is no accident that most of the complaints about multiple choice concern items where the discrimination called for is allegedly too fine or is reckoned to be non-existent. Consider, for instance, the following 'O' level English Language comprehension item set by the London Board in June 1975 which came in for some criticism in the correspondence columns of the *Guardian* and *The Times Educational Supplement*.

The item refers to the following sentence which was part of a longer passage:

> The distinction of London Bridge station on the Chatham side is that it is not a terminus but a junction where lives begin to fade and blossom again as they swap trains in the rush hour and make for all regions of South London and the towns of Kent.

The item was as follows:

> The statement that London Bridge is a place 'where lives begin to fade and blossom again' is best explained by saying that it is a place where people:
>
> A Grow tried of waiting for their trains and feel better when they have caught them.
> B Flag at the end of their day and revive as they travel homeward.
> C Leave behind the loneliness of the city and enjoy the company in a crowded carriage.
> D Escape from the unhealthy atmosphere of London and flourish in the country.
> E Forget about their daily work and look forward to enjoying their leisure.

According to one critic (*Guardian*, 17 June 1975), there are 'rules that pertain to this type of question. One answer must clearly be perceived to be correct and evidence must be forthcoming why this is so'. In his view, the London Board broke that 'rule' with this item, and indeed others in the same paper. The crux of the matter is obviously the word 'clearly' and here is where I part company with the critic. The examiners have set candidates an item which calls for rather closer attention to the text than might generally be the case. But is this so wrong? A test where the right answer jumped out every time would be a very dull test. As it happened, the reason why statement B was considered to be the best answer was explained very nicely by another correspondent to the *Guardian*. This is what she said:

> The candidate does not need to read the examiner's mind, if he reads the question. In the sentence you are not told:
>
> A   Whether the people grow tired of waiting, or whether
> C   The city is lonely, or whether
> D   London is unhealthy, or whether
> E   They will forget their work.
>
> You are told that 'lives begin to fade and blossom again' and statement B best explains this by saying London Bridge is a place where people flag at the end of their day and revive as they travel homeward. (*Guardian*, 24 June 1975)

Backwash

I would like to distinguish two kinds of backwash. The first concerns the effect of an examining technique on the way subject matter is structured, taught and learnt, the second concerns the way candidates prepare and are prepared for the technique in question. In the case of multiple choice this involves developing what the Americans call 'test-wiseness' — the capacity to get the most marks from a test by responding to cues, knowing how to pace oneself and so forth. In the case of essay tests, the comparable behaviour would be knowing how to 'spot' questions, how long to spend on questions and generally knowing how to maximize one's chances.

Providing it is not overdone, the second kind of backwash need not be taken as seriously as the first. After reviewing eighty or so studies, Mellenbergh (1972) observed that 'there seems to be no evidence that study habits are strongly affected by the type of test that students are expecting in examinations'.

Vernon (1964) offers the view that 'so long as the objective questions are reasonably straightforward and brief, we know that the amount of improvement brought about by coaching and practice is limited ... However, it is possible (though there is little direct evidence) that facility in coping with more complex items is more highly coachable and that pupils who receive practice at these may gain an undue advantage'. When we come to look at the more complex item types, readers may feel that Vernon has a point. The sort of coaching which is more likely to go on involves the collections of items I referred to somewhat disparagingly in the Introduction. Teachers may believe that having their students work through these productions is the best way of preparing for the examination, but they may be deluding themselves. Covering the subject matter is one thing, mastering the technique another. These collections of items may leave the candidate short of both objectives.

Reviewing the impact of multiple choice on English Language testing in three African nations, Ghana, Nigeria and Ethiopia, Forrest (1975) maintained that the most regrettable effect everywhere is the amount of time teachers give to working objective questions in class, but added that better trained teachers find that multiple choice gives them scope for better teaching — it is the weaker ones who resort to undesirable methods. Whether the net result of multiple choice coaching activity is any more serious in scale or effect than the preparations which are made for essay and other kinds of tests one simply does not know. There is a greater need for coaching in writing skills if the comments of examiners are anything to go by.

Coming now to the backwash which affects learning, it is sometimes claimed that multiple choice perpetuates false concepts or, what amounts to the same thing, over-simplifies events and relationships through the limitations of the format. 'If you teach history with a view to circulating some idea of the toleration of the other person's point of view, not only does multiple choice not test this but it tends to have the opposite effect, with harmful effects on the proper study of history' was the comment of one teacher in the discussion following Nuttall's (1974) paper. This comment, of course, harks back to the earlier discussion of the relativity of knowledge, and the varying degrees of sophistication with which it can be handled. I can understand this particular teacher feeling sore at having to suffer what he would regard as a regression to 'black and white' judgments, but I wonder if he was triggered off by one or two clumsily phrased items which I am afraid are often the ones the public sees.

Whether or not multiple choice actually *reinforces* wrong answers is a moot question. Taking as his point of departure Skinner's (1961) dictum that 'every wrong answer on a multiple choice test increases the probability that a student will someday dredge out of his memory the wrong answer instead of the right one', Preston (1965) attempted to test the influence of wrong answers (and right answers) upon students' grasp of vocabulary within the same hour. The conditioning effect of wrong selections of items was demonstrated for some words but not for others. Karraker (1967) obtained a more positive result when he found that a group exposed to plausible wrong responses *without being told the correct answers* made more errors on a later test than another group who were told the correct answers. Eklund (1968), having carried out a thorough experimental study of the question, maintained that the use of multiple choice in the earlier stages of the learning process may involve considerable risks of negative effects but that later on these risks seem to become much less marked. This is interesting when we consider the terminal nature of examinations and the fact that they often signal discontinuities in learning. How much candidates remember after examinations is in any case debatable. Miller and Parlett (1974, p. 107) put forward the idea that examinations actually serve to clear the memory rather than reinforce existing knowledge, correct or incorrect. This may sound an odd function of an examination but Miller and Parlett claim that, unless 'rehearsed' or used, detailed recall of factual information drops rapidly after an examination, a claim we might all echo from our experience.

The best way of mitigating forgetting is to give immediate feedback of results. In what is rare unanimity, the sundry studies in this area (Berglund, 1969; Zontine, Richards and Strang, 1972; Beeson, 1973 and references there in; Strang and Rust, 1973; Betz and Weiss, 1976(a) and 1976(b)) all claim that immediate knowledge of results, item by item or at the end of the test, enhances learning. Even if it is not feasible in connection with public examinations, in the classroom, where diagnosis and repair are the critical activities, immediate feedback is certainly possible and should always be given.

I have not mentioned what for many people is the real objection to multiple choice — the opportunity it offers for blind guessing. That a candidate can deceive the examiner by obtaining the correct answer when in a state of ignorance cannot be denied — there is no way of stopping it — but as I shall make clear, I do not see this as a grave impediment. Besides, the opportunity for guessing exists with the traditional type of questions, although this is seldom remarked upon. In particular, traditional essays invariably require the candidate to guess which parts of his knowledge are going to appeal to the examiner (Cross, 1972).

As in other instances, multiple choice tests are vulnerable to the guessing charge because statistical evidence can be adduced, whereas for essay papers it is so much harder to come by.

Critics of multiple choice testing are inclined to apply double standards. Not only do they expect multiple choice to be something it is not, but they subject it to tougher criteria than they apply to other techniques. Dudley (1973), for instance, in the medical context, criticizes multiple choice on the grounds that it fails to test adequately all aspects of an individual's knowledge. This is about as fair as complaining about a stethoscope because it cannot be used to examine eyes and ears. I do not say that multiple choice is above reproach; what I do say is that it must be viewed in context, and fairly. American critics are entitled to be worried about what they see as the adverse effects of multiple choice in the USA, but when criticism turns into crude caricature and obsessive vilification we should know when to part company.

Summary

1   Just as the multiple choice test originated in the USA, so most of the strongest criticism has come from there, particularly from Banesh Hoffman and Jacques Barzun. One reason for this is the exclusive use of multiple choice in school and college testing programmes which deprives students of the opportunity to express themselves in writing.

2   The British situation is quite different. If anything, too much emphasis has been given to writing. Multiple choice seldom attracts as much as 50 per cent weighting in external school examinations; generally the figure is in the region of 30 to 40 per cent.

3   Multiple choice serves a distinct assessment function. It makes the candidate concentrate on thinking about problems without requiring the extended writing which can often be irrelevant and worthless, given the time-trial conditions of examinations. Yet critics want it to be something it is not, complaining that it cannot measure things like 'toleration of the other man's point of view', when no one ever claimed that it could. Multiple choice has faults but so do other techniques. One point in its favour is that it leaves the candidate in no doubt about what he has to do, unlike the essay test where he has to guess what the examiner expects from him.

4   Multiple choice is criticized for encouraging students to think of knowledge as cut and dried and for penalizing clever students who see ambiguities their duller colleagues do not. It should be remembered, however, that knowledge is always provisional and that what is a sophisticated viewpoint to one group is simple-minded to a more mature group. Examinations codify what is accepted as 'approved' knowledge at any given time. Because examiners reveal themselves more openly through multiple choice, it provides a convenient target for critics who resist the idea that knowledge is packaged in standardized form.

5   Concerning the 'backwash' effects of multiple choice, few 'hard' data are available. We simply do not know if multiple choice helps to perpetuate false concepts and misinformation and leads to more superficial learning than would have occurred otherwise. Nor do we know how much coaching of multiple choice answering techniques goes on nor what payoff accrues. Information on these matters is not necessarily required but those who pontificate on the baleful effects of multiple choice ought to realize how little is known.

References

ALKER, H.A., CARLSON, J.A. and HERMANN, M.G. (1969), 'Multiple-choice questions and students characteristics', *Jour. Educ. Psychol*, 60, pp. 231–43.

BARZUN, J. (1959), *The House of Intellect*, New York, Harper and Row.

BEESON, R.O. (1973), 'Immediate knowledge of results and test performance', *Jour. Educ. Res.* 66, pp. 224–6.

BERGLUND, G.W. (1969), 'Effect of knowledge of results on retention', *Psychol. Sch.* 6, pp. 420–1.

BETZ, N.E. and WEISS, D.J. (1976(a)), 'Effects of immediate knowledge of results and adaptive testing on ability test performance', *Research Report, 76–3*, University of Minnesota, Psychometric Methods Program.

BETZ, N.E. and WEISS, D.J. (1976(b)), 'Psychological effects of immediate knowledge of results and adaptive ability testing, *Research Report 76–4*, University of Minnesota, Psychometric Methods Program.

BRITTON, J., BURGESS, T., MARTIN, N., MCLEOD, A. and ROSEN, H. (1975) *The Development of Writing Abilities (11–18)*, Schools Council Research Studies, London, Macmillan Education.

BROWN, J. (1966), *Objective Tests; Their Construction and Analysis: A Practical Handbook for Teachers*, London, Longman.

CROSS, M. (1972), 'The use of objective tests in government examinations', *Vocational Aspect.* 24, pp. 133–9.

DAVIDSON, K. (1974), 'Objective text', *The Use of English*, 26, pp. 12–18.

DRIVER, R. (1975), 'The name of the game', *Sch. Sci. Rev.* 56, pp. 800–5.

DUDLEY, H.A.F. (1973), 'Multiple-choice tests', *Lancet.* 2, p. 195.

EKLUND, H. (1968), *Multiple Choice and Retention* Uppsala, Almqvist and Wiksells.

FORREST, R. (1975), 'Objective examinations and the teaching of English', *Eng. Lang. Teach. Jour*, 29, pp. 240–6.

FRY, E. (1971), 'The orang-outang score', *Read.Teach.* 24, pp. 360–2.

HOFFMAN, B. (1962), *The Tyranny of Testing*, New York, Crowell-Collier.

HOFFMAN, B. (1967(a)), 'Psychometric scientism', *Phi Delta Kappa.* 48, pp. 381–6.

HOFFMAN, B. (1967(b)), 'Multiple-choice tests', *Physics Educ.* 2, pp. 247–51.

HONEYFORD, R. (1973), 'Against objective testing', *The Use of English.* 25, pp. 17–26.

KARRAKER, R.J. (1967), 'Knowledge of results and incorrect recall of plausible multiple-choice alternatives', *Jour. Educ. Psychol.* 58, pp. 11–14.

KUHN, T.S. (1962), *The Structure of Scientific Revolutions*, Chicago, University of Chicago Press.

LA FAVE, L. (1966), 'Essay versus multiple-choice: Which test is preferable?', *Psychol. Sch.* 3, pp. 65–9.

MACINTOSH, H.G. and MORRISON, R.B. (1969), *Objective Testing*, London, University of London Press.

MELLENBERGH, G.J. (1972), 'A comparison between different kinds of achievement test items'. *Nederlands Tijdschrift voor de Psychologie en haar Grensgebieden.* 27, pp. 157–8.

MILLER, C.M.L. and PARLETT, M. (1974), *Up to the Mark: A Study of the Examination Game*, London, Society for Research into Higher Education.

NUTTALL, D.L. (1974), 'Multiple-choice objective tests — A reappraisal', in *Conference Report 11*, London, University of London University Entrance and School Examinations Council.

PEARCE, J. (1974), 'Examinations in English Language', in *Language, Classroom and Examinations*. Schools Council Programme in Linguistics and English Teaching Papers Series II, Vol. 4, Longman.

PRESTON, R.C. (1965), 'Multiple-choice test as an instrument in perpetuating false concepts', *Educ. Psychol. Measmt*, 25, pp. 111–6.

RAVETZ, J.R. (1971), *Scientific Knowledge and its Social Problems*, Oxford, Oxford University Press.

SKINNER, B.F. (1961), 'Teaching machines', *Scientific American*, pp. 90–102.

STRANG, H.R. and RUST, J.O. (1973), 'The effects of immediate knowledge of results and task definition on multiple-choice answering', *Jour. Exper. Educ.* 42, pp. 77–80.

VERNON, P.E. (1964), *The Certificate of Secondary Education: An Introduction to Objective-type Examinations*, Examinations Bulletin 4, London, Secondary Schools Examinations Council.

WASON, P.C. (1970), 'On writing scientific papers', *Physics Bulletin.* 21, pp. 407–8.

WOOD, R. (1976), 'Barking up the wrong tree? What examiners say about those they examine', *Times Educational Supplement*, 18 June.

ZONTINE, P.L. RICHARDS, H.C. and STRANG, H.R. (1972), 'Effect of contingent reinforcement on Peabody Picture Vocabulary test performance', *Psychol. Reports*, 31, pp. 615–22.

Paper 6: Inhibiting Blind Guessing: The Effect of Instructions*

Introduction

The idea of curbing blind guessing on multiple-choice items by the post hoc imposition of a penalty based on a proportion of incorrect answers has been in vogue for many years. Hamilton (1950) dates it back at least to 1920. He also points out its dubious theoretical footing. Another correction of similar vintage, although less often used, seeks to inhibit guessing by encouraging candidates to omit items about which they are totally at a loss. Recently, this approach has received fresh study (Traub and Hamilton, 1972; Waters and Waters, 1971). By awarding a score of 1/m for each item omitted, where m is the number of choices contained in the item, candidates are credited with the score they would presumably have obtained had they guessed blindly at the items they omitted. The operative word here is 'presumably'. Lord (1975) has queried whether the instructions are always adequate and cites research by various workers, notably Slakter (1968), which concluded that examinees tended to omit items on which they could actually do better than chance. He also quotes studies by Mead and Smith (1957) and by Ebel (1968) which reported that when examinees felt completely uncertain of an answer, their forced responses to items they had omitted were little better than random. However, Lord noted that these studies used true-false items only and recommended that they should be repeated with multiple-choice items, stressing the importance of phrasing the instructions so as to bring about the desired effect among candidates. The study reported here falls into this category.

Test Materials, Student Samples and Test Administration

Two mathematics achievement tests, designed for 17 and 18-year-old students, were used in this investigation. One is referred to as mathematics and the

---

*Reprinted from *Journal of Educational Measurement*, (1976) 13, pp. 297–307.

other, being more advanced, as further mathematics. Both tests consisted of forty-five five-choice items. Half were standard multiple-choice items while the rest was made up of varying item types, such as the one below. The time allowance was one-and-a-half hours.

Directions. Each of the following questions consists of two statements (in some cases following very brief preliminary information). You are required to determine the relationship between these statements and to choose

A   if 1 always implies 2 but 2 does not imply 1
B   if 2 always implies 1 but 1 does not imply 2
C   if 1 always implies 2 and 2 always implies 1
D   if 1 always denies 2 and 2 always denies 1

E   if none of the above relationships holds

1   The curve $y = f(x)$ has a point of inflexion at $x = a$
2   $f''(a) = 0$

From among those students about to take examinations in the two subjects, samples of 331 and 195 for mathematics and further mathematics, respectively, were drawn. Numbers of further mathematics, being a less popular subject, were bound to be lower.

Three sets of instructions, designated A, B and C were prepared. They are reproduced below.

A   There are 45 questions in this paper and you should try to answer all of them. For each question there are five suggested answers. Read each question carefully. When you have selected what you believe to be the correct answer, mark your choice on the answer sheet.
WORK CAREFULLY AND ATTEMPT AS MANY QUESTIONS AS YOU CAN. YOUR RESULT WILL CONSIST OF THE TOTAL NUMBER OF CORRECT ANSWERS YOU GIVE.
Do any necessary calculations and rough work on the paper provided. It is important that you write the letter 'A' on the top right hand corner of your answer sheet.
B   There are 45 questions in this paper and you should try to answer all of them. For each question there are five suggested answers. Read each question carefully. When you have selected what you believe to be the correct answer, mark your choice on the answer sheet.
IF YOU ARE TEMPTED TO GUESS, YOU SHOULD BEAR IN MIND THAT AN INCORRECT GUESS WILL NOT GAIN YOU

ANY MARKS. WHILE EVERY QUESTION YOU OMIT WILL GAIN YOU ONE FIFTH (1/5) OF A MARK.

Do any necessary calculations and rough work on the paper provided. It is important that you write the letter 'B' on the top right hand corner of your answer sheet.

C   There are 45 questions in this paper and you should try to answer all of them. For each question there are five suggested answers. Read each question carefully. When you have selected what you believe to be the correct answer, mark your choice on the answer sheet.

IF YOU ARE TEMPTED TO GUESS, YOU SHOULD BEAR IN MIND THAT AN INCORRECT GUESS WILL LOSE YOU ONE-QUARTER (1/4) OF A MARK, WHILE EVERY QUESTION YOU OMIT WILL SIMPLY BE SCORED ZERO.

Do any necessary calculations and rough work on the paper provided. It is important that you write the letter 'C' on the top right hand corner of your answer sheet.

Sheets bearing the instructions were inserted into the test booklets and these were distributed in the sequence ABC, ABC, etc. Random allocation might have been better, but this was ruled out on administrative grounds. The numbers answering each form were not quite the same because of attrition and some uneven distribution.

Candidates were asked to study their instructions and to act accordingly. Supervisors were requested to handle this part of the briefing — particularly any questions — as discreetly as possible so as not to draw attention to the existence of different instructions, while at the same time doing all in their power to make sure that the instructions registered with the students. In any event, it is certain that some, perhaps most, candidates realized that different instructions were in operation, but there seems no good reason to suppose that this knowledge spoiled the experiment in any material way.

Results and Interpretations

1   With reference to tables 1 and 2, which show summary statistics, both tests proved hard, especially further mathematics. In fact, this last test was so hard that the effects it produced cannot be accepted as a sound guide to what could happen in an operational examination.

2   A is associated with most rights (and wrongs); C with fewest wrongs. Omits for B and C are, to all intents and purposes, identical.

3   It is evident that the instructions took hold. The harder test brings about more B and C omits, as would be expected. On the face of it, B and C seem to exert much the same effect on students; whether this is true across the board is something to be looked into.

4   It is interesting that the differences in mean rights between A and B are almost explained by the difference in mean omits divided by 5, which is, of course, the amount B-takers would be credited with, on average, after adjustment. This suggests that B has done its job. The same is true of C, although the calculation has less meaning.

Table 1   Mean scores and standard deviations (   ) by type of instruction and quality of response: mathematics.

	A	B	C
Rights	20.21	18.89	20.02
	(7.75)	(6.77)	(6.90)
Wrongs	23.03	19.18	18.09
	(7.99)	(7.13)	(7.18)
Omits	1.76	6.93	6.89
	(3.65)	(6.01)	(6.94)
N	109	110	112

Table 2   Means scores and standard deviations (   ) by type of instruction and quality of response: further mathematics.

	A	B	C
Rights	16.80	13.68	14.40
	(5.81)	(5.86)	(7.21)
Wrongs	26.61	20.75	20.38
	(6.86)	(7.07)	(8.02)
Omits	1.59	10.57	10.22
	(3.33)	(7.40)	(7.22)
N	63	71	61

To compare the effects of B and C with A we need to look more closely at the data. The question we should really like to answer is whether these instructions work uniformly across the score range. It may be, for instance, that C (the penalty) has an inhibiting effect on the better candidates or it may be that B encourages the same group to adopt a 'lazy' strategy, to their detriment.

Figures 1 and 2 are barycentric plots[1] of the rights, wrongs and omits for B (x's) and C (o's) responses. Each point represents a particular right-wrong-omit combination. The three vertices represent all items right, all items wrong and all items omitted, and are labelled as such. All the points sitting on the base line represent respondents who omitted nothing. The uppermost point in figure 1 (11-8-26) stands for the respondent with the most omits. Contrast this with the rightmost point on the baseline (10-35-0) which signifies slightly fewer rights, many more wrongs, but no omits. The two points in the lower left-hand corner signify the same number of rights (40), the difference being that the baseline point represents 5 wrongs and 0 omits and the other 3 wrongs and 2 omits. Note that in figure 1 every other observation has been plotted so as to avoid congestion, and that in both the figures the A response profiles have not been plotted at all because the low omit rate would have compressed the points at the base of the triangle and the picture would have been confused.

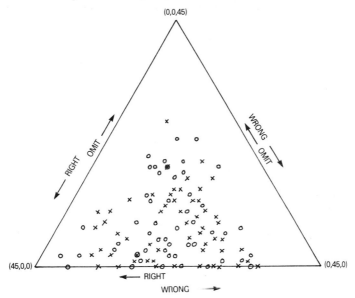

Figure 1   Mathematics data: rights, wrongs and omits (R, W, O) for groups B and C

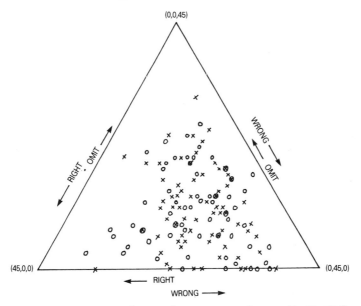

Figure 2   Further Mathematics data: rights, wrongs and omits (R, W, O) for groups B and C

It should now be possible to see that in figure 1 (mathematics) the low scoring C students tended to omit more than their B counterparts while the high scoring C students did less omitting than did their B counterparts. This suggests that the best C students were not put off by the punitive instructions and 'had a go', with some success, whereas most of the best B students ducked the challenge and took the credit for omits. At the other end of the ability range, the B and C instructions had much the same effect.

For further mathematics the picture is much the same, perhaps a little exaggerated. Notice that the shapes of the two plots are different, reflecting the difference in difficulty of the tests. Among high scorers the C members are conspicuous and the better B students show even more propensity to omit. Otherwise, there is nothing much to choose between the two groups in terms of omitting behaviour.

Evidence concerning response behaviour was obtained from a questionnaire administered immediately after the tests were worked. One of the questions was intended to elicit incidence of guessing.

About how many times did you make a sheer guess at an answer?
Not more than 5 times
Up to 10 times
More than 10 times.

A measure like this is open to criticism but it does provide a guide to *relative* frequencies of blind guessing. It is reassuring to see from tables 3 and 4 that the numbers falling into each guessing category for the three groups are in line with what would be expected. Other points to note from tables 3 and 4 are:

1   Not surprisingly, reported guessing is more extensive in the A group than in the others. The difference is much more striking in Table 4 reflecting the greater difficulty of the further mathematics test.

2   Reported guessing frequencies for B and C are almost identical across the three categories.

3   Looking at table 3, only in the group reporting least guessing — which also obtains the highest scores — are there noticeable differences in number right. The differences of average omits between A and B and between A and C — five or so points — are compatible with reported guessing frequencies, but do not explain — as they did before — the discrepancies in number right when the notional addition of $\frac{1}{3}$th × number of omits is made. That is to say, the A group has gained more from answering the extra items than would have been predicted on a random guessing model.

This last result runs contrary to Taylor's (1966) finding that differences in instructions did not lead to differences in mean scores. However his instructions — reproduced below — which were meant to inhibit the propensity to guess (A), to encourage it (C) and to be neutral in respect to guessing (B) are

Table 3   Mean scores in terms of reported frequency of guessing: mathematics

Reported guessing frequency		A	B	C
Not more than 5 times	Rights	24.28	19.94	21.19
	Wrongs	18.63	17.81	16.33
	Omits	2.09	7.25	7.48
	N	57	83	82
Up to 10 times	Rights	16.43	15.41	16.57
	Wrongs	27.41	22.32	23.21
	Omits	1.16	7.27	5.22
	N	37	22	23
More than 10 times	Rights	14.53	14.60	14.33
	Wrongs	28.94	27.20	28.17
	Omits	1.53	3.20	2.50
	N	15	5	6

Table 4   Mean scores in terms of reported frequency of guessing: further mathematics

Reported guessing frequency		A	B	C
Not more than 5 times	Rights	19.87	14.17	16.17
	Wrongs	20.20	18.76	16.98
	Omits	4.93	12.07	11.85
	N	15	41	40
Up to 10 times	Rights	16.58	11.83	11.93
	Wrongs	27.34	23.88	24.54
	Omits	1.08	9.29	8.53
	N	24	24	15
More than 10 times	Rights	14.38	13.50	11.17
	Wrongs	30.41	23.67	30.50
	Omits	0.21	7.83	3.33
	N	24	6	6

not as distinctive in terms of implied action as the ones used in this study, and so one is not surprised to find no effects.

A   *Do not* record an answer until you have studied the question carefully and *do not record an answer unless you are certain it is correct.*

B   *Your aim should be to do as well as you can.*

C   It is important that you get as many right as possible. In order to do this you may need to guess what the answer is. *Don't be afraid to guess and to have to go at every question.* (Taylor, 1966, p. 2)

Tables 3 and 4 suggest that ability and blind guessing frequency are more likely to be negatively than positively related. Correlations between number right and reported number of blind guesses are shown in table 5. In sign and size, the pattern is the same for both tests.

Table 5   Product moment correlations between number right and reported number of guesses

Form	Maths	Further Maths
A	−0.52	−0.43
B	−0.28	−0.13
C	−0.32	−0.27

The message of table 5 would seem to be that those who know least guess most and vice-versa. Since the number of rights includes the fruits of guessing, it must be concluded that the returns from guessing diminish along with ability. This supports the conclusion arrived at by other writers that the most able do not guess blindly any more then anyone else. Ebel (1968) reported a correlation of − .21 between number right and number of blind guesses while Choppin (1975), using the Ziller index of guessing tendency, reported essentially zero correlations between ability and guessing behaviour.

From figures 1 and 2 and tables 3 and 4, it appears that the reward for omitting seems to exert most attraction among the better candidates. A closer analysis bears this out. Below are total rights (R), wrongs (W) and omits (O) for upper and lower score groups (16 cases) from the A, B and C score distributions for the mathematics test only.

Group	Response	Upper	Lower
A	R	545	163
	W	165	529
	O	10	28
B	R	501	162
	W	155	359
	O	64	163
C	R	512	156
	W	156	354
	O	52	210

For the upper groups, it is apparent that the B and C cumulative profiles are quite similar and that both differ from A in rights and omits. Number wrong is much the same in all three groups. If the discrepancy in number right is divided by the discrepancy in omits, the result is a rough measure of the chances of B and C takers obtaining correct answers had they attempted those questions they omitted. Calling these statistics P_B and P_C we get,

$$P_B = (44/54) \simeq 0.8 \text{ and } P_C = (33/42) \simeq 0.8$$

This means that there is about an 80 per cent chance of a correct answer in both cases, very different from the 20 per cent derived from a random guessing model. But this is really no surprise; we expect the best candidates to have distinctly better than chance probabilities of arriving at correct answers. What is revealing is that in both the B and C groups, particularly B, some of the best students passed up opportunities to score, being put off either by promise of automatic reward or by fear of attracting a penalty. A good example would be two C cases with 29-6-10 profiles, who, had they worked the A form, might well have scored 35 or 36. For the lower scoring group the picture is very different. This time there is little or no difference between the groups in number correct but the discrepancies in omits between A and B and A and C are just as great as before. This indicates that the chances of low scorers getting items right when in a state of uncertainty are quite small, certainly less than the random model would allow, as calculation of P_B and P_C will show. Just as good candidates are good 'guessers', so the reverse seems to apply to poor candidates.

Discussion

If the last observation is true, it might appear that, for poor candidates, it makes little difference which instructions are operative. But this is not true; the B-type instructions will favour them most. By omitting items and accepting one-fifth or some fraction of a mark each time, they can improve on what their position would probably have been under non-restrictive (A-type) instructions. Conversely some of the best candidates will be under-rewarded by the bonus for omits. In view of the fact that their chances of arriving at a correct answer are nearly always better than chance, sometimes considerably so, able candidates ought to thrive best on instructions which encourage them to answer all questions. Choppin (1975) finds it surprising that high ability candidates do not indulge more in guessing strategies but the answer seems to be that they have little need of *blind* guessing although they make plenty of use of informed hunches.

When a test is of appropriate difficulty — an important qualification — there is little to choose between standard A-type and C-type instructions, except that the latter seem to have an inhibiting effect on some of the better candidates. Under guess-limiting instructions examinees whose guessing tendencies are high ignore the warnings and receive additional credit for partial knowledge, while timid examinees heed them and receive no such credit.

What of the criticism that lack of a guessing correction puts teachers in the invidious position of 'having' to advise their students to guess randomly at the answers to items they are completely stumped by? (Schofield, 1973; Wood, 1974). The seriousness of the criticism depends on how often students will find themselves so placed. When the test is of appropriate difficulty — as it should be — many candidates may never be *totally* at a loss with any item, especially as they will generally have enough time to consider all items. Generally, candidates will be drawing on their resources and endeavouring to find a solution by means of elimination or whatever. They will be following the precept that hunches should be played, for they are right with frequency greater than chance, except among the poorest candidates where hunches are grotesquely off-beam and are worse than chance. That is why some teachers still advise their students to attempt all questions even when they believe a guessing correction to be in operation, a behaviour which perplexed Schofield.

The question we started with concerned the power of instructions to persuade candidates to omit only those items they are totally at a loss with. The results obtained indicate that the instructions have only been partially successful. Having said that, it must be asked whether *any* instructions could persuade candidates to attempt items for which their probabilities of success would be effectively less than chance. Those who understand the significance of the scoring method will be quite content to accept credit for omits. The basic objection to any scheme which requires respondents to differentiate between guessing and knowing, as if these were qualitatively different processes, is that factors extraneous to testing obtrude. As Gritten and Johnson (1941) noted, any guessing correction is properly called a correction for individual differences in confidence. It is applied because some people attempt more items than others. Encouraging everyone to answer all items does not always work, as can be seen from tables 1 and 2, but under the right ocnditions it does reduce omitting to a point where individual differences in confidence cannot exert any real distorting effect.

Extract from *The School Science Review* 56, pp. 79–80, 1974.

Guessing on Objective Type Test Items

Dear Sir,

I have just seen Schofield's article concerning guessing on multiple-choice test items (S.S.R., 1973, 190, 55, 170–2). Since he alludes to this board as proposing to experiment with corrections at A level and since the results of that experiment are now available, I thought your readers might like to hear what the outcome was, in potted form.

Three scoring methods thought to have differing effects on response behaviour in a state of uncertainty were compared for effect on performance using groups undertaking A-level mathematics multiple-choice pretests. A method which induces respondents to omit items when uncertain by offering a reward — Schofield's correction (*b*) — was found to 'under-reward' the better students and 'over-reward' the weak ones. A method which exacts a so-called penalty for guessing — Schofield's correction (*a*) — appears to inhibit the better candidates from making full use of their abilities. Only the rubric currently used by the London board — 'attempt all questions' — seems to have this desirable effect while not offering any noticeable gains to weaker candidates who might be expected to take advantage of it.

The drawback with the reward strategy, which is promoted by one of your correspondents (S.S.R., 1974, 192, 55, 607) and which I favoured myself before the experiment, is that it appears to encourage what I can only describe as laziness in certain able candidates. The crux of the matter is that good candidates are good 'guessers'; poor candidates are poor 'guessers'. This means that in opting for one-fifth of a mark by omitting an answer, a bright candidate is accepting less than he could get by attempting such items. Conversely, my data indicate that the chances of low scorers getting items right when in a state of uncertainty are extremely small, much less than chance, which, of course, means such people gain by omitting items. This is what I meant above by over- and under-rewarding.

As far as the penalty for guessing is concerned, the situation appears to be this: when the test is of appropriate difficulty — an important proviso — there is little to choose between standard and penalty instructions, except that the latter seem to exert an inhibiting effect on some of the better candidates. This is a matter of personality. Under guess-limiting instructions, examinees whose guessing tendencies are high ignore the warnings and receive extra credit for partial knowledge, while timid candidates heed them and receive no such credit.

The virtue, as it seems to me, of the injunction to answer all questions is that it maximizes the opportunity for candidates to reveal all they know. Mr. Schofield claims that 'science teachers have institutionalized guessing as an activity'. Even if true, this does not necessarily mean, of course, that much blind guessing among candidates goes on. It must be remembered that when the test is of appropriate difficulty many candidates may never be *totally* at a loss with an item, especially as they will generally have ample time to consider all items. In these circumstances it is surely preferable to encourage candidates to persevere and find a solution; certainly your correspondents, Miss Siggers and Mrs Sneezum (S.S.R., 1974, 192, 55, 606–7) seem to think so. As has often been said, hunches should be played for they are right with frequency more than chance. This explains why some teachers still advise their candidates to attempt all questions even when they believe a guessing correction to be in operation. Such advice does not turn the examination into a game situation, as Mr. Schofield contends, and my results indicate that the scores are more reliable, in the technical sense, using standard instructions than using the other two strategies.

I can accept that teachers are confused about board practices concerning guessing, but we try to make our policy clear in our various publications. Perhaps we have not done enough. I would say, though, without being disrespectful, that questionnaires could probably turn up many facts concerning examinations of which 25 per cent of teachers are ignorant, not that too much reliance should be placed on Mr. Schofield's figure. No excuse, maybe, but worth bearing in mind.

As long as objective testing is thought to be a worthwhile measurement technique, it must be accepted that some marks will be obtained fortuitously.

No one can legislate against this. The problem really is that the able and less able — perhaps all candidates — need different instructions. Since this is not realistic, the fairest policy for all, based on the results of this experiment, is to stick with the board's standard instructions to attempt all questions. As long as the board's multiple-choice tests continue to be easy rather than hard, are adequately timed, and have 5 choices per item, there is little to worry about.

Yours faithfully,
R. Wood.

Extract from The School Science Review, 58, 1976.

Guessing in Objective Tests

Dear Sir,

Mr. Forsyth (*S.S.R.*, 1975, 198, 57, 195–6) takes issue with my views on guessing (*S.S.R.*, 1974, 194, 56, 179–80) and widens his remarks into an attack on objective tests. As far as guessing is concerned, the significant point is that Mr. Forsyth finds 16-year-olds using reasoned guesses when not sure of an answer. This, of course, is the age group I dealt with and the conclusion I reached.

More generally, it seems to me that if so many of his students can obtain the right answer by incorrect reasoning this says more about his items and his teaching than about the shortcomings of objective tests. At least his experiment will have alerted him to learning difficulties experienced by his students.

The point about objective testing in the classroom is that it should be used flexibly and informally. With papers being marked by the teacher I see no reason why students should not be asked to write down their reasons for the choices they make.

Yours faithfully,
R. Wood.

Schools Examinations Department,

Note

1 Points (x, y, z) can be represented as barycentric coordinates whenever $x + y + z = c$, c being a constant (see Mosteller and Tukey, 1968.)

References

CHOPPIN, B. (1975) 'Guessing the answer on objective tests', *British Journal of Educational Psychology*, 45, pp. 206–13.

EBEL, R.L. (1968) 'Blind guessing on objective achievement tests'. *Journal of Educational Measurement*, 5, pp. 321–5.

GRITTEN, F. and JOHNSON, D.M. (1941). 'Individual differences in judging multiple-choice questions', *Journal of Educational Psychology*, 30, pp. 423–30.

HAMILTON, C.H. (1950) 'Bias and error in multiple-choice tests', *Psychometrika*, 15, pp. 151–68

LORD, F.M. (1975) 'Formula scoring and number-right scoring', *Journal of Educational Measurement*, 12, pp. 7–11.

MEAD, A.R. and SMITH, B.M. (1957) 'Does the true-false formula scoring work. Some data on an old subject', *Journal of Educational Research*, 51, pp. 47–53.

MOSTELLER, F. and TUKEY, J.W. (1968) 'Data analysis including statistics' in LINDZEY, G. and ARONSON, E. (Eds.), *Handbook of Social Psychology*, Reading, MA, Addison-Wesley Publishing Co.

SCHOFIELD, R. (1973) 'Guessing on objective type test items', *School Science Review*, 55, pp. 170–2.

SLAKTER, M.J. (1968) 'The penalty for not guessing', *Journal of Educational Measurement*, 5, pp. 141–4.

TAYLOR, P.H. (1966) 'A study of the effects of instructions in a multiple-choice mathematics test', *British Journal of Educational Psychology*, 36, pp. 1–6.

TRAUB, R.E. and HAMBLETON, R.K. (1972) 'The effect of scoring instructions and degree of speededness on the validity and reliability of multiple-choice tests', *Educational and Psychological Measurement*, 32, pp. 737–58.

WATERS, C.W. and WATERS, L.K. (1971) 'Validity and likeability ratings for three scoring instructions for a multiple-choice vocabulary test', *Educational and Psychological Measurement*, 31, pp. 935–8.

WOOD, R. (1974) 'Guessing on objective type test items: A reply to Schofield', *School Science Review*, 56, pp. 79–80, and in this volume.

V   Latent Trait Theory

Comments

I would like to be able to offer a synoptic paper covering this area but I would have to write the sort of paper I wrote in 1970 (Bock and Wood, 1971), and I do not feel up to that. No question of reproducing that paper, even if I wanted to, because of course it has been officially pensioned off by virtue of subsequent reviews. The last time I had an opportunity to say exactly what I thought of latent trait theory or, what amounts to the same thing, item response theory (IRT), was in 1982 when Ron Hambleton asked me to be discussant of a collection of papers he was putting together. When I realized that I could not avoid being rude to most of the other contributors, I pulled out — which was pretty tender-minded of me. Actually, the paper I would not have been hard on, by Ross Traub (1983), said most of what I would have said, so there really was no point. Traub is very good on what I call counter-perspective in paper 8 and on the positions modellers commit themselves to by virtue of choosing a model.

The next opportunity to pontificate on latent trait theory will almost certainly be the book I am writing with Harvey Goldstein where we are dealing with all the theory and models circulating in educational measurement and psychometrics, past and present (Goldstein with Wood, in preparation). At this point I would say that IRT tends to induce in practitioners blindness to real-world significance, leading to mathematizing for its own sake and trivializing of problems. More categorically, I would say that it is dangerous to be so dependent on a particular family of probabilistic models when the fit problem remains obstinately uncracked.

As for the papers here, the first I thought a decent contribution at the time. For an update on most of the matters I raised, and others besides, Bejar (1983) is a good reference. The two papers on Rasch reflect my exasperation at what was going on in his name, and the paper on Lawley is a genuine tribute to a fine statistician who, I am sure, would be quite bemused to find himself in the pantheon of psychometric greats. Rasch also belongs there, and I would like to have written a tribute to him too, but I am afraid his followers produced too much cognitive dissonance for that.

References

BEJAR, I.I. (1983) *Achievement Testing: Recent Advances*, London, Sage Publications.
BOCK, R.D. and WOOD, R. (1971) 'Test theory', *Annual Review of Psychology*, 22, pp.193–224.
GOLDSTEIN, H. with WOOD, R. *Test Theory Models and Educational Practice*, Oxford, Pergamon Press.
TRAUB, R.E. (1983) 'A priori considerations in choosing an item response model', in HAMBLETON, R.K. (Ed.) *ERIBC Monograph on Applications of Item Response Theory*, Vancouver, BC, Educational Research Institute of British Columbia.

Paper 7: Trait Measurement and Item Banks*

This paper falls into three parts. In the first I will try to establish what kind of measurement we should look for from item banks. This involves me in a direct comparison of the generalizability and latent trait models of response behaviour. These models are contrasted in their capacity to cope with response-contingent testing (Wood, 1973) which, in my view, offers the most imaginative measurement application for item banks. The second part of the paper deals with what is entailed in calibrating item banks so that desirable measurement strategies can be implemented with the necessary accuracy and precision. In the final section I shall consider the implications for trait definition and validation of fitting different latent trait models, specifically the Rasch and normal ogive models.

Generalizability and Latent Trait Models

Original Item Banking Work

I continue to think of an item bank as an all-purpose measurement system capable of meeting any testing requirement, group or individual, and rooted firmly in latent trait or item characteristic curve theory (Wood, 1974). Recently, however, I have been obliged to reconsider my position in the light of some strong statements about the future of achievement testing which envisage item banks being used in a rather different way. I have in mind David Shoemaker's recent paper (Shoemaker, 1975) in which he argues that domain-referenced measurement is the only way forward for achievement testing. It is reminiscent of Anderson (1972) who maintained that except for purposes of extreme selection, criterion-referenced testing and achievement testing are coterminous. In this conception item banks are evisaged as constituting the

---

*Reprinted from *Advances in Psychological and Educational Measurement*, (1976) London, John Wiley and Sons Ltd.

domains from which items will be sampled with the associated measurements being handled within the generalizability framework.

When Skurnik and I did our work on item banking between 1966 and 1968 (Wood and Skurnik, 1969) the notion of criterion or domain-referenced testing — I shall use the two terms interchangeably — was just beginning to surface. Osburn's (1968) ideas about universe-defined tests had recently become available and we gave them plenty of space. We even quoted his attack on trait measurement approvingly:

> In the absence of an unambiguous basis for generalization to a well-defined universe of content we resort to statistical and mathematical strategies in an attempt to generalize beyond the arbitrary collection of items in the test (Wood and Skurnik, p. 161).

Yet we were not thoroughly convinced by Osburn — 'the effect of these conflicting views is to place us in something of a quandary' (*op. cit.*, p. 181) — and in the end we couldn't go along with him. In the first place, we couldn't see that breaking down mathematics achievement into many small domains would be worth the extra information, even supposing we could do it. Nor could we swallow the notion of random sampling or even stratified random sampling of items (Wood and Skurnik, *op. cit.*, p. 162). It wasn't just that random sampling strained credulity; it was alien to the whole idea of the bank, which was for teachers to select what, funnily enough, were essentially criterion-referenced tests, although we didn't call them that. The most compelling objection, however, was on the measurement front. Our purpose was to develop a mechanism for establishing comparability between scores obtained on any set of items drawn from the bank. This meant taking into account the difficulty and discrimination of the items. Universe scores, being regression estimates based on number correct, were of no help to us, while item characteristic curve theory gave us a handle on the problem.

Content and Constructs

For these reasons, although with some reluctance, for operational definition of grades appealed to us (*op. cit.*, p. 163), we parted company with the domain-referenced or generalizability framework. And that is more or less still my position. But the generalizability framework is more elastic than I thought at first. Certainly there are still those who insist on the necessity of defining very specific and ultra-homogeneous domains but if you read what Cronbach has written you find there is provision for broad domains, as broad as you like — 'nothing in the logic of content validation requires that the universe or test be homogeneous in content' (Cronbach, 1970, p. 44). Cronbach went on to cite our old friend the driving test (where would we be without it and I say that as someone who has used it himself) as an example of a universe containing diverse elements:

To make a decision about an applicant for a license, it is necessary to know whether he would pass a certain proportion of the items belonging to the universe defined by the code. If the items have low correlations (or if they vary in difficulty), it will take a larger sample of items to be confident that the subject's universe score reaches the required level. But, no matter how heterogeneous the universe, with enough items one can estimate the universe score as precisely as desired. Low item intercorrelations do not necessarily imply failure of the test content to fit the definition (Cronbach, pp. 44–5).

Now this is the kind of formulation I can live with. But I would like to know how achievement in a heterogeneous domain is to be described. As far as I can see, it is impossible to avoid using what we ordinarily call traits or constructs, whether it be driving ability or whatever. This, of course, is the very practice Osburn so violently objected to. Not that he is alone; the view that constructs have nothing to do with educational measurement is held by many. I wish they would read Messick's (1975) paper which has helped enormously to clarify my thinking on this subject. He challenges the belief that in educational measurement, unlike psychological measurement, constructs should be considered unimportant or even irrelevant. He notes that many of the terms used to characterize common educational tests such as scientific reasoning, reading comprehension, knowledge, synthesis and so forth clearly imply process intepretations. 'In short', Messick writes, 'whenever one's interpretations depart from the strict behavioral language of task performance, one is apt to employ constructs' (Messick, 1975, p. 958).

From this position Messick develops the idea that all tests should be *construct-referenced*. Content must be relevant, of course, but that is a commonsense requirement anyway. What Messick objects to in the notion of content validity, and I share his view, is that it inheres in instruments instead of in scores or responses, which are after all the fundamental data to be interpreted. Not only that, the meaning of a measurement arising from a particular collection of items is made to depend heavily on the artificial mechanism of random sampling from the larger domain of items.

Random Sampling

Perhaps random sampling has been a straw man ever since Loevinger (1965) savaged it. Those who stand by it tend to offer rather half-hearted rationalizations. Fhanér (1974), for instance, concedes that selection of items is typically casual rather than random but argues that the idea of random sampling is a 'useful idealization of the situation'; useful, that is, from the statistical point of view.

These days the idea of stratified sampling is supposed to make everything all right. Certainly Cronbach and Shoemaker are prepared to admit just about any degree and kind of stratified sampling whether the strata be content, difficulty, item type, response mode or whatever. It seems to me that with so much latitude permitted for stratification, it is only a short step to argue that given a test constructed on the basis of expert judgment, or even a blend of judgment and statistical criteria, there could be said to exist a unique stratification plan which, if implemented, would result in a test corresponding more or less exactly with the test as compiled. That is really just another way of saying that intensive stratification leads ultimately to an almost determined sample, the point about experts being that they embody an extremely complicated stratification through which their beliefs about what constitutes achievement are expressed. This strikes me as a good illustration of Brunswik's ideas, discussed by Loevinger, which stress the necessity of *representative* rather than systematic design as the foundation for psychological generalization (see also Eysenck, 1975).

Those who believe that to rely on 'experts' is magical and backward will repudiate this principle, I know, their object being to outlaw value judgments but they might at least query the relevance of randomness in education, which is above all purposeful activity. It strikes me as ironical that in a testing system so closely identified with child-centred instruction the test of what has been learned should be decided by an *aleatory* device when none of the so-called norm-reference systems I am familiar with would dare to operate such a procedure. Loevinger (*op. cit.*, p. 148) is surely right when she claims that everyone who has a serious investment in applied testing seeks optimal and not random testing conditions. The teacher knows this; any teacher worth his salt will try to individualize his questions. Despite what the doctrinaires say, he is not necessarily interested in 100 per cent mastery at any particular time; rather he wants to find out as much as he can as quickly as he can. This is only being intelligent. One of the features of criterion-referenced testing I find hard to stomach is its *exhaustiveness* when in practice there has to be selection, usually severe. Individualized testing strategies take short cuts based on assumptions about what is already known; in this way they constitute both an *acceleration* and a *compression* of criterion-referenced procedures (Wood, 1976a).

Individualized Measurement

This brings me to what really interests me and that is those alternatives to conventional testing for which item banks are specially suited. So far I am quite comfortable with generalizability theory but naturally I want to know how well it deals with response-contingent testing, where by this term I do not necessarily mean exact tailoring but what has been called 'unmatched' testing, that is, any form of testing where the possibility exists for an individual or group of individuals to take a different although not necessarily exclusive set of items.

The first thing to ascertain is whether individualized testing is admissible in the generalizability system. Since the term 'unmatched' originated in that tradition, the answer must be yes. Generalizability theory does provide explicitly for each individual to receive a different set of items; in the jargon of the Cronbach (1972) book, items are nested within persons in an $i : p$ or perhaps an $i \times j : p$ design.

In this kind of design, the point estimate of an individual's universe score, U_i, is given by Truman Kelley's classical regression formula,

$$U_i = \hat{p}^2 X_i + (1 - \hat{p}^2)\bar{X}$$

where X_i is the observed score, $\bar{X}$ is the observed mean for the group to which the individual is said to belong and $\hat{p}^2$ is the estimate of reliability or the coefficient of generalizability. The same value of $\hat{p}^2$ is used for all cases on the grounds that each test administration draws a large although not necessarily equal collection of items (Cronbach, *et al.*, 1972, pp. 74, 106). In reality, error variance is most unlikely to be the same from person to person, particularly if the number of items administered is not large and varies considerably from person to person. A way round this is to use Jackson's (1972) expressions for true and error variance based on assumptions of heteroscedastic error and unequal replications although Jackson warns that estimates of individual error variance, and therefore of $\hat{p}^2$, are likely to be themselves unreliable given anything but large numbers of replications.

But this is a minor issue. The basic point is that the universe score depends essentially on observed score. No allowance is made for set-ups where by design one individual has received easier questions than another, as would happen in individualized testing. What it boils down to is that no comparisons among individuals are possible in terms of actual performance nor can individuals be judged in absolute terms with respect to some mastery level. Like classical test theory, to which it is identical in this particular case (Cronbach *et al.*, 1972 p. 17), generalizability theory is inadequate for scoring the results of individualized testing.

For workable scoring methods, it is necessary to turn to item characteristic curve theory (Lord, 1974). Being a theory about what governs individual item responses, items are liberated from belonging to test forms. Moreover, and this is what makes latent trait theory so useful for individualized tests, any subtest of items will yield estimates of ability which can be expressed in a common metric. Direct comparisons are therefore possible as, of course, are absolute decisions in terms of a common criterion.[1]

The question now arises, what substantive meaning can be attached to latent trait estimates derived from individualized testing? In the first place, these estimates are estimates of how the individuals concerned would have performed on the entire bank of items (Lord, 1974). Thus they are conceptually equivalent to universe scores. Functionally, each item response is related explicitly to the trait or ability or construct being measured. Given multiple item responses, inferences about how much of the ability an individual possesses can be made. The substantive meaning which can then be attached to an ability estimate depends entirely on how well the ability has been explicated. Regrettably it is all too common to find abilities in a primitive state of explication and validation, thus giving substance to Osburn's criticism. I shall return to this subject in the last section.

Merging Generalizability and Latent Trait Theory

I daresay I have given the impression that I am hostile towards the generalizability model. This is not so. I am happy to use it in the right setting, which means situations where one can be comfortable with the sampling assumptions, where the universe is relatively well-defined and where components of variance are the objects of interest rather than universe scores. In particular, I have found it useful in the kind of data collection set-up where you have numbers of raters, occasions and traits, and where the interactions are as interesting as anything else (Wood, 1976c). It just happens that the generalizability model, as presently developed, does not provide the wherewithal for estimating scores from individualized tests. According to Cronbach (this symposium) there is no competition, different models suit different situations.

Not that everyone takes this friendly point of view. Strong statements have been made, for instance by Guttman (1969) in his review of Lord and Novick's book, also Ross and Lumsden (1968). By way of reply Cronbach and his colleagues were quite categorical:

> Complex kinds of estimation such as Lord is currently investigating ...
> may ultimately be of practical value, but they cannot be accommo-
> dated within the present techniques of generalizability analysis. (p. 24)

Given this firm statement, it was very interesting to hear Cronbach in this symposium spell out how generalizability and latent trait theory can be merged and, in particular, how tailored testing can be made to dovetail with generalizability theory. If observations are collected according to some design, say $i : p$, and scored by a latent trait or conceivably some other method, then the resulting scores can be slotted back into the generalizability model to produce universe scores and estimated components of variance.

There is, in fact, a paper which shows how this can be done. Novick (1969) sketched out an individualized testing procedure which depends on a group of individuals being tested separately but simultaneously. The estimation procedure is based on Kelley's regression formula but with latent trait parameters appearing as arguments. Individual ability estimates are updated by this formula after every item, each person's provisional estimate being used as collateral information to compute a group mean at every step. As the information about individuals grows and firms up, the group mean is given less and less weight. This is as it should be, which is the beauty of Kelley's formula. Novick concluded that regression-type estimates may be found in logistic, normal ogive and other quantal response models of interest to testing practice. He also noted that 'these results again confirm that estimates based solely on the individual observed scores are not optimum' (p. 8). Of course, the idea of regressing towards a particular group mean, so that a person's ultimate score depends on the company he keeps, is controversial, as the Cronbach book admits. Doubtless, some people would reject generalizability theory on that score alone. All the same it is a pity that Novick's ideas in this area do not appear to have been picked up for here is a clear opportunity for creative synthesis.

Calibrating Item Banks

I want to turn now to more technical matters, in particular, I want to consider the problem of calibrating items in a bank so that accurate and precise latent trait estimation is possible.

Invariance

The availability of trustworthy item parameter estimates is essential for any measurement application of item banking but especially for tailored testing procedures where repeated poor matches between estimated ability and item difficulty estimates, compounded by distorted discrimination estimates, would defeat the purpose of the exercise. Likewise two-stage testing strategies could be ruined if the specifications of either routing of measurement tests or both were awry.

Apart from the problem of getting accurate estimates in the first place — the calibration problem — there is the continuing problem of making sure that for every item the parameter estimates are appropriate for any person or persons to whom the item is to be administered. Much play is made of the 'invariance' of item parameter estimates in latent trait models but supportive evidence is conspicuous by its absence. In fact, this is one of the greyest areas of test theory.

Gulliksen (1950, p. 392) identified invariance as an outstanding problem and suggested that whoever elucidated it would have made a significant contribution to item analysis theory but since he wrote no one seems to have been too keen to make a name for himself in this direction. The more recent work such as Lord and Novick (1968, pp. 380–1), and Henrysson (1971, p. 148), is not a great deal of help. In both cases, it is contended that linear relationships between estimates of items parameters for the same items administered to different samples *should* hold but neither cites empirical studies in support of this statement.

With the increasing popularity of the Rasch model, the subject of invariance has come in for more study (for example, Anderson *et al.*, 1968; Willmott and Fowles, 1974; Whitely and Dawis, 1974) and invariance for the single parameter model has been demonstrated under certain conditions. All the same I think it is fair to say that there have not been too many attempts to work out and substantiate what is entailed in the calibration and updating process. I don't think we treated the subject adequately in the original item banking report (Wood and Skurnik, *op. cit.*, p. 124). I may also have given the impression in a more recent publication (Wood, 1974) that calibration is a routine matter. Perhaps my attitude was infectious for I find a recent report of Rasch model work (Willmott and Fowles, 1974) continuing to take calibration more or less for granted. To find people who really do take the problem seriously you have to go to the Psychometric Methods Group at the University of Minnesota and I shall come back to their work a little later.

Sample-Freeness

Although much is made of the property of 'sample-freeness', there exist accounts of work with the Rasch model which neglect to give any explanation of the term's statistical foundation. Empirical demonstration is thought to be sufficient. For those who are bewildered by the model — any model — in the first place this serves only to heighten the magical effect already created by extravagant promises of what it will do. Analogies with detergent advertisements come to mind, with sample-freeness as the new wonder ingredient.

The property of sample-freeness derives from the use of regression analysis to estimate item parameters, a course of action which follows directly from the wish to calibrate items on an arbitrary collection of individuals rather than on a sample from a defined population, in which case a *correlational* method of estimation would be appropriate (Bock and Wood, 1971, p. 121). Although from the point of view of obtaining efficient item parameter estimates, particularly of the slope or discrimination, it is preferable for the distribution of the independent variable to cover the whole ability range in a more or less uniform manner, just about any distribution of points which fits the linear regression model will do. Thus, though extrapolation would be necessary, a cluster of points at either of the extremes should give the same estimates of difficulty (the intercept) and discrimination providing the item does not behave in an odd manner elsewhere in the range. This is the basis of sample-freeness and invariance.

There are circumstances, however, where sample-freeness breaks down. Should there be interaction effects between samples and items, so that items behave differently in different samples, whether because of cultural or sex bias or whatever, then invariance ceases to hold. The same applies to items which discriminate differentially across the ability range, as represented by the rectified item characteristic curves in Figure 1 (p indicates proportion correct at ability level θ; Φ^{-1} is the inverse normal deviate transformation).

If items like these were to be calibrated on either high or low ability samples, the extrapolation of the regressions would give a quite misleading picture of how the items behave. Unfortunately, interactions may not show up

Figure 1

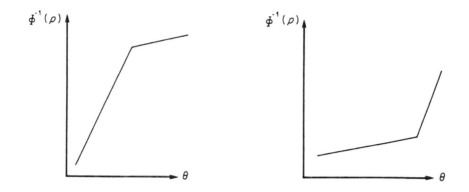

until serious measurement is underway, making the original calibration untrustworthy. This effect could be particularly serious in individualized testing situations where interactions might not show up at all.

Anchoring

Strictly speaking, it is not correct to say that the latent trait models provide invariant item parameter estimates. Only if a common scale for the ability, θ, is used from group to group will this be true. In general, the metric of θ is likely to differ from group to group so that the item parameters have to be transformed to those for a standard reference group. This makes it necessary to administer a certain number of 'anchor' items along with the items which are to be calibrated. If Lord and Novick and Henrysson are right, the values of a_g and b_g, denoting discrimination and difficulty respectively, should show a linear relationship from group to group. A plot of the values for the anchor items provides the check. If all is well a_g and b_g values for each new group of items can be transformed into the anchor set metric. With the Rasch model, of course, there is only one parameter which makes the procedure simpler to carry out.

But, as I keep saying, the operative word here is 'should'. Various empirical investigations of the Rasch model seem to have verified that for items which fit the model the translation of difficulty parameters from one scale to another by a constant shift works well enough, although it is often the case that a number of items have to be discarded before the linear relationship holds. What, though, of the three parameter models such as the normal ogive? These interest me more because I prefer to try and fit as many items as possible. I have some results which bear on this issue.

The context is a 70-item physics achievement test answered by 388 candidates. Two distinct sets of twelve items were drawn, both fitting the normal ogive and Rasch model. Three samples of ninety candidates were selected. The first was a random sample, the second consisted of the forty-five highest and the forty-five lowest scorers on the test and was labelled an 'extremes' sample, and the third was a 'grab' group, comprising all the candidates from a particular school, the sort of group which ought to provide perfectly good item parameter estimates if sample-freeness is working. Naturally the samples were not exclusive although the overlap was very small. The two item sets were calibrated on the three samples and, of course, on the population. The resulting mean values of the item parameters and the correlations between them are shown in table 1.

Evidently the item sets had rather different characteristics even though both fitted the two models. For some reason the typical negative relationship between difficulty and discrimination was not found in the second set. The mean values show that the second set was somethat easier than the first which would usually mean higher discrimination values, yet the mean discrimination estimates were not really very different, except for the 'grab' group.

Among the various estimates of difficulty there is plainly a very high correlation. The recommended method for transforming parameter values would work with any pair of these groups and either of the item sets. The same cannot be said of the discrimination estimates. For both item sets the lowest correlation is between the random and grab groups, a result which raises doubts about the advisability of calibrating one kind of sample on the other although I suppose some might prefer to interpret it as a vindication of the policy of avoiding random samples and preferring non-normal samples of subjects for the purposes of securing efficient and stable estimates of discrimination parameters.

Whatever the interpretation, these results, slender though they are, suggest that the discrimination parameter, and also the biserial correlation of which it is a function, is quite *volatile* and cannot be claimed to be invariant as a matter of course. A close reader of Lord and Novick's book might raise his eyebrows at this observation. 'The biserial is widely used because it is hoped that the biserial will demonstrate a type of invariance from one group of examinees to another not provided by the point-biserial' (Lord and Novick, 1968, p. 341). However, Lord and Novick went on to remark (p. 342) that biserial invariance is necessarily a matter for empirical investigation and *that they are not aware of definite empirical studies of this question* (my italics). My own experience has been that biserials for items tested on ostensibly equivalent pretest groups can vary considerably, beyond what would be expected from sampling theory.

One thing is clear; any attempt to transform the item parameter values repeatedly by starting with one group, say, the random in this case, and working round until the same group is reached again — in symbolic terms $R \rightarrow E \rightarrow G \rightarrow P \rightarrow R$ — would not succeed in recovering the original discrimination values even if the same item set was used as an anchor, and especially if the anchor was varied. That there will be *slippage* every time there is a recalibration seems unavoidable.

What effects this slippage is likely to have on measurement can only be guessed at. If the discrepancies between current estimates of item parameters and the 'true' values are more or less constant then no great harm is done; the same items are likely to be chosen for individualized testing sequences. If, however, the shift is not constant, as appears likely, different item sequences could be selected according to whatever the current parameter estimates happen to be. Since the size of the discrimination estimate plays an important part in tailored testing item selection strategies and measurement, the consequences could be serious.

Table 1   Item set I

Variable	Mean	S.D.	Correlations							
			1	2	3	4	5	6	7	8
1. 'Random' b_g	0.14	0.34								
2. 'Extremes' b_g	0.12	0.40	0.89							
3. 'Grab' b_g	0.04	0.54	0.89	0.91						
4. 'Population' b_g	0.11	0.39	0.93	0.94	0.93					
5. Random a_g	0.49	0.23	−0.21	0.04	0.04	0.01				
6. Extremes a_g	0.89	0.34	−0.66	−0.53	−0.46	−0.51	0.73			
7. Grab a_g	0.57	0.42	−0.64	−0.56	−0.40	−0.45	0.53	0.83		
8. Population a_g	0.55	0.24	−0.21	−0.02	0.09	0.01	0.86	0.81	0.68	

Item set II

Variable	Mean	S.D.	Correlations							
			1	2	3	4	5	6	7	8
1. Random b_g	0.28	0.46								
2. Extremes b_g	0.32	0.37	0.93							
3. Grab b_g	0.26	0.51	0.93	0.89						
4. Population b_g	0.28	0.48	0.96	0.95	0.94					
5. Random a_g	0.50	0.19	0.68	0.74	0.74	0.69				
6. Extremes a_g	0.86	0.25	0.30	0.38	0.46	0.35	0.73			
7. Grab a_g	0.72	0.28	0.30	0.41	0.51	0.35	0.68	0.82		
8. Population a_g	0.57	0.20	0.32	0.47	0.54	0.42	0.79	0.92	0.90	

Some interest has been shown in the problem of individualized testing with fallible item parameter estimates. Lord (1974, p. 120) writes that 'an outstanding current problem is how to carry out individualized testing using test items characterized by a variety of inaccurately estimated item parameters'.

My own limited experience within the context of Bayesian tailored testing (Wood, 1976b) suggested that the consequences would not be too serious. But I was not dealing with quite the situation I have been talking about where repeated slippage may introduce distortions of unknown size.

A Plan for Proper Calibration

Evidently the only way to reduce slippage is to carry out every updating as carefully as possible. As I said before, this is an area which has been rather glossed over, perhaps because no one has run a calibrated item bank designed for practical measurement long enough to have come to terms with the updating problem.

One outfit which seems to have ambitions in this direction is the Psychometric Methods Group at the University of Minnesota which has published reports dealing with various aspects of adaptive and two-stage testing. One of these papers (McBride and Weiss, 1974) deals specifically with the calibration and updating of an item bank. It leaves no doubt about the amount of work a proper calibration entails. Seven basic steps are envisaged. They are:

1 Define the population of interest.
2 Compile an initial development test and norm it on a representative sample from the population.
3 On the basis of the norming data, construct a calibration/criterion subtest.
4 Construct several long secondary development tests incorporating the calibration/criterion subtest.
5 Norm these development tests on large representative samples from the population.
6 Perform item analysis of the development tests, employing calibration/criterion subtest scores as the criterion.
7 Select items for the item pool on the basis of the item analysis data.

Points to note here are that great care is necessary in the construction of the anchor test. McBride and Weiss think the test might need to be as long as forty–sixty items which would place quite a burden on groups who would have to take the anchor test in addition to other tests, particularly as the 'norming' tests contemplated by McBride and Weiss would themselves have to be long. A further, not-easy-to-meet demand is that the norming tests must be administered to 'very large samples from the population' in order to achieve stability of the item parameters.

McBride and Weiss also insist on the necessity of verifying the unidimensionality of item banks. They maintain that items must be administered in sufficient combinations so that it is possible to compute a total item intercorrelation matrix. This is a tall order. Multiple matrix sampling may be of some use although there are problems here as we found out in the original item banking project. Evidently huge samples of subjects would be needed in order to achieve the desired inter-correlations based on samples of roughly equivalent size. Even supposing the correlations could be obtained there would still be the problem of factor analyzing a very large matrix. McBride and Weiss's solution of splitting the matrix into manageable portions looks rather dubious.

Apart from problems of size, interpretation of the results of factor analyses of binary data is far from straightforward as McDonald and Ahlawat (1974) have reminded us recently. They believe that the so-called 'difficulty' factors, which have been the object of so much controversy in the past, stem from items showing differential curvature in the relationship between proportion correct and ability. Examples would be those plots I presented earlier. My own feeling is that a rigorous check on unidimensionality in large item banks is not a realistic proposition, if it is even necessary. The fit of an item to the model and its appropriateness on substantive or theoretical grounds ought to be sufficient grounds for deciding whether it should be banked.

Perhaps the McBride and Weiss scheme for calibrating item banks is too fussy. No doubt short cuts will be discovered by the people who have to do the job. Even so, I am persuaded that calibration needs devotion, effort and good psychometric practice. Calibration and updating schemes based on the casual use of odd groups of subjects are likely to come to grief.

Item Fit and Trait Validation

Implicit in what I just said is that an item can only be calibrated and accepted into a bank if it fits whatever statistical response model is favoured. This means that new items must be 'conformal' with the anchoring items and, by extension, with the rest of the bank. What is not absolutely clear to me, although I suppose it could be proved, or at least demonstrated empirically, is whether just because an item fits in one company, it will always fit in any other, even though the anchoring items are present on both occasions. Whitely and Dawis (*op. cit.*, p. 177) point out how important the assumption of local independence is for individualized testing. The administration of a given item must not influence the subject's response to subsequent items. They remark that the degree to which test items interact will have to receive systematic study if individualized testing is to be successful.

By virtue of their response consistency, conformal items may be said to be measuring something in common, what we call a trait or ability or construct. It follows that it ought to be possible to learn something about these traits from an examination of the items that fit and, more importantly, fail to fit the model being used. Attractive though this notion is, it has certain drawbacks.

In the first place, as Levy (1973, p. 23) notes, the manifest content of an item may not always give the right clue as to process. Items which apparently call for a certain kind of reasoning (for example, geometrical) may be soluble by other means (for example, algebraic). And we are all familiar with items allegedly tapping comprehension which turn out to be solved by rote memory.

It is small wonder that items fail to fit models for no apparent reason and conversely, fit when it would appear they shouldn't.

These item response models seem to be remarkably elastic considering the motley collections of items they will fit. Of course, fit is a relative term, being usually decided by referring a X^2 value to tables and using a conventional level of significance. In practice what one is looking for are *tendencies*.

To illustrate the elasticity of these models, I might mention that with the normal ogive model, using the simultaneous ability and item parameter estimation procedure programmed by Kolakowski and Bock (1973), we were able to fit all but three of the items in the seventy-item physics achievement test I referred to earlier, a test which contained five different item types, one of which, the assertion-reason type, was quite different from the rest, and three distinct syllabus sections, heat, light and electricity. Like many achievement tests, the intercorrelations of the items were low — of the order of 0.10 — so that the item-test biserials were also low, in the main, although with some variation. However, low discrimination is no problem in itself, because of the inclusion of a discrimination parameter in the normal ogive model. Being without this parameter, the Rasch model will generally fit fewer items, but even so sixty of the seventy items were fitted in this particular case.

The search for causes of lack of fit is complicated by the fact that items will fit one model but not another. With the Rasch model it is often hard items which fit least well. In these cases poor fit is unlikely to be attributable to item content *per se* but rather to individuals who indulge in guessing or whatever one likes to call response behaviour in a state of uncertainty. On the other hand, there are cases of low discrimination which are not necessarily attributable to individuals. I am thinking of items which just about every subject knows the answer to, the sort of item you would be likely to find in a criterion-referenced test. On the face of it, there seems no reason why this kind of item should be regarded as measuring some other trait; it is simply a very easy item. This problem does not arise with the normal ogive model although if guessing on certain items is pronounced, it will also reject those items.

The items that tend not to fit the normal ogive model are those with non-linear item-trait regression lines such as those presented earlier. Again, content or item type do not appear to be significant factors; the left hand item discriminates in the lower part of the ability range only, the right hand in the upper range only. While it would certainly be worth enquiring into why there should be such differential rates of mastery of the material involved, there seems no reason to separate out these items and postulate different traits to explain the subjects' performance on them.

One reason for items like these turning out as they do could be that the population of subjects being tested is a mixture of two or more populations. If this is suspected, fit might be contrived by separating the two populations, always supposing this can be done (analytical solutions I have seen generally require some knowledge of the proportions in which the populations are mixed), and fitting each section of the item-trait regression line separately.

Piecewise regression techniques (Wainer, 1971) are also relevant, as is the nonlinear probit analysis procedure developed by Maritz (1965). Whatever method is used, and they will all make heavy programming and machine time demands, the ability range for which an item is validly calibrated must be carefully demarcated for, as I argued earlier, blind extrapolation on the basis that the items behave uniformly across the ability range is liable to give misleading results.

The principle of calibrating items on suitable samples is an important one. Responsibility for lack of fit may lie in individuals as much as in items. Choppin's (1969) advice, that it is sensible to use clever pupils to calibrate difficult items, and foolish pupils for easy items, is as relevant as ever.

Data Editing

Where it is suspected that the calibration sample is not quite appropriate, steps can be taken to, in Tukey's phrase, 'vacuum clean' the observations by editing the data so that dubious observations are removed, thus improving fit. By 'dubious observations' I mean items answered correctly by those whose chances of doing so are calculated on the basis of the model to be very small (say, less than 0.05) or alternatively items answered incorrectly by those whose chances are calculated as being very high (say, greater than 0.95). Waller (1974, 1975) has developed techniques for data editing in the context of the Rasch and normal ogive models and has shown that a significant improvement in fit can result. We have tried these procedures and agree that they can bring about improved fit. However, a note of caution should be sounded against over-zealous data editing which can easily turn into fudging. The danger is that genuine observations may be deleted, genuine because the low scoring individual who is assumed to be guessing may actually possess 'pockets' of knowledge which he is able to turn into correct answers. By the same token, the high scoring individual may have pockets of ignorance, especially given the sort of achievement test where a broad syllabus has to be covered and individuals or schools may opt to omit certain sections to make examination preparation more manageable.

How Far Should Abilities Be Measured Separately?

It looks as if, by one means or another, heterogeneous collections of items can be made to fit response models even though inspection suggests strongly that the items are not congruent, as where groups of items call on psychologically distinguishable processes — different item-types, for instance. What are we to make of this sort of outcome? Levy (1973), who has a penetrating discussion on the subject, seems to be arguing that if we are seriously interested in pure trait measurement we should keep apparently different groups of items separate. But would there be much point in practice?

Experience shows that correlations between trait measures among adolescents are often high, the likely reason being, as Levy (1973, p. 6) himself points out, that children developing in a particular culture are likely to accrue knowledge, processes or whatever at different rates but in a similar order. Correlations between individual items may be low, as noted, but they are likely to be no higher within *a priori* domains as across domains, a source of frustration to those who hope to define distinctive traits (Wijnen, 1974). Levy (1973, p. 11) offers the idea that ostensibly different items may be behaviourally equivalent, that is, there are alternative routes through what he regards as the simplex of development. This notion may, or may not, have some validity. It is not clear how one would ever know one way or the other.

The fact must be faced that fit to a statistical model is not necessarily informative about traits. Moreover, whatever inferences are made will depend on the model being used. The Rasch model leads to narrower trait definition because it imposes more stringent fit criteria. Which poses a dilemma: do you tighten up fit criteria and shrink domains or do you stick with broad classes of items? At this point statistics are irrelevant. You must decide on pedagogic or logical grounds whether and how to compartmentalize. Just because scientific reasoning and comprehension scores correlate highly is no reason to suppress the distinction between them (Cronbach, 1970). Likewise, some skills may be relatively undifferentiated at a certain stage of development whereas it is known that they become more differentiated later on. On the other hand there is probably no good reason for differentiating between objective item types.

All these decisions imply the existence of trait theories which are tested out by the data. Here we come to the heart of construct validation, in particular what has been called *substantive* validity which Messick (*op. cit.*) characterizes as involving a confrontation between content representativeness and response consistency. Representative items are included in an item pool on the basis of theoretical conceptions of a behavioural domain, including theories of the processes that produce the behaviours. These theories are examined in terms of items which fit (and don't fit).

That looks good on paper but theory generation has not been a strong point in educational measurement. Levy (*op. cit.*, p. 36) complains that classical procedures for construct validation in psychological measurement are flabby and *post hoc* and the same must be true of educational measurement, even more so. He calls for tests constructed to test hypotheses and fewer hypotheses about tests. Likewise, Whitely and Dawis claim that what impedes wider use of the Rasch model is the dearth of substantive trait theory.

My own view is that generation of trait theory must proceed from an analysis of the way learning and therefore achievement cumulates. This is an area which, as far as I can see, is more or less *terra incognita*. Whether we should follow Guttman and Levy and erect the simplex as the basic model of growth I do not know, but I am sure where the analysis must start.

Whatever the theoretical position taken it is evident that a serious attempt at trait validation would represent a considerable undertaking on the part of those concerned with running item banks. No doubt some will argue that this sort of work has nothing to do with the business of an item bank. The question to be resolved is this: should we regard an item bank as a continually evolving measurement system in which construct validation is a permanent activity (cf. Cronbach, 1975) or should we see it as a resource which remains in a more or less fixed state without any responsibility for verifying what it claims to be offering, if indeed it makes any claims at all? My future interest in item banks is very much tied up with the answer to this question.

Note

1 In passing, it may be noted that ability scores derived from the Rasch model can be used as indices of success on a specified group of items in exactly the same way as number correct since the two are correlated perfectly. To this extent ability scores lend themselves to criterion-referenced interpretation (Whitely and Dawis, 1974, p. 169). This is only true, however, in conventional group testing situations. Ability estimates derived from the three-parameter models may also be used for the same purposes although, of course, these estimates will generally not be correlated perfectly with number correct.

References

ANDERSON, R.C. (1972) 'How to construct achievement tests to assess comprehension', *Review of Education Research*, 42, pp. 145–70.

ANDERSON, J., KEARNEY, G.E. and EVERETT, A.V. 'An evaluation of Rasch's structural model for test items', *British Journal of Mathematical and Statistical Psychology*, 21, pp. 231–8

BOCK, R.D. and WOOD, R. (1971) 'Test theory', *Annual Review of Psychology*, 22, pp. 193–224.

CHOPPIN, B.H. 'An item bank using sample-free calibration', in WOOD, R. and SKURNIK, L.S. (1969) *Item Banking*. Slough, National Foundation for Educational Research.

CRONBACH, L.J. (1970) 'Validation of educational measures', in *Proceedings of the 1969 Invitational Conference on Testing Problems*. Princeton, NJ. Educational Testing Service.

CRONBACH, L.J. (1975) 'Beyond the two disciplines of scientific psychology', *American Psychologist*, 30, pp. 116–27.

CRONBACH, L.J., GLESER, G.C., NANDA, H. and RAJARATNAM, N. (1972) *The Dependability of Behavioral Measurements: Theory of Generalizability for Scores and Profiles*. New York, Wiley.

EYSENCK, H.J. (1975) 'Who needs a random sample?', *Bulletin British Psychological Society*, 28, pp. 195–8.

FHANÉR, S. (1974) 'Item sampling and decision-making in achievement testing', *British Journal of Mathematical and Statistical Psychology*, 27, pp.172–5.

GULLIKSEN, H. (1950) *Theory of Mental Tests*. New York, Wiley.

GUTTMAN, L. (1969) 'Review of Lord and Novick's' *Statistical Theories of Mental Test Scores*', *Psychometrika*, 34, pp. 398–404.

HENRYSSON, S. (1971) 'Gathering, analyzing and using data on test items', in THORNDIKE, R.L. (Ed.) *Educational Measurement*. Washington, D.C., American Council on Education.

JACKSON, P.H. (1973) 'The estimation of true score variance and error variance in the classical test theory model', *Psychometrika*, 38, pp. 183–201.

KOLAKOWSKI, D. and BOCK, R.D. (1973) *NORMOG: Maximum Likelihood Item Analysis and Test Scoring — Normal Ogive Model*. Chicago, National Educational Resources.

LEVY, P.H. (1973) 'On the relation between test theory and psychology', in KLINE, P. (Ed.), *New Approaches in Psychological Measurement*, New York, Wiley.

LOEVINGER, J. (1965) 'Person and population as psychometric concepts', *Psychological Review*, 72, pp. 143–55.

LORD, F.M. (1974) 'Individualized testing and item characteristic curve theory', in ATKINSON, R.C., KRANTZ, D.H., LUCE, R.D. and SUPPES, P. (Eds.) *Contemporary Developments in Mathematical Psychology*. Volume II: Measurement, Psychophysics, and Neural Information Processing. San Francisco, Freeman.

LORD, F.M. and NOVICK, M.R. (1968) *Statistical Theories of Mental Test Scores*. New York, Addison Wesley.

McBRIDE, J.R. and WEISS, D.J. (1974) 'A word knowledge item pool for adaptive ability measurement', *Research Report*, 74–2. Psychometric Methods Program, University of Minnesota.

McDONALD, R.P. and AHLAWAT, K.S. (1974) 'Difficulty factors in binary data', *British Journal of Mathematical and Statistical Psychology*, 27, pp. 82–99.

MARITZ, J.S. (1965) 'Nonlinear probit analysis and its application to psychometric data', *Psychometrika*, 30, pp. 31–8.

MESSICK, S. (1975) 'The standard problem: Meaning and values in measurement and evaluation', *American Psychologist*, 30, pp. 955–66.

NOVICK, M.R. (1969) 'Bayesian methods in psychological testing', *Research Bulletin*, 69–31, Princeton, Educational Testing Service.

OSBURN, H.G. (1968) 'Item sampling for achievement testing', *Educational and Psychological Measurement*, 28, pp. 95–104.

ROSS, J. and LUMSDEN, J. (1968) 'Attribute and reliability', *British Journal of Mathematical and Statistical Psychology*, 21, pp. 251–64.

SHOEMAKER, D.M. (1975) 'Towards a framework for achievement testing', *Review of Educational Research*, 45, pp. 127–48.

WAINER, H. (1971) 'Piecewise regression: A simplified procedure', *British Journal of Mathematical and Statistical Psychology*, 24, pp. 83–92.

WALLER, M.I. (1974) 'Removing the effects of random guessing from latent trait ability estimates', *Research Bulletin*, 74–32. Princeton, Educational Testing Service.

WALLER, M.I. (1975) 'Estimating parameters in the Rasch model: Removing the effects of random guessing', paper presented at the Annual Convention of the American Educational Research Association Washington, D.C.

WHITELY, S. and DAWIS, R.V. (1974) 'The nature of objectivity with the Rasch model', *Journal of Educational Measurement*, 11, pp. 163–78.

WIJNEN, W.H. (1974) 'Formative evaluation and educational practice', in CROMBAG, H.F. and de GRUIJTER, D.N. (Eds.). *Contemporary Issues in Educational Testing*, The Hague, Mouton.

WILLMOTT, A.S. and FOWLES, D.E. (1974) *The Objective Interpretation of Test Performance: The Rasch Model Applied*, Slough, National Foundation for Educational Research.

WOOD, R. (1973) 'Response-contingent testing', *Review of Educational Research*, 43, pp. 529–44.

WOOD, R. (1974) 'Question banking', in MACINTOSH, H.G. (Ed.), *Techniques and Problems of Assessment*. London, Edward Arnold.

WOOD, R. (1976a) 'A reaction to Harvey's "Some thoughts on norm-referenced and criterion-referenced measures"'. *Research in Education*, 15, pp. 69–72.

WOOD, R. (1976b) 'Adaptive testing: A Bayesian procedure for the efficient measurement of ability', *Programmed Learning and Educational Technology*, April.

WOOD, R. (1976c) 'Halo and other effects in teacher assessments', *Durham Research Review*, 7, pp. 1120–6 and in this volume.

WOOD, R. and SKURNIK, L.S. (1969) *Item Banking: A Method for Producing School-based Examinations and Nationally Comparable Grades*. Slough, National Foundation for Educational Research.

Paper 8: Fitting the Rasch Model — A Heady Tale[*]

It is shown that the Rasch model fits simulated coin-tossing data very well. An explanation is offered and in the ensuing discussion issues concerning the fitting of latent trait models are raised.

Introduction

In addition to fitting cognitive data, the Rasch model has been shown to fit affective data (Anderson, 1976*a*) and personality data (Anderson 1976*b*). Fischer (1976) mentions other spheres of application including industrial medicine and communications theory. How does a model as versatile as this cope with the results of tossing a coin?

It will be recalled that the Rasch model postulates that the probability of a correct item response is a multiplicative function of the ability of the individual and the difficulty of the item, or else an additive function of the log of the ability and the log of the difficulty. Nothing else enters into it. Thus in a coin-tossing context the outcome of tossing a coin can be seen as a function of the ability of the tosser and a property of the coin which might be called its bias. An unbiased coin gives equal numbers of heads and tails over the long run while bias leads to a preponderance of heads or tails. It is axiomatic that someone who is 'headstrong', i.e. good at producing heads, is better able to deal with a tail-biased coin than someone who is, to coin a phrase, 'weak in the heads'.

Data and Analysis

Using RANDU from the IBM scientific subroutine package 50 coin tosses for each of 500 individuals were simulated. The resulting 500 × 50 response

---

[*]Reprinted from *British Journal of Mathematical and Statistical Psychology* (1978), 31, pp. 27–32.

matrix was tested for fit using Choppin's (1974) calibration procedure. Although the approach is different, experience shows that the person and item calibrations and tests of fit give similar results to those obtained using the simultaneous maximum-likelihood solution of Wright and Panchapakesan (1969).

Results

There is nothing absolute about fit, of course. As Choppin (1976) observes, 'Eventually every item will show discrepancies; every item can be discarded; no item fits the model exactly'. Tendencies are all we can observe, using some formal statistical test as a basis for judgment. Using the chi-square test of item fit provided in Choppin's program it transpired that for the fifty simulated items or tosses, forty-two had values less than the 90th percentile point of the chi-square distribution, five lay between the 90th and 95th percentiles, two lay between the 95th and 97.5 percentiles and only one value exceeded the 97.5 percentile point.

By conventional standards, then, the fit is more than adequate. As to why a few tosses should have produced larger chi-square values, various possibilities suggest themselves. The coin might be caught by a gust of wind at the wrong moment (cf. the 'lawn-mower' effect in achievement testing) or else the coin might be tossed with an extra vehemence which could be said to introduce extraneous factors, such as physicality, into the proceedings. Another less frequently observed reason for lack of fit occurs when a 'smart' tosser inexplicably fails with certain tosses. The reasons for this are not always obvious; sometimes it is overconfidence, as when the coin is tossed too casually; sometimes the tosser shouts too soon and what would ordinarily have been a head becomes a tail. Because this behaviour introduces 'noise' into the data it is sometimes necessary to delete these untoward outcomes in order to make the data fit the model for, as champions of the Rasch model are fond of saying, 'It is not a question of the model fitting the data but the data fitting the model' (Willmott and Fowles, 1974, p. 24).

Prospects

Once 'sample-freeness' is established and it is known that coins will behave in the same way when tossed regardless of who tosses them, exciting possibilities open up. One is that the ratio scale property of the Rasch model enables us to make statements like 'gambler X has twice as much coin-tossing ability as gambler Y'. Another is the construction of a 'bank' of coins on which prospective coin-tossers such as cricket captains can draw, knowing that the properties of the coins they choose are calibrated. For once 'bank' is the *mot juste*. Nor is it too far-fetched to imagine constructing a bank of coins to suit not just an ability range but an age range also. To quote Willmott and Fowles (1974, p. 55), 'If a trait is able to be determined in children of age 10, is the same trait identifiable in children of 11, 12, 13, etc?' Needless to say, any such enterprise should articulate with developmental theories concerning the growth of coin-tossing ability, from the moral opportunism of 'best out of 3' to the mature understanding of 'the long run'.

Explanations, Contradictions

To see why the Rasch model fits random data with barely a hiccup, we might start with Birnbaum's two-parameter logistic model:

$$P_g(\theta) = \{1 + \exp[-Da_g(\theta - b_g)]\}^{-1}, g = 1, 2, \ldots, n.$$

Here $P_g(\theta)$ is the probability that an examinee with ability θ answers item g correctly, a_g and b_g are parameters for item g and n is the number of items in the test. The parameter b_g is usually referred to as the index of *item difficulty* and represents the point on the ability scale at which the slope of the item characteristic curve is a maximum. The parameter, a_g, called *item discrimination*, is proportional to the slope of $P_g(\theta)$ at the point $\theta = b_g$. Finally, D is a scaling factor usually taken to be 1.7 to bring the logistic and normal ogive models into harmony.

Now the Rasch model can be viewed as a special case of Birnbaum's model in which all the items are assumed to have equal discriminating power so that the rate at which the probability of passing the item increases with total score will be the same for all items and the only difference between the items will be in terms of difficulty. The easiest way to get from the Birnbaum to the Rasch model is to let each $a_g = 1$ and $D = 1$, giving

$$P_g(\theta) = \{1 + \exp(b_g - \theta)\}^{-1}.$$

This is what Birnbaum (1968, p. 402) does, but that seems to me too convenient; a_g is seldom as high as one and D is set at 1.7 for a purpose. More to my liking is Hambleton and Traub's (1973) approach which is to write the model as follows:

$$P_g(\theta) = \{1 + \exp[-D\bar{a}(\theta - b_g)]\}^{-1},$$

where $\bar{a}$ is the common level of discrimination for all items, estimated by the observed average value of a_g.

What the last equation does is to make it clear that when θ is estimated, it is always scaled by a factor $D\bar{a}$. This means that, contrary to what was said in the introduction, the Rasch model is not simply additive; but the existence of these other terms is seldom if ever mentioned by presenters of the Rasch model. It is also apparent that providing values of a_g are not far removed from $\bar{a}$, so that the assumption of equal discrimination is more or less met, the *size* of $\bar{a}$ is immaterial. Due to variations in item difficulty across the score range, items may still fail to fit the model, even when $a = \bar{a}$, but it will not be because $\bar{a}$ is too low or too high.

In a way there is no more to be said; the coin tosses fit the model because they are equivalent within sampling (i.e. error) variation even though if they were items they would be quite useless for measurement purposes. But perhaps there is more to be said about $\bar{a}$. In the first place, why is each a_g, and therefore $\bar{a}$, not zero when the data are random? The answer lies in the spurious inflation given to the biserial correlation by the item itself being included in the total score. In these circumstances it turns out (Guilford, 1954, p. 439) that the value of the biserial correlation for each item is a constant, $1/\sqrt{n}$, where n is the number of items. Letting r_g stand for the biserial, application of the formula $a_g = r_g/\sqrt{(1 - r_g^2)}$ gives a constant value for a_g of $1/\sqrt{(n - 1)}$. With $n = 50$ for the coin-tossing data, a_g and therefore $\bar{a}$ turns out to be 1/7 or 0.14, which may be compared with the observed range of values for a_g of 0.09 to 0.25.

Now the values of a_g should really be corrected for spurious inflation although this is seldom, if ever, done in the latent trait estimation probably because it usually makes little difference. In this case, of course, it matters crucially, but there is no point in applying a correction formula because we know that the a_gs and $\bar{a}$ should be zero. The upshot is that the set of 50 coin tosses corresponds to 50 item characteristic curves, all parallel to the abscissa or θ axis, so that estimation of θ is impossible. This can be seen explicitly in Birnbaum's (1968, p. 458) formula for the maximum-likelihood estimator of θ,

$$\hat{\theta} = b + \frac{1}{D\bar{a}} \log \left(\frac{\bar{u}}{1 - \bar{u}} \right),$$

where $\bar{u} = \Sigma_{g=1}^{n} u_g/n$ and u_g are item responses, scored 0 or 1. Since for these data $\bar{u}$ is always $\frac{1}{2}$ (without error variation), then providing $\bar{a} \neq 0$, $\hat{\theta} = b$ but if $\bar{a} = 0$, $\hat{\theta}$ goes to infinity.

So much for what happens to $\bar{a}$ with random data, but otherwise does it have any rôle to play in the Rasch model? Wright and Panchapakesan (1969, p. 25) state categorically, first, that 'if a given set of items fit the model this is evidence that they refer to a unidimensional ability, that they form a conformable set' and then that 'fit to the model also implies that item discriminations are uniform *and substantial*' (my italics). Whether the last claim is based on some kind of circular reasoning — if items fit the model they form a conformable set, therefore they must be highly correlated — is not clear but nowhere is proof offered of the connection between 'substantial' discrimination values and fit to the model. On the contrary, Wright and Panchapakesan are at pains to point out that while conventional item selection procedures reject items of low reliability or validity the only criterion for fit to the Rasch model is conformability.

If fit to the Rasch model does not guarantee a substantial $\bar{a}$, then, in one referee's opinion, it will have to be regarded as a necessary condition for fit over and above statistical fit. Coin tosses, he points out, may fit the model but will have zero reliability — which they do — when what is wanted is a common discriminating value which is high enough that *'the test reliability is acceptable'* (my emphasis). But how high do biserials or item intercorrelations have to be before the statistical fit can be taken seriously? There is no answer to this question, just as there is no answer to the question, 'Is this test homogenous enough, or is it too heterogenous?' This was demonstrated some years ago by Ebel (1968) and Horn (1968) in a stimulating exchange about the value of internal consistency where achievement tests are concerned. Ebel put the case that tests must be internally consistent if they are to discriminate and what is the good of a test which does not discriminate, that interdependencies in the structure of competence tend to bring about moderately high internal consistency, anyway, that measures of internal consistency give reasonably good estimates of reliability (although he conceded that a test could be perfectly reliable, in the variance ratio sense and yet have zero internal consistency) and that lack of reliability impairs the value of any measurement, whatever it is used for. To this Horn countered that what matters above all in achievement test is representativeness of content and that internal consistency is a secondary consideration. The chips must be allowed to fall where they may and if that means no score variance, so be it. Horn even went further and suggested that in some circumstances high internal consistency may even be a counter-indication of validity. Now Horn and Ebel had to agree to disagree, but in practice achievement test constructors invariably find themselves torn between the conflicting claims of homogeneity and heterogeneity and in the process become thoroughly mixed up. On the one hand they want to 'cover the syllabus' by sampling content according to a specification, while on the other they worry about biserials being above a certain notional figure. The result is an uneasy compromise, leading to estimates of internal consistency of around 0.85 which are recognized as so-so but are not low enough (being in the 80s) for the test to be branded as unreliable or rather, too heterogeneous.

Of course, life is a lot simpler if you believe in homogeneity and in the possibility of realizing it. I am an infidel where unidimensionality is concerned, but Lumsden (1976) is one who takes the view that by constructing items carefully and deliberately high internal consistency can be achieved. More than that, he maintains (Lumsden, 1978) that providing they are constructed so as to be unidimensional tests are bound to be perfectly reliable — it is people who are unreliable. In this scenario homogeneity, unidimensionality, test reliability, uniform item characteristic curves and fit to the Rasch model imply and are implied by each other. It is a closed system of measurement with all the assumptions and consequences laid out for all to see. Whether it is realistic is another matter. In general it seems to me that applied workers seeking to use the Rasch model for non-trivial purposes will be unable to escape the Ebel-Horn dilemma and will have to deal with it as best they can.

Concluding Remarks

There are so many issues concerning the nature and purpose of measurement to be attended to that fit to the Rasch or any other latent trait model is almost irrelevant. Nothing is necessarily to be deduced from items fitting — or not fitting — although I would not expect Wright, the person most closely identified with the Rasch model, to agree with that statement. His position, which has much in common with that of Lumsden (1978), is uncompromising. If a set of items all bear on a single common latent variable, then the Rasch model is the necessary and sufficient conceptualization. If they do not, then the set of items contains a mixture of variables and there is no simple, efficient or unique way to know their utility for measuring anything (Wright, 1977, p. 224). The choice is a stark one but thanks to Wright (1977) and especially to Whitely (1977) the issues are now out in the open and those who have flirted with the Rasch model must make up their minds where they stand; the time for aimless fishing expeditions with whatever items are to hand, followed by what Choppin (1976) calls 'the witch-hunt for non-conformable items', is past. It comes down to this. By narrowing the scope of the tests in order to fit the Rasch model we may run the risk of throwing out the baby with the bath water, even though the measurements have desirable, perhaps even necessary, properties, but by insisting on heterogeneous, content-rich tests, and rejecting the properties of the Rasch model, are we thereby denying ourselves the possibility of *any* coherent measurement? I am persuaded by Lumsden (1978) that two- and three-parameter models are not the answer — 'test scaling models are self-contradictory if they assert both unidimensionality and different slopes for the item characteristic curves' — apart from which weighting marks according to discrimination is likely to harm content validity. So what is left? Adding marks together, I suppose, which leaves Wright with the last laugh, 'Everyone who is content to use test scores which are unweighted by item discrimination and/or uncorrected for guessing, the practice followed by nearly all practitioners, is assuming that their items are in fact working in just the way modeled by Rasch, whether they realize and capitalize on that assumption or not' (Wright, 1977, p. 220). Perhaps tossing a coin may be necessary after all!

Acknowledgement

I would like to thank the referees and the editor for prodding me into writing the final two sections.

References

ANDERSON, L.W. (1976a). 'Affective data analyzed with the Rasch model', paper given at the annual meeting, of the American Educational Research Association, San Francisco.

ANDERSON, L.W. (1976*b*). 'Using the Rasch model to measure the development of self-concept', paper given at the annual meeting of the American Educational Research Association, San Francisco.

BIRNBAUM, A. (1968). 'Some latent trait models and their use in inferring an examinee's ability', in LORD, F.M. and NOVICK, M.R. (Eds.), *Statistical Theories of Mental Test Scores*, Reading, MA, Addison-Wesley.

CHOPPIN, B.H. (1974). *Rasch/Choppin Pair-wise Analysis: Express Calibration by Pair-X*, Slough, NFER.

CHOPPIN, B.H. (1976). 'Recent developments in item banking: A review'. in de GRUITJER, D.N.M. and van der KAMP, L.J. Th. (Eds.), *Advances in Psychological and Educational Measurement*, London, Wiley.

EBEL, R.L. (1968). 'The value of internal consistency in classroom examinations', *Journal of Educational Measurement*, 5, pp. 71–4.

FISCHER, G.H. (1976) 'Some probabilistic models for measuring change', in de GRUITJER, D.N.M. and van der KAMP, L.J. Th. (Eds.), *Advances in Psychological and Educational Measurement*, London, Wiley.

GUILFORD, J.P. (1954) *Psychometric Methods*, New York, McGraw-Hill.

HAMBLETON, R.K. and TRAUB, R.E. (1973). 'Analysis of empirical data using two logistic latent trait models', *British Journal of Mathematical and Statistical Psychology*, 26, pp.195–211.

HORN, J.L. (1968). 'Is it reasonable for assessments to have different psychometric properties than predictors?', *Journal of Educational Measurement*, 5, pp. 75–8.

LUMSDEN, J. (1976) 'Test theory', *Ann. Rev. Psychol.* 27, pp. 251–80.

LUMSDEN, J. (1978) 'Tests are perfectly reliable', *British Journal of Mathematical and Statistical Psychology*, 31, pp. 19–26.

WHITELEY, S.E. (1977). 'Models, meanings and misunderstandings: Some issues in applying Rasch's theory', *Journal of Educational Measurement*, 14, pp. 227–35.

WILLMOTT, A.S. and FOWLES, D.E. (1974). *The Objective Interpretation of Test Performance: The Rasch Model Applied*, Slough, NFER.

WRIGHT, B.D. (1977). 'Misunderstanding the Rasch model', *Journal of Educational Measurement*, 14, pp. 219–25.

WRIGHT, B.D. and PANCHAPAKESAN, N. (1969). 'A procedure for sample-free item analysis', *Educational and Psychological Measurement*, 29, pp. 23–45.

Paper 9: The Rasch Model and Modelling

The item below appeared in the *Education Guardian* of 15 June 1982 under the headline 'Rasch judgement'. It tickled me pink, above all the gossip columnish way with personalities. That a psychometric model should be written about in this breathless way was too much. I was glad my name was missing when it could so easily have been there among the critics, but I was keeping my head down in Jamaica. Anyway the upshot was that I was stimulated to write a piece on modelling. *New Society* didn't want it (I had hoped to capitalize on a remark by the then editor, Paul Barker, to the effect that behavioural scientists didn't have to carry the can for their mistakes whereas architects and engineers did) and I didn't try anywhere else.

> One of the most gruelling heavyweight contests educational research has seen this decade has just ended. Millions of pounds have been spent here and in the US, Canada, and elsewhere: statisticians have slogged it out in seminars around the world and outside the ring allegations of shifty behaviour and non-scientific politicking have circulated.
>
> But in Britain at least, the fight is over. The statistical technique that some statisticians and politicians hoped was the magic weapon that would transform testing in our schools — the Rasch model — has been officially discredited ...
>
> The National Foundation for Educational Research and the Government's Assessment of Performance Unit plunged in and half a million was quickly spent. But the critics of Rasch were also organising, notably Professor Harvey Goldstein of the London Institute and Professor Desmond Nuttall of the Open University. Rasch was put to the question in London, New York, and elsewhere, and in many eyes was found wanting.
>
> The NFER's Deputy Director, the redoubtable Dr. Clare Burstall, changed sides and came out against Rasch and Professor Goldstein was invited in as statistical adviser. The NFER's main Rasch user, Dr. Bruce

Choppin, upped and left for California (where the Rasch model is still is use).

The Rasch model was formulated by a Danish mathematical statistician, Georg Rasch. He was working in a psychological milieu, and the first thing to say is that psychologists have shown little interest in his model, or rather models. Rather Rasch has been used, abused and argued over largely by people in education, especially the quantitative types. The number of genuine psychological applications of the Rasch model can, I suspect, be counted on fingers and toes. Rasch would have been disappointed. Of his several models, the Poisson-based model for misreadings is particularly interesting.

So the finger cannot really be pointed at psychologists this time. True, the psychologists behind the British Ability Scale backed the Rasch model. Where do they stand now? Elsewhere in Europe, the Nordic part of it at any rate, there seems remarkable unanimity that the Rasch model is a good thing. Scandinavia, perhaps inevitably, Holland, West Germany, Austria — these countries together represent a rump for Rasch. Other psychometric work coming out of these countries suggests that they are carrying on in the finest brass-ruler tradition, refusing to let reality testing spoil things. Does anyone have any idea why this is? In the US battle-lines were drawn but the argument has never come to a head as it has done in the UK. The people who run the National Assessment program were wise enough to keep off Rasch.

Having been involved in the Rasch story off and on since 1967, when I sent data to Chicago from England (NFER as it happens) to be fitted to the model, I have found much to ponder in the whole episode. My thoughts fan out from specific aspects of the Rasch model to general considerations of modelling and modellers.

For the uninitiated, Rasch demands an unusual philosophical commitment which takes some getting used to. Data must fit the model, rather than the other way round, which some of us had got into the habit of believing. But that was rigid of us. After all, if a model fails to fit a body of data then it is not hard to imagine that by disaggregating it will be possible to find somewhere a parcel of data which fits the model. The question then is 'What does the fit mean?' Presumably there is little scope for generalization. So it is with the Rasch model in certain applications, especially the measurement of educational achievement.

It is precisely this application which has caused all the fuss. Psychometricians are notoriously insensitive to the distinguishing characteristics of achievement and usually treat aptitude, ability and achievement as interchangeable. That did not matter for a time, and besides we were all rather bowled over by the audacity of the model, the existence of measurement problems to which the model seemed to hold solutions and the bravura presentations of the man who became identified with the RAsch model — Benjamin Wright of the University of Chicago. Not until the NFER thought to use Rasch on national assessment data did the balloon go up. A crucial assumption underpinning Rasch or, what comes to the same thing, a requirement of the model — that the relative difficulties of items should remain the same regardless of sample, classroom, time etc — was suddenly exposed. A new psychometrics textbook, by no means hostile to Rasch, states, as an express condition necessary for Rasch to work, that items should reflect general growth in some attribute rather than specific instruction (Thorndike, 1982). In measures of academic achievement, Thorndike says, focused instruction could be expected to shift radically the relative difficulty of items involving a topic that had just been taught, to which might added that such 'focused' instruction might be precisely what is needed as a matter of urgency or even on a routine basis. As Goldstein, among others, has pointed out, the essence of many educational systems is the diversity of approaches whose actual aim is to create differential attainments among otherwise similar children, for example, by way of the order of teaching or as a result of different pedagogical objectives (Goldstein, 1979). That smart cookie, Maurice Holt, spotted straight away that the pedagogical implications of the Rasch model are unacceptable. He was especially dismissive; it (the Rasch model) should never have been allowed to stray outside a test technician's laboratory (Holt, 1981, p. 68).

A consequence of the unorthodox philosophical stance is that it takes a great act of will to reject the model, much greater than if the model were presented in the conventional way. The attitude has been 'Here is a model you can use. If you don't like it, don't use it but don't complain about it.' Probably because of this attitude, there has been an absence of what has been called 'counterperspective', or just simply devil's advocacy on the part of those promoting the model. This was to be expected given the way the model was announced or rather reannounced in its popularized form by Ben Wright (Wright, 1968). The language he used then was distinctly boosterish and his supporters caught the habit. It has been irritation with intemperate language and immoderate claims which, as much as anything, led to the denouément reported in the *Guardian*. My own reaction was, first, to draw parallels with the selling of soap powder, and then to publish a lampoon in a serious journal (Wood, 1978); this last effort was not appreciated among the ranks of the true believers. (A rather serious Swede was very severe on me but he may have missed the humour, which I grant was out of place.) Meanwhile the hype goes on. There are still plenty of audiences ripe for Rasch. When I went to the Caribbean I was disturbed — but not surprised — to find that talk of Rasch was in the air. The inevitable promotional article had already been written in language which was horribly familiar, down to the rhetoric. Here is the last sentence of the article. Note the strongly pointed implication that to ignore the Rasch model is to remain backward. 'It remains to be seen if bodies such as the Caribbean Examinations Council decide to take the task of testing and measurement seriously, or if they decide to let it remain at the level of a "cottage industry"' (Mathias, 1980).

Modelling seems to be out of vogue in psychology, if it was ever in. Sociologists have the habit more. Overt modelling, that is; there is plenty of covert off-the-peg modelling, so covert you hardly notice it is happening. I'm talking about regression, analysis of variance, even correlation. Such models are seldom stated in formal symbolic language; instead the reader has to cope with calculations. It is, of course, quite brave to write down a model; you might lose half your readers there and then.

Econometric modellers build cumulative models comprising hundreds of equations. Psychologists don't, which some might think a good thing; I doubt if we want 400-equation models of the psychology of bereavement even if there is no problem getting data. What happens instead is a bit of tinkering; there seems to be no ambition to build anything to take care of contingencies, never mind expand them over the years. Perhaps Cronbach's admonition 'Generalizations decay' has been taken too much to heart. More likely there is a profound queasiness about the whole enterprise of modelling. Consider the one branch of modelling which is ambitious, structural modelling, of which path analysis is the best known example. (This is sociologist's territory really, but psychologists get involved.) It is *extremely* ambitious, as ambitious as 'drawing up causal pathway maps as complete and complex as the real world setting', as one recent text puts it. Readers will have their own reactions to this programme; for me it evokes J.L. Borges' exquisite fragment 'Of Exactitude of Science' which describes how cartographers, dissatisfied with maps of provinces the size of cities, 'evolved a Map of the Empire that was of the same Scale as the Empire and that coincided with it point for point'. Models which make explicit what one knows about a real-world causal nexus are, of course, unmanageable statistically; too many parameters, not enough degrees of freedom. Their value is disciplinary and heuristic. Perhaps there is a heroic element too; they tell us what might be possible if only we could crack the statistical problems.

What, though, of models that are manageable statistically, or are made to be so? The getting out of estimates is taken to be the first order of business but at what cost? Reduced complexity, wholesale elimination of plausible causal connections, omissions which render most of the conclusions suspect; these are the results of the pressure to come up with a model permitting estimation. Here is an example, quite disarming really. 'This model (of school achievement) had to leave out the effects of intelligence, past academic achievement and the potential influence of school district administration. The latter can be of crucial importance to the distribution of both personnel and supplies.' Elsewhere the writer owns up further, 'Pupil attitudes were limited to an index of self-concept development for use in the Ugandan context' (Heyneman, 1976).

Evidently the first casualty of modelling is sophistication. You cannot remain sophisticated *and* say the inane things modelling for statistical convenience forces on you. If I were discussing with someone the determinants of educational achievement I would be sure to introduce all the relevant factors and make all the necessary qualifications, but since I am modelling I will have to do it this way. And this way is embarrassing! I have to say things like 'this model assumes that the quality of a child's environment at age 3 has the same effect on achievement at age 18 as it does on achievement at age 3' and because I am not brazen enough to leave it at that, I have to add 'A strong assumption!'. The exclamation mark is my way of saying 'I don't believe this either but what can you do? We all do this sort of thing so give a fellow a break, won't you?' Naturally there are superior ways of bringing this off which, I suppose, is where the lost sophistication is reinstated. My favourite is the writer who simply refers the reader elsewhere; 'Widmerpool (1976) has the apologies'. Truly, we are different creatures when we are modelling.

Of course the practice of keeping models manageable is defended on impeccable gradualist grounds, and rationalization levels are high. Start with the simplest model and work outwards. Results from early modelling are highly provisional and should not be taken seriously etc. It is interesting, though, how often this injunction is overlooked. Hardly any writer will resist the temptation to draw some conclusion based on his modelling experience even if only of the mildly negative variety, like 'It should not be assumed that what is true of the US is true of Uganda', which could have been said anyway, at any time, without need of proof.

It is interesting, too, how some models never seem to get beyond the primitive stage. Occasionally there are giveaway signs that workers would rather not trade in their simplified models if they can avoid it. Having noted that no direct and stringent test of their model was possible, two American sociologists went on to 'point to some modifications obtained at a price of having to deal with more complicated models, but possibly realizing a gain of a more valid specification' (Sørenson and Hallinan, 1977). Psychologists write in the same defensive vein: 'Thus some detailed modification of the present Maxwell-Boltzmann scheme would perhaps be necessary, yielding a more accurate description of this subsidiary aspect of the data (if indeed it is a reliable one), though possibly at significant cost to the present elegance of the model' (Jones, 1982, p. 125). The perceived need to protect the *elegance* of models seems to be deep-seated.

If elegance is regarded as being the same as parsimony, and I think it is, although it need not be, then this attitude is understandable, for were we not all brought up to believe in parsimony, to carry with us and to wield Occam's razor at all times? There is something disconcerting about the hostility to ultra-simple models. Is there some new strain of anti-rationalism abroad, what Isaiah Berlin meant when writing of Schelling and other German thinkers of the Counter-Enlightenment 'for whom the seamless whole of reality in its unana-lysable flow is misrepresented by the static, spatial metaphors of mathematics and the natural sciences?'. To dissect is to murder and so on (Berlin, 1981, p. 9). Such a strain of thought, which has probably always been represented in the social sciences — 'illuminative evaluation' has more than a touch of it although it too wishes to dissect although not quantitatively — would, of course, be hostile to any modelling enterprise and might even be more friendly to ultra-simple models on the grounds that they are so obviously inadequate. For what the critics are saying is that the simple models cannot possibly fit complex data so that more complicated models must be sought or else, perhaps, the subject, for example, educational achievement is unmodellable and should be left alone. On this they are not clear. They would, however, say as a corollary to 'simple models cannot fit complex data' that if they do something must be wrong.

I do not want to get into what constitutes 'fit' here. It is a technical matter on which statisticians are far from being agreed. But more needs to be said about the surprise element of fitting, indeed it is worth analyzing as a little piece of psychology in itself. Now when I mention 'surprise' I am not talking about anything as improbable as Rutherford's elephant bouncing off a piece of confetti (his own description of his particle theory); it is rather the everyday experience modellers have when their greatly simplified models fit data tolerably well. The question though is 'Why'. The fit needs interpretation, just as a high correlation would. The alternative is to surrender to a black box mentality. Too many people who have fitted data to the Rasch model, especially under the flag of robustness, have been too pleased with the fit to bother about asking why, or for how long, or, as I have indicated, what pedagogical view allegiance to the model might commit them to. This is true even when, as is now happening, people are going to the trouble of commencing articles with a list of all the reasons why Rasch should not fit. When fit materializes, the reasons melt away. If this sounds like dishonesty then I have to add that those who seize hold of it, like those who seize hold of favourable correlations, may barely be aware of what they are doing. I.J. Good put it beautifully when he said that the statistician rationalizes by 'pretending he has a train to catch' (Good, 1965).

I do not think that anti-rationalism is responsible for hostility to modelling. The severest critics of Rasch go in for modelling themselves, for example, Goldstein. No, it is as I said. It is the claims made for models which offend, not the models themselves. Evidently the trick is not to become visible. There is no such thing as tentative publicity. Perhaps the greatest irony attaching to the Rasch model is that it is probabilistic in character, which suggests that we should have been judging it in those terms, but that has not happened. In spite of using such ludicrous language, the *Guardian* piece manages to suggest quite accurately how models come to grief for all sorts of reasons, mostly personal and political. (For a very much more interesting companion piece on the world of econometric modellers, see 'The model that crashed', *New Society*, 12 August 1982.)

I had wondered whether the Rasch model brouhaha illustrated any truths concerning modelling. I think it does. I think it illustrates the wish to cling to simple models and to protect them and their elegance against ephemeral and questionable data. Never mind all the humbug about the gradualist tradition, which I suppose most people would have said they belonged to, if they thought about it at all. Why shift when you have got something that looks good? Essentially people find or develop a model they like and stick to it, especially if their thinking is motivated by adversarial challenge. Taste and style and temperament count, as in all things.

References

BERLIN, I. (1981) *Against the Current*, Oxford, Oxford University Press.

GOLDSTEIN, H. (1979) 'Consequences of using the Rasch model for educational assessment', *British Educational Research Journal*, 5, pp. 211–20.

GOOD, I.J. (1965), quoted by WISE, M.E. in GOOD, I.J. (Ed.) *The Scientist Speculates*, New York, Capricorn Books., p. 374.

HEYNEMAN, S.P. (1976) 'Influences on academic achievement: A comparison of results from Uganda and more industrialized societies', *Sociology of Education*, 49, pp. 200–11.

HOLT, M. (1981) *Evaluating the Evaluators*, London, Hodder and Stoughton.

JONES, G.V. (1982). 'Letter transpositions in words; Application of a fixed-constraint model', *British Journal of Mathematical and Statistical Psychology*, 35, pp. 117–27.

MATHIAS, B. (1980) 'Objectivity of measurement: An introduction to the Rasch model of test calibration', *Caribbean Journal of Education*, 7, pp. 193–202.

SØRENSON, A.B. and HALLINAN, M.T. (1977) 'A reconceptualization of school effects', *Sociology of Education*, 50, pp. 273–89.

THORNDIKE, R.L. (1982) *Applied Psychometrics*, Boston, MA, Houghton and Mifflin.

WRIGHT, B.D. (1968) 'Sample-free test calibration and person measurement', in *Proceedings of the 1967 Invitational Conference on Testing Problems*, Princeton, NJ, Educational Testing Service, pp. 85–101.

WOOD, R. (1978). 'Fitting the Rasch model — a heady tale', *British Journal of Mathematical and Statistical Psychology*, 31, pp. 27–32 and in this volume.

Paper 10: D.N. Lawley and the Convergence of Factor Analysis and Latent Trait Theory

A Tribute to Lawley and a Tantalizing Synchronicity

D.N. Lawley, who retired in 1982 but is happily still with us, made seminal contributions to factor analysis and to latent trait theory; in fact he laid the basis for modern latent trait theory. Lord (1968), to whom the honour is often given, was quite clear that credit for laying the basis of modern latent trait theory belonged to Lawley (1943). Baker's (1965) little history makes the same attribution. When, as a very green beginner (1967), I sought his advice on a practical application of latent trait theory (Wood and Skurnik, 1969), I found Lawley to be very modest about his pioneering work. In the factor analysis sphere, Lawley's name is, of course, firmly bracketed with the development of maximum likelihood methods of estimation.

Nothing said here is meant to demean Lawley's achievements. Rather I am intrigued by a certain historical conjunction: at the time of Lawley's seminal work, roughly 1939–44, he was developing — apparently simultaneously — latent trait theory and factor analysis. We know now how close the parallels are, much of the credit for that going to McDonald (1967, 1981 and 1985) who assimilated both systems into his general non-linear factor analysis, but also to Labouvie (1972). Did Lawley, much earlier, seem to be aware of the parallels? The answer, I think, is no. Although he worked with both systems in the same paper (Lawley, 1944) nowhere is the telling conceptual join to be found. But more of that later.

The Parallels Between Factor Analysis and Latent Trait Theory

It occurs to ask why factor *analysis* and latent trait *theory*, or item response theory as it is being called these days? One might as well say factor *theory* and item response *analysis*, for all the truth conveyed. Perhaps factor analysis has more claim to be a theory; it does, at least, do something about item/test-specific variance, and to that extent offers more of an *explication* (although this hardly amounts to theory) of what explains performance. Pertinent, too, is McDonald's charge that, in contrast to factor analysis, latent trait theory has not yet been developed to the point where it routinely supplies reasonable decisions as to the dimensionality of data sets (McDonald, 1981, p. 103). Indeed it could be argued that latent trait theory, simply by virtue of its Procrustean preoccupation with single factor solutions is, ipso facto, less sophisticated than factor analysis. It will be remembered that Lord and Novick's (1968) theories were statistical, not psychological (Wolins, 1978).

But the parallels, what are these? They are, of course, the informal connections between factor and trait, which are after all just two members, all more or less interchangeable, of a family extending to faculty, capacity, characteristics, etc. Shared, too, are the infelicities of interpretation committed by factorists and by latent traitists. Goldstein (1983) has noted that the kinds of arguments fashionable among the proponents of the Rasch model echo surprisingly well the sentiments of Spearman after he had discovered 'g'. Lord and Novick (p. 538) advance the proposition that the latent trait is the only important factor and once a person's value on the trait is determined the behaviour is random, in the sense of statistical independence. When McDonald argues (1985, p. 203) that common factor analysis is essentially a special case of latent trait theory based on the principle of local independence, the empirical reality of one trait being 'extracted' against several factors must be borne in mind.

The formal parallels between factor analysis, models and latent trait theory or rather stochastic models of test item behaviour are best seen in Labouvie's (1972) paper, produced, according to McDonald (1981), independently from himself. What Labouvie does is to consider the regression of an item trace line (here borrowing from Lazarsfeld's latent structure model) on a set of latent continuous variables i.e. factors or traits. This is precisely what we get when we linearize, by transformation, a normal ogive or logistic item characteristic function, except, of course that there is only one trait (factor).

For Labouvie, then $f_j(x) = a_{j0} + a_{j1}x_1 + \ldots a_{jm}x_m$

where $f_j(x)$ can be read as the proportion of individuals with a given x responding positively to item j, and x is an m-dimensional vector of m latent continuous variables. The variance-covariance matrix for all $f_j(x)$ is derived, also the correlation matrix. Labouvie then invites us to perceive the similarities between his equations and those encountered in factor analysis. It turns out (although Labouvie does not actually show this, as he promises in the synopsis) that the factor loadings can be interpreted as parameters of item trace lines. To the objection that the traditional factor model cannot cope with discrete or qualitative data such as item responses, he offers the defence that providing you are willing to accept that the response of an individual to a dichotomous item is not all-or-nothing but rather the expression of the 'stronger' tendency at a given time, the scale on which the 'tendency' is expressed can be considered continuous over the range [0, 1] and the solutions go through.

This is also what Christofferson (1975) and Muthén (1978) do. Note, however, that these workers, who are otherwise doing the same thing as Labouvie — factor analysis of multivariate binary data — do not invoke item characteristic functions, and so choose not to make the connection. Incidentally, Labouvie managed to do without specific factors, which McDonald (1981) makes much of.

Lawley's Attempt at Unification

McDonald has talked about the 'essential unity' of factor analysis and latent trait theory — 'the term *latent trait* carries essentially the same meaning as the term *common factor*' (McDonald, 1985, p. 203). The unity is in the formal structure of the models, which are equivalent, as are the explanatory ambitions. But presenting an application of factor analysis in a latent trait context does not necessarily imply unity. As a matter of fact, this is what Lawley did and perhaps if we contrast that with Labouvie's formulation the point will be made.

Let us note immediately that Lawley *did* claim that he had established a connection between the two systems. 'The object of the present enquiry is to extend the preceding method of approach to problems in which more than one test is concerned and where the tests are measuring different abilities. The subject of item selection is in this way connected with that of factorial analysis' (Lawley, 1944, p. 74).

It would appear that Lawley was striving to achieve commensurability between the two systems. Lawley works throughout at a test score level although he claims at the end that all his results would apply to items. This, for reasons already mentioned, would not have been so. He starts with what we would now call the test characteristic function expressed in normal ogive form, that is to say the expected proportion of items correctly answered by a given person on the ith test. Let it be $F_i(x)$ where x_i is one ability measured by the test, of which there are n in all. Lawley was interested in the correlation between $F_i(x_i)$ and $F_j(x)$, as was Labouvie, but unlike Labouvie he did not conceive of $F(x)$ in terms of factorial decomposition.

The upshot is that he had to do the correlation between F_i and F_j the hard way — explicitly. But perhaps he enjoyed that. At the end of it all he had an expression for the variances and covariances of F_i.

Next, he introduces factor analysis. Suppose, he says, that the ability x depends upon a number of factors, $f, g, \ldots$ then we may write

$$x_i = \lambda_i' f + \mu_i' g + \ldots,$$

where λ', μ' are loadings in the usual way. Where Labouvie merely converts traits into factors, Lawley wants to factorize traits! Obviously there is no need.

Would Lawley have done the same had he motivated the problem in terms of items rather than tests? I think probably not, and he might then have been led to Labouvie's formulation. Incidentally, Lawley only managed to get results from his factor analysis — the presence of a difficulty factor — by assuming a single common factor.

What is interesting, though, about Lawley's factoring of a trait is his willingness to break with unidimensionality, or perfect scalability. Perhaps he had in mind something like Hunt's formulation that psychometric unidimensionality does not ensure that only a single psychometric function is being tested (Hunt, 1982, p. 235), but it does ensure, at least, that all items on a test are being approached by use of a strategy that emphasizes each of the underlying functions in roughly the same way.

Actually, I have trouble with that formulation. 'Ensure' is too strong and what can 'roughly the same way' mean? Dimensionality is proving a stubborn term to break down. McDonald (1981), who took upon himself the mission of clearing up the mess created by importunate use of the terms homogeneity, internal consistency and unidimensionality, nevertheless manages to leave the impression that dimensionality is a property of items, or tests. (Nor did he nail it in his recent book.) It is no such thing. Dimensionality is a joint property of items and people, a specific set of items and a specific set of people. It is situation specific, as Bejar (1983) says, and is subject to the usual requirements of generalizability.

Factor Indeterminacy and Latent Traits

It would be astounding if Lawley had managed to come up with Labouvie's formulation. That he did not is due in part to the old preoccupation with tests. The switch to the item as the unit of analysis came much later with Frederic Lord. Nor, at that early stage of development, would Lawley have been looking for synthesis, although he did try in his 1944 paper to connect factor analysis and latent trait theory.

If the 'essential unity' between factor analysis and latent trait theory can be said to hold, then there is at least one distressing consequence for latent trait or item response theory and that concerns the identifability problem (rotational indeterminacy). If the canker in the factor analytic rose is indeterminacy, what, then, of latent trait theory? It must share this basic problem yet only Guttman (1977, p. 103), as far as I can see, has spotted this. The only place indeterminacy in latent trait theory crops up at all noticeably — and even then it can easily be missed — is in Rasch model analysis where, in order to solve explicitly for the item and score group parameters, the sum of the item difficulties is taken to be zero. McDonald is inclined to be sanguine about factor score indeterminacy (McDonald, 1985, p. 168), on the grounds that known alternatives will be no better. But he does not extend his comments into latent trait theory. McDonald is the man who has made the connection between factor analysis and latent trait theory forty years after Lawley, and so it is pleasing to read in the introduction to his book (p. x) that his thinking was equally influenced equally by Louis Guttman and D.N. Lawley.

References

BAKER, F.B. (1965) 'Origins of the item parameters X_{50} and β as a modern item analysis technique', *Journal of Educational Measurement*, 2, pp. 167–80.

BEJAR, I.I. (1983) 'Introduction to item response models and their assumptions', in HAMBLETON, R. (Ed), *Applications of Item Response Theory*, Vancouver, BC, Educational Research Institute of British Columbia.

CHRISTOFFERSON, A. (1975) 'Factor analysis of dichotomized variables', *Psychometrika*, 40, pp. 5–32.

GOLDSTEIN, H. (1983) 'Review of *The Mismeasure of Man* by S.J. Gould', *British Journal of Mathematical and Statistical Psychology*, 36, pp. 159–60.

HUNT, E. (1982) 'Towards new ways of assessing intelligence', *Intelligence*, 6, pp. 231–40.

LABOUVIE, E.W. (1972) 'Stochastic models and factor analysis', *British Journal of Mathematical and Statistical Psychology*, 25, pp. 121–7.

LAWLEY, D.N. (1943) 'On problems connected with item selection and test construction', *Proceedings of the Royal Society of Edinburgh*, 61, pp. 273–87.

LAWLEY, D.N. (1944) 'The factorial analysis of multiple item tests', *Proceedings of the Royal Society of Edinburgh*, 62, pp. 74–82.

LORD, F.M. (1968) 'An analysis of the verbal scholastic aptitude test using Birnbaum's three-parameter logistic model', *Educational and Psychological Measurement*, 28, pp. 989–1020.

LORD, F.M. and NOVICK, M.R. (1968) *Statistical Theories of Mental Test Scores*, Reading MA, Addison-Wesley.

McDONALD, R.P. (1967) 'Nonlinear factor analysis', *Psychometric Monographs*, No. 15.

McDONALD, R.P. (1981) 'The dimensionality of tests and items', *British Journal of Mathematical and Statistical Psychology*, 34, pp. 100–17.

McDONALD, R.P. (1985) *Factor Analysis and Related Methods*, Hillsdale, NJ, Lawrence Erlbaum Associates.

MUTHÉN, B. (1978) 'Contributions to factor analysis of dichotomized variables', *Psychometrika*, 43, pp. 551–60.

WOLINS, L. (1978) 'Interval measurement: Physics, psychophysics and metaphysics', *Educational and Psychological Measurement*, 38, pp. 1–9.

WOOD, R. and SKURNIK, L.S. (1969) *Item Banking*, Windsor, National Foundation for Educational Research in England and Wales.

VI   Testing, Including Achievement Testing

Comments

The main paper here (referred to as the 'Unit') was written for the Open University. It is a straightforward account of testing, educational and psychological, set in historical and social context. I have included it because I thought it might appeal to lecturers who need to have a basic treatment of testing in their courses. The fact that I have retained some of the activities which OU students are asked to attempt, may increase its value in this regard. The more novel material comes at the end in the paragraphs on organization of learning.

As a sequel to the treatment of sex-linked discrimination in the Unit, I have included a script I wrote for a follow-up cassette which was, to the best of my knowledge, not used. The piece is right up-to-date as far as my views on the subject are concerned.

The paper on criterion-referencing also backs up and amplifies the relevant paragraphs in the Unit. At times in the past I could easily have put my name to an article with the title 'Criterion-referenced testing as fools' gold'.

The test review (paper 14) is there because it supplements, in a practical way, the more didactic treatment in the Unit. By delving into the guts of a test, and the claims made for it, it is possible to bring out aspects of validity and reliability and especially utility, which would otherwise not emerge. My other piece in that volume is more respectful (of Alice Heim) and is perhaps less useful on that account.

The little paper on Cronbach and Gleser was written for a newish occupational psychology journal intended to have popular appeal. I wanted to pay tribute to Lee Cronbach, although what is there is small enough, and also to give decision theory a dusting off. I did not dare introduce it into the Unit.

The piece called 'Achievement Tests' is an encyclopedia article written in mid-1982. The references to other articles have been left in for those who are interested. Themes were introduced which surface elsewhere. I had discovered Vygotosky not long before and was trying to fit in his ideas. The problem of what can be inferred from the single item (Robert Gagné) had bothered me for some time. The Anderson article — what of all the question we might ask, shall we ask students? — is, as far as I am concerned, one of the 'golden oldies' and is certainly part of the agenda for theory-building, whose absence Akeroyd was complaining about (Section IV).

Paper 11: Testing[*]

Introduction

A theory of intelligence must be a theory of individual differences. (Campione *et al*. in Sternberg, 1982, p. 473)

Only a society of mechanical robots could be physically and intellectually alike. Biological creatures reliably vary. Therefore, no matter how intelligence is defined, we may expect people to differ in the degree to which they possess it. . . . One implication of this heterogeneity principle is that programmes should not attempt to change children to fit into a uniform mould. . . . Another implication of heterogeneity is that no single programme or treatment is necessarily the best solution for all persons with a particular problem. (Zigler and Seitz, in Sternberg, 1982, p. 610)

As Zigler and Seitz say, no matter how intelligence is defined (excluding perverse definitions), we may expect people to differ in the degree to which they possess it. The trouble is that if we are ever to measure individual differences in intelligence, intelligence itself has to be defined in such a way as to create a series of tasks that will reveal such differences — the problem of operationalization. This is far from being a straightforward and uncontroversial matter. There is no point, at this stage, in trying to devise a generally acceptable definition of intelligence; it is better to beg the questions and look instead at how individual differences in intelligence have been and are being studied, and at some of the educational consequences of such studies. But first, it will help to refresh your memory about the approaches that psychologists have taken to intelligence.

A Brief Review

Three major approaches to the study of intelligence can be identified, the psychometric (coming out of differential psychology), the information

---

[*]Reprinted from Unit 21 of Course E 306, Open University Press, 1985.

processing (coming out of cognitive psychology) and the developmental, which owes much to the ideas of Piaget. The psychometric approach treats intelligence as a set of quantifiable dimensions along which people can be scaled and ordered. It is the 'strength' model; people have a lot or a little of 'it'. At one extreme 'it' has been conceived of as a single general intellectual capacity (for example, Spearman's 'g'), and at the other as having many dimensions (for example, Guilford's 120 distinct abilities, which go to make up his so-called 'structure-of-intellect' model). Generally speaking, however, a relatively small number of abilities are held to be responsible for observed variation among individuals on general intelligence tests. To find these sources of variation in test data, correlational techniques are used and, in particular, factor analysis whose purpose is to produce a parsimonious solution. Factor analysis is very closely identified with the psychometric model.

The psychometric approach to studying intelligence held sway from the turn of the century to the early 1970s, although not without criticism. Sigel (1963), for instance, complained that intelligence tests limit understanding of the nature of intellectual functioning whenever scoring systems reduce everything to a single score such as IQ or Mental Age. Sigel argued that more attention should be paid to *how* children arrive at the answers they do and in this regard he advocated that valuable information could be gained from analyzing the *errors* made in answering test items. (This is not a new idea; in the 1920s the young Piaget analyzed the errors made by children on Binet's intelligence test).

Eventually, impatience with the psychometricians' apparent inability to answer these sorts of criticisms took the form of a challenge from the information-processing wing of cognitive psychology and, in particular, Earl Hunt. Hunt was critical of the absence of a theoretical basis to intelligence testing, test items being selected because they work rather than because they are related to a theory of cognition (Hunt and Lunneborg, 1973). He therefore set out to study the *processes* of cognition rather than the products themselves by correlating scores on psychometric tests with measures such as 'encoding speed' or 'time to solution' which related to a particular model of cognition.

Robert Sternberg also adopts a cognitive approach but this differs in certain respects from that of Hunt. Sternberg looked at possible higher-order cognitive skills assessed by tests, such as 'planning strategy' and 'monitoring strategy'. Both cognitive approaches attempt to look beyond test scores to see what thinking processes might be going on. All this sounds promising but you ought to be aware that those committed to an information-processing approach to the study of intelligent behaviour still have many questions to answer. Is information represented in a linguistic form, in an imaginal form or in some other kind of form? Is most processing conducted in parallel or serially? Is the overall system best conceived in terms of separate memory-storage units such as immediate, short-term and long-term memories or in terms of a single system whose parts undergo varying degrees of activation at any one time? And so on.

The third major approach to the study of intelligence — the Piagetian — comes from Jean Piaget's philosophical quest for the nature of human knowledge. It, too, is concerned with process; Piagetians show little interest in quantification and therefore differences between persons (although some scales have been constructed); the approach is much more concerned with qualitative aspects of intelligence and with establishing universal patterns such as invariant orders of acquisition. How do children come to understand basic categories of space, time and causality? How similar is children's reasoning across different contexts?

No single approach to the study of intelligence will do

Despite the inadequacies of each approach considered individually, the combination of psychometric, information-processing and Piagetian perspectives has resulted in a relatively clear and comprehensive picture of intellectual development (Siegler and Richards, in Sternberg, 1982). Just as, in many cases, there is no single definition that fits well all exemplars of a concept, so there may be no single approach that it well suited to studying all aspects of intellectual development.

But even if there is no royal road to the study of intelligence, the fact remains that it is the psychometric approach that, in terms of educational practice, dominates most discussions of 'intelligence' and achievement. Orthodox testing practice is firmly rooted in the psychometric approach and that is unlikely to change quickly. The other approaches may never lend themselves to presentation in a sufficiently practical and readily understandable form. They would need to achieve this if they were to provide an irresistible alternative to the prevailing orthodoxy for their vast clientele, which uses tests not only for research but also for making decisions about people. After all, one of the great attractions of IQ testing has been its simplicity; no theory of any complexity to grasp and one single product to deal with: IQ. Consequently we must continue to pay attention to tests of mental abilities.

From Binet to Streaming and Grouping

Binet's scale

The original purpose of Binet's scale was to identify children with special educational problems and needs, an important point to remember in the light of what came afterwards. It is also necessary to realize that Binet's approach to test construction was pragmatic; the tests were loose collections of samples of scholastic ability chosen for their effectiveness at distinguishing between children according to their teachers' judgments of who was 'bright' and who was 'dull'. Thus, intelligence was defined, operationally and conceptually, almost solely in terms of *educational* criteria (Snow and Yalow, in Sternberg,

1982). After Binet's death in 1911 the scene changed from Paris to California. Intelligence testing was never to be the same again.

Lewis Terman and the California experience

The translator (and reviser) of the Binet-Simon scale (Stanford-Binet) was Lewis Terman who became the spearhead behind the use of intelligence tests in California and subsequently throughout the US. He was a strong believer in the influence of heredity on intelligence and he would probably not have objected to being called an élitist. Like Binet, Terman first explored (in 1911) the use of tests to identify 'abnormal' children, both those who were retarded and those who showed signs of unusual ability. Following the latter became Terman's lifelong passion. He also predicted a much wider application of tests as a means of modifying school curriculum so as to suit individual abilities:

> Now that the individual treatment of pupils in the schools has begun, there is no stopping short of this ideal. Tests must be developed which will enable us to differentiate all degrees of intellectual ability and all kinds of intellective unevenness. (Terman, 1911, quoted in Chapman, 1981, p. 703)

America's entry into the First World War in 1917 provided a massive boost to intelligence testing. The Army Alpha, a pencil-and-paper test that could be completed by a group of people in one sitting, was used to classify some 1.7 million recruits to the services. This experience demonstrated to the general public and educationists alike the practical value of such tests for classifying large numbers of people. Terman and some colleagues were given financial support from the Rockefeller Foundation to 'develop an intelligence scale for the group examination of school children' and in the years that followed he consistently advocated that intelligence tests had value, not only in theoretical studies of intelligence but as a practical tool for school administration. Using the slogan 'a mental test for every child' he proposed a systematic programme of intelligence testing. Test results would be used to sort children into 'homogeneous class groups' within the framework of a 'multiple-track plan' that would provide for five ability groups. Table 1 shows how Terman saw these five groups distributed within a typical elementary school of 2,000 pupils. You will see that the percentages in table 1 approximate to a normal distribution curve.

The five groups were suited to different courses of study, said Terman. The 'bright' and 'gifted' groups should be prepared for advanced work in college whilst the 'slow' group was destined for vocational careers. A system of educational and vocational guidance based on intelligence tests would help in the decision making. Terman had translated more than Binet's scale, he had transformed the Frenchman's limited intentions into a universal programme.

Some of the wider changes that had prompted Binet's activities were also to be found in Terman's California, in particular, legislation that made education compulsory. The structure and function of schools was changing, the

Table 1   Terman's 'multiple-track plan'

Group	Number in each group		Remarks
Gifted	50 pupils	(2.5%)	Two classes, 4 grades in each
Bright	300 pupils	(15%)	One class per grade
Average	1300 pupils	(65%)	Four to five classes per grade
Slow	300 pupils	(15%)	One class per grade
Special	50 pupils	(2.5%)	Three ungraded classes

Source: Chapman, 1981, p. 704.

curriculum moving from an emphasis on classical education to one concerned with preparation for life. Furthermore, there had been a large migration from the countryside to the cities and towns with a corresponding leap in school enrolments and these school populations spanned a wide range of ethnic groups. This was the educational scene in cities such as Oakland and San Jose where the educational administrators were in close touch with Terman at nearby Stanford University. The following account of how they were influenced draws heavily on the historical research of Chapman (1981).

When Virgil Dickson, a trainee of Terman, came to Oakland in 1917 he proposed a three-pronged plan for testing the work of the schools. There would be retardation studies, achievement testing, and psychological examinations. His plan called for 'segregation' of the 'mentally superior' for accelerated work, and the 'mentally deficient' for special class work. For those with ability who have 'fallen behind', and those who 'work very slowly', he recommended 'opportunity' classes. Dickson's proposals were well received by administrators and teachers; the principals of the two largest elementary schools, which also contained the highest concentration of immigrants, reported that ability groups based on tests reduced discipline problems and that teachers and pupils alike seemed 'happier'. Teachers reported a 'deeper and more sympathetic understanding of the child' and new respect for individual differences. Although there is some risk in interpreting these statements since they were solicited by Dickson, the indications are that both school administrators and teachers found intelligence tests of immense practical value. By 1922, Dickson could report that a 'three-track-plan' of classes for bright, average and slow students 'prevails throughout the entire city' (Chapman, 1981, p. 708).

In 1920, San Jose had a high immigrant population; over half of the 40,000 residents were first or second generation immigrants. That year at Stanford a student of Terman's named Kimball Young was analyzing the 'mental differences in certain immigrants'. Having tested all 12-year-olds in the schools, Young discovered that 42 per cent of them were retarded, or behind their grade level, and that students of South European descent were farthest behind. He was in no doubt what these data meant. He dismissed the idea that language handicap could be held responsible to any great extent and instead concluded that 'the true difficulty is one of mental capacity, or general intelligence, which makes the Latins unable to compete with the children of North European ancestry in the mastery of the traditional American public school curriculum' (quoted in Chapman, 1981, p. 710). To solve the problems in the San Jose schools, Young called for a 'new educational policy' according to which 'standardized tests should be applied throughout the elementary schools' as a preliminary step toward regrouping students on the basis of ability. There should be three tracks for the superior, the average and the backward, each with its own form of instruction and course of study, in order to 'fit the levels of capacity of the pupils' to 'their future requirements in adult society'. Young's proposals were well received and by 1922 San Jose had initiated a major reform of public education based on testing, classification and guidance.

Why Were Intelligence Tests Well Received?

Why were intelligence tests adopted so rapidly in the California schools? Were they seen as a welcome contribution of applied psychology to social and educational progress or were they foisted upon the schools by people seeking to promote a particular social philosophy and to protect their own self-interest? Second, what was the relationship between testing on the one hand and ability grouping or 'streaming' (or 'tracking' as it is called in the US) on the other? Did the adoption of intelligence testing lead directly to a comprehensive system of ability grouping or had schools already developed a systematic means of treating students differently? Or was the historical relation between testing and streaming more complex than these interpretations? Chapman's analysis of the available information indicates some central themes:

> In each instance tests were introduced by a network of university psychologists and school administrators. The reforms they proposed met with quick acceptance, in good part because intelligence testing and tracking reinforced some central values of the Progressive Era — efficiency, science, and nativism. In Oakland and San Jose especially, the publication of group intelligence test scores seemed to validate widespread assumptions about the inferiority of certain ethnic groups. The most important cause of the testing movement, however, may well have been the problems the schools faced — mushrooming size, increasing diversity, and a new role for education in a complex, industrial world. The school systems in their cities had already begun to differentiate their curricula and overall structure before the development of intelligence tests. Even without intelligence tests, these schools probably would have sorted students using other means, such as achievement tests and teachers' judgements. Nonetheless, the impact of the tests served as a powerful catalyst for the rise of ability grouping. The invention of intelligence tests and the rise of ability grouping in California schools early in the nineteenth century thus

heralded a new role in society for schools as sorters. (Chapman, 1981, p. 714)

As a postscript you may find it ironic that in 1974 California became the first American state to prohibit the use of the individual standardized tests in determining eligibility for special education placement when Judge Peckham temporarily barred the use of IQ assessments for black children. The law now requires that the absolute numbers of children in special classes from all ethnic groups reflect the state proportions. Terman would have been appalled.

Ability grouping or 'tracking' has been a standard practice in American schools since the 1920s and special education has never really developed the truly alternative instructional treatments originally envisaged. As Snow and Yalow (in Sternberg, 1982, p. 505) see it, progressive ideas seeped into the elementary school but practical economics preserved the thirty-children classroom. Learners were divided into ability groups for subjects such as reading and mathematics on the basis of measured or perceived ability levels, but the genuine alternative instructional treatments did not materialize. And that really is the crucial question to ask of any grouping arrangement: is the instruction varied to take account of those within the groups? We will return to this question in a later section, when we consider the British version of tracking, streaming, and its antithesis, mixed ability grouping, still a lively issue.

Not all of the factors that shaped American practice presented themselves in Britain, yet what do we find? In America, intelligence tests were put to work sorting children; in Britain the same thing happened, only here the first order of business was conceived to be that of sorting children into *institutions*, after which further sorting *within* institutions could take place, and usually did. This is the theme of the next Section. Obviously there is a direct correspondence between the two kinds of sorting or grouping (to use the more polite term) both in terms of the motives behind them and methods used; indeed the results that are used to effect one can be used to effect the other.

Selection, Its Assumptions and Its Effects

'Selection' is the term used for the process of allocating people to different kinds of institution where they will receive education supposedly fitted to their needs or, as is sometimes said, their ability to profit from it. I say 'supposedly' because it is not at all clear that this is what happens in practice. The question in the penultimate paragraph of the previous Section applies: having differentiated people, do you then provide them with appropriate and genuinely alternative instructional treatments? Of course, if Zigler and Seitz are right that 'no single program or treatment is necessarily the best solution for all persons' — and it is hard to disagree — why expect that an institution of type A will cater properly for all those admitted to it any better than institution B or C?

The strong implication of this argument is that sorting by institution fails to deal with the real problem. But, as we shall see, those who shaped British education in this century did not take their thinking that far.

Selection does not have to be by test. After all, if the object of the exercise is to match students to institutions according to need, why should test results contain all, or anything like all, the information required to do that job properly? Be that as it may, the most famous (perhaps notorious) system of selection based on testing known to us is still the 11 +, and we make that the major case study of this Section. If any justification is needed, it is that the 11 + still exists, in pockets here and there. In 1981 it was reported in Parliament that thirty-nine of ninety-seven English LEAs still had at least one school to which entry was made on a selective basis.

The 11 + : Theory and Practice

The educational (and social) policy for which the 11 + examination was the cutting edge of enactment is expressed in the 1944 Education Act but its roots can be traced back at least to the Hadow Report of 1926, which proposed the distinction between primary and secondary education that is familiar to us today. The principle from which all else has been derived is 'equality of educational opportunity'. It has always been a slippery customer to deal with, and it still is. A recent sociological study (Garnier and Raffalovich, 1984), defined it as 'independence of the child's educational attainment from social origins' but you might just as well define it as 'provision of equal life chances'. In 1922 a committee convened to examine whether education for boys and girls should be differentiated, found itself agreeing, simultaneously, that equality meant *sameness*, expressed in the view that practically all children were eligible for secondary education, but also *differentiation*, inasmuch as the principle of equal opportunity required full recognition of various aptitudes, interests and inclinations in each individual pupil, as well as his or her academic ability. Out of this collision, the Committee formulated the novel concept of equality as 'equal cultivation of different capacity'. Henceforth equality should not necessarily be compatible with identity or sameness, but should depend upon the fuller recognition of individual differences.

Reading (Allow about 1 hour)

'Intelligence tests and educational reform in England and Wales in the 1940s' by Deborah Thom (the Reader, Reading 4.2) explores, from a social historical perspective, the various factors leading to the 1944 Education Act and, in particular, the role of psychologists and psychometrics. Thom's research forms part of a larger study of the place of mental testing in English education; the period 1880–1940 has been described and analysed by Sutherland (1984).

As you read this chapter notice that in England and Wales, as in

California, there was an alliance between academic psychologists and educational administrators but on this side of the Atlantic the role of psychologists was more ambivalent.

You will also see how the 'equal but different' formulation was interpreted and put into practice, in terms both of children and schools. In this last connection you should ask yourself whether secondary modern schools (and latterly, comprehensives) were ever 'separate but not inferior', in Hadow's phrase. Were the different paths by which all children were to go forward equally well prepared and kept? If 'equal cultivation of different capacities' is anything other than cant, the programme it implies is massive, and still to be completed. What do *you* think it means, and what does it entail?

Equality for All?

Thom's article takes us up to the end of the 1940s but the 11+ continued to be used throughout the 1950s and early 1960s. Most authorities claimed to be allocating pupils to the 'most suitable' form of education, yet the proportions suited to a particular form of schooling varied considerably between different areas on a scale that went far beyond any explanation in terms of the social composition of the population. As a British Psychological Society enquiry of 1957 noted:

> By 1954 the proportion of grammar school places of all types was close to 20 per cent in England and 33 per cent in Wales. ... But it ranged from just over 9 per cent in Gateshead to nearly 39 per cent in Gloucester, and from some 14 per cent in Nottinghamshire and Northumberland to 42 per cent in Westmorland and 60 per cent in Merioneth. (Vernon, 1957, p. 17)

There were inequalities in terms of gender too. Eleven-year-old girls did better on average than boys on the predominantly verbal tests used in 11+ selection procedures, a difference that is to be found on most similar tests of ability or attainment. The explanation usually given for this difference is the earlier maturing of girls, but what to do about their superiority has presented dilemmas that persist to this day. One widely adopted solution was to apply different cut-off points to boys and girls in any selection procedure so that, in order to obtain a grammar school place, girls had to obtain a higher mark than boys. This implied that girls' superior test results should not be taken to mean an intrinsically greater capacity to benefit from grammar school places. A survey carried out by the National Foundation for Educational Research (NFER) in 1972 found that 67 per cent of LEAs were treating the sexes separately in this way and 25 per cent were treating them together by making reference to the same pass mark when allocations were made (the remaining 8 per cent treated them together in the case of mixed schools but otherwise separately) (Hill, 1972). It is interesting to note that had the 1975 Sex Discrimination Act been in existence at the time, those 25 per cent of LEAs would have been in step and the 67 per cent would have been acting illegally.

By 1978 the Equal Opportunities Commission (EOC) had in front of it a number of cases of alleged sex discrimination arising from 11 + testing. In some of the LEAs that had adjusted for boys' deficiencies by applying a lower cut-off for selection or, what comes to the same thing, permitted different or even equal quotas of boys and girls to be selected, there were complaints from the parents of girls who scored higher than boys yet, unlike those boys, were not awarded grammar school places. The Act says that there is such a thing as *indirect* discrimination, when a condition or a requirement, not justifiable regardless of sex, means that a smaller proportion of one sex than another could comply with the requirement. The EOC agonized over what indirect discrimination might mean in this context. If the boys at age 11 do score lower, on average, than the girls is it indirect discrimination *not* to weight the tests somehow in their favour? By 1979, the Commission had decided where it stood. Commenting on an example of separate treatment that had been brought to its attention (from Avon LEA) it judged that the following contravened the Act:

(a)   the use of tests incorporating the adjustment factor for one sex;
(b)   the preparation of separate lists of boys' and girls' test scores;
(c)   a sex-quota allocation system;

Although the EOC delivered an unequivocal judgment the matter is by no means dead, and it is understood that in the early 1980s the Ombudsman was called upon to deal with a similar case. Consider some of the issues. The Avon case could only be brought because the decision area was so clear-cut. Make the selection variable less obvious or blur the edges of the decision area and charges become more difficult to substantiate and people are deterred from making them. This is amply demonstrated by the experience of the LEA that replaced tests with a combination of school records and parental choice and found that protests dried up. Notice that the nub of the problem — whether later academic achievement or ability to benefit from a grammar school education can be predicted with any certainty — is left untouched, since there is no good reason to think that the new procedure, especially parental choice, is any better than the old. But how do you get to grips with school records and parental choice? It would be interesting to know the relative proportions of girls and boys selected by the new procedure. We must ask, too, whether the argument on which separate treatment was based — that girls are no more likely than boys to benefit from grammar school education — is adequately met by the 1975 Act and the EOC's ruling. To examine that, we need to look at the efficiency of the 11 + as a predictor of later scholastic performance.

Efficiency of the 11 + as a Predictor

It is conventional psychometric practice to evaluate tests used for selection in terms of their predictive efficiency. Of any two tests, the one that is more accurate at predicting future scholastic and career achievements will generally be more highly regarded. For the early proponents of the use of IQ tests in the 11 + examination, it was important to establish that performance on the tests at age 11 correlated, to a sufficiently impressive degree, with performance on subsequent measures of academic achievement, above all with performance in public examinations at age 16. If a strong positive correlation could be established, then the use of IQ tests to select at age 11 would be vindicated; the right decisions had been taken. Such was the reasoning, and early work promised well. McClelland's study sought to establish the predictive value of teachers' estimates, ordinary exams, IQ tests and standardized scholastic attainment tests. It confirmed 'the view that intelligence will tell in the end, and that IQ rises in predictive value relative to other measures as the years go on' (McClelland, 1942, quoted in Evans and Waites, 1981, pp. 97–8). But it also indicated that both teachers' estimates and ordinary exams were more reliable predictors of junior-school children's later scholastic careers than were IQ tests. On its own, an IQ score of a junior-school child had the lowest predictive value, although its inclusion in any battery of tests improved the battery's value. That, as Evans and Waites (1981) observe, could be and was taken to mean that including an IQ test was essential if the best possible battery of tests was to be produced.

Following this research in the 1940s, several empirical studies reported data on the predictive efficiency of the 11 + examination. The correlations were reasonably impressive but people were beginning to question the assumptions upon which this demand for prediction was based. Indeed, as early as 1950, the authors of the first NFER survey of allocation procedures had more or less rejected the whole idea, giving no fewer than seven reasons for their view:

(a) It (the 11 +) ignores the qualities that are not easily examinable and that ought to play a part in secondary school success.
(b) It assumes that school progress is mechanically determined, and that variations in teaching, school environment, discipline and children's home conditions and changing interests affect achievement to an insignificant extent.
(c) It assumes that the same examination results may safely be used as a measure of both secondary school instruction and the success of allocation.
(d) It fails to tell us anything about those children who just miss allocation to the school in which the examination used as a criterion is taken.
(e) It has been applied to children who have been selected by a

competitive examination or test whereas allocation must now have regard to all children and employ qualifying examinations or tests.

(f) As used so far, it does not allow sufficiently for uncompensated brilliance in one or two subjects only; instead, it favours all-round mediocrity.

(g) It has the unfortunate effect of seeming to imply that the junior school curriculum must be such as to prepare children for an examination that will forecast secondary school achievement at 16+. (Watts and Slater, 1950, p. 19)

The point made in (d) has a methodological significance that is often overlooked. Since the people you discard do not, by and large, go on to produce comparable evidence of future achievement, they cannot figure in the correlation calculation and so the true predictive value can never be ascertained. This shortcoming, which cannot be righted short of schools, universities and employers selecting applicants at random, has marred all studies of predictive efficiency. Among other things, it means that any accusation of bias in selection against any particular group can never be properly evaluated. The underlying statistical point is that the value of the correlation coefficient is always depressed by any restrictions in the range of either variable; if one selects only those with a score in the top 20 per cent, say, the restriction of range in their scores compared with the population is bound to lower the correlation of their scores with the criterion. Thus the true predictive efficiency will always be higher than the one reported from just the restricted group who were selected, which is one reason why reported predictive values for 'O' and 'A' levels look so unimpressive.

Watts and Slater (1950) went on to suggest that the appropriate procedure, in line with the requirements of the 1944 Education Act, would be to allocate children to secondary school places in accordance with their possession of the minimum qualifications for tackling successfully the kind of work recommended for them, and to review the results at thirteen plus. Children, they said, are not automata whose subsequent performances can be accurately forecast. They are complex creatures and often develop differently from what may reasonably be expected of them. Besides, schools vary in their power to secure the best efforts from each and every one of their pupils. And so on; no doubt you can supply other reasons why it was (and is) absurd to suppose that the 'ability to profit from a grammar school education' can be predicted with any success for any particular individual. (Remember that prediction is evaluated on a group basis but it is the individual who is affected, and it is always harder to predict for an individual than for a group.)

Social and Personal Consequences of Selection

In his account of the Spens Committee's deliberations, Kang (1983) claims that the minutes show explicitly that committee members were aware of the probable danger of social discrimination arising from a strong differentiation at 11. Yet, he says, it seemed that the educational desirability of differentiation on the basis of ability was given a higher priority than the avoidance of social stigma. That selection has been the cause of stigma, pain and anger hardly needs to be demonstrated. The grammar school that I attended in north-east England in the 1950s was cheek by jowl with the secondary modern to which the 'discards' had been sent, and the attendant tensions and abuse, even violence, which came out of that juxtaposition are still vivid in my memory. I also recall how, arriving on our first day at the grammar school, we were sorted into four streams (A, B, C and D) on the strength of the 11+ scores.

The tensions associated with these sorts of classification remain today, despite changes in the reorganization of secondary schooling. For example, Gray *et al.* interviewed Scottish children divided within the same schools into certificate and non-certificate groups and found evidence of considerable resentment mixed with a perceptive awareness of how the system operated. Observing that some schools were thought by pupils to be too ready to consign non-certificate classes to what pupils saw as the irredeemable status of 'remedial', Gray *et al.* (1983) quote a non-certificate boy who found that a label had stuck:

> So you see, if there was no such a thing as a remedial class, then there would have been no such thing as the common thicky. (p. 167)

And, this, from a certificate boy:

> School is still geared to the academically minded child and some teachers think the rest are all nit-wits! The chosen few are still catered for. (p. 165)

It is customary, even fashionable, these days to explain achievement, high or low, either as a product of the student's relationship with the teacher, in which case the notions of the teacher expectation, the self-fulfilling prophecy, and labelling are invoked, or as a product of the student's own perception of him or herself *vis-à-vis* his or her peers, in which case attribution theory is invoked. Teacher expectation, in particular, has come to be regarded as an especially powerful determinant of learning outcomes: 'He thinks I'm thick, he tells me I'm thick, I'm thick'. However, several of the Scottish students' testimonies reported by Gray *et al.* do not bear this out. Rather, they are saying, 'they acted as if I was thick, but I'm not' or as one non-certificate girl put it, 'teachers tend to underestimate pupils. I'm quite intelligent really but you just don't get a chance to show what you can do' (Gray *et al.*, 1983, p. 167).

It is not only amongst the ranks of academic psychologists that belief in a fixed endowment of intelligence is to be found: it is a view shared by teachers, if one is to judge by studies that suggest teachers evaluate children from an early age in terms of perceived intelligence (which may mean IQ). But I do not know that anyone has ever asked teachers, the people who count most in this matter, where they stand on the nature versus nurture question.

One authoritative view has been offered by Denis Stott at the end of a commentary on a published debate about intelligence between H.J. Eysenck (a proponent of the hereditarian viewpoint) and Leon Kamin (a leading environmentalist) (Eysenck and Kamin, 1981):

> We cannot deny that genetic differences may play some part in the observed differences in people's mental capabilities. But the complexity of successive gene-gene and gene-environment interactions — with the possibility that any one of them can set the individual's development on a new course in which a different array of genes becomes effective within a different environment — will for ever nullify attempts to calculate the 'contributions' of heredity and environment by a mathematical model.
>
> The value of the debate, as I see it, is that it has exposed the fruitlessness of the search for the determinants of 'intelligence' and of academic ability in terms of separable genetic versus environmental 'contributions'. It has removed a compulsion from our minds which has misdirected research effort over two generations like some alchemist's search for the means of making gold. Twin and adoption studies can no longer be seen, simplistically, as natural experiments in apportioning the roles of nature and nurture. It is not a question of bigger and better studies. We shall never be able to place twins from birth in separate environments randomized in a manner that meets the canons of scientific acceptability. Likewise we shall never be able to find adopted children whose true mothers have life-histories typical of the population as a whole, nor could the children be placed with randomly selected foster-mothers. (Stott, 1983,.p. 49)

It hardly needs adding that educational policy-makers, administrators and teachers cannot change genetic endowment, so the only rational policy is to take people as they are and do what you can with them — back to equal cultivation of different capacities.

What is a Test?

This unit does not contain a comprehensive treatment of tests, or testing. The aim is to bring to your attention some major considerations and issues you need to be aware of, but without doing so in any technical detail. For instance, you will find no instructions on how to evaluate different kinds of reliability coefficients, only an explanation of why reliability is important.

In 1983 the British Psychological Society established a working party to consider competence in psychological testing. This was done in the context of a debate over whether there should be licensing of non-psychologists who use psychological tests. The working party needed to define a psychological test; here is their initial attempt:

The term 'Psychological Test' refers to a procedure for the evaluation of psychological functions. Psychological tests involve those being tested in solving problems, performing skilled tasks or making judgments. Psychological test procedures are characterized by standard methods of administration and scoring. The results of psychological tests are usually quantified by means of normative or other scaling procedures but they may also be interpreted qualitatively by reference to psychological theory.

Included in the term psychological tests are tests of varieties of:

intelligence;
ability;
aptitude;
language development and function;
perception;
personality, temperament and disposition;
interests, habits, values and preferences.

Excluded from the term psychological test are:

tests of educational or occupational attainment;
tests of scholastic aptitude, designed for use by school teachers;
checklists or rating scales used in observing specific behaviour interview schedules;
non-standardized attitude inventories;
tests of sensory function;
diagnostic procedures used to give a general indication of impairment.
(p. 192)

Note that tests of educational attainment and scholastic aptitude have been excluded; their administration is considered to require no more than minimal psychological knowledge or skill. Examinations are also excluded, as are teacher-made criterion-referenced tests, checklists and inventories, which are just the kind of assessment devices on which we might rely to make grouping decisions in the classroom. This cordoning-off of the educational application illustrates once again the intermittent, non-interpenetrating and ultimately fickle relationship between psychology and education. Terman installed psychological tests in schools before anyone knew what was happening; now, the tests educationalists use or want to use are not to be regarded as *psychological* tests. But at least we know where we are and this sort of formulation provides some support for my own efforts at differentiating educational from psychological measurement (Wood, 1986).

Activity (allow about 10 minutes)

Take a few minutes to consider whether an examination such as 'O' level is or is not a psychological test (leaving aside the administration aspect), as defined by the BPS in the second paragraph of this section.

Comment

The argument is far from being open and shut. Examinees are expected to solve problems, perform skilled tasks (as in practical examinations) and make judgments. Examinations (above all) are characterized by standard methods of administration and scoring, and the results are quantified by means of normative procedures. What, then, is missing? Examinations would appear to fit the description of a psychological test without needing psychologists to administer them. In order to exclude examinations the working party needs to borrow from the American Psychological Association what is probably its most important standard, 'for each test there should be a test manual ... to provide enough information for a qualified user to make sound judgments regarding the usefulness and interpretation of test scores' (American Psychological Association, 1974, p. 5). You do not find examination boards supplying manuals although examination results must affect the life chances of far more people than do psychological test scores.

'A procedure for the evaluation of psychological functions' si a very dry attempt at a definition of a test. It sounds like the psychological equivalent of a stool analysis. By contrast, a definition offered by Frederiksen (1984) is more congenial and informative: 'A test may be thought of as any standardized procedure for eliciting the kind of behaviour we want to observe and measure' (p. 199). If we want to measure spelling ability, says Frederiksen, we can dictate words to spell. If we want to measure ability to repair TV sets, we can present TV sets needing repair. If we want to measure medical diagnostic ability, we can provide simulations of medical problems, and so on. The whole point in these situational or performance tests is to obtain as close a correspondence as possible between the tasks on the test and the behaviour of interest. Unfortunately, such tests tend to be costly to develop and administer and there are technical problems of scoring and interpretation, which are not readily soluble. So, 'pencil-and-paper' tests are used instead, even though we know that the relationship between the tasks on such tests and what we would really like to know about people is often tenuous and sometimes misleading. Consequently, attention is focused on what is *easiest* to test and a lot of interesting behaviour is ignored because we cannot test it or cannot afford to test it. The implications for teaching are obvious, which is why critics complain that what gets taught is what is easiest to test, and it is a charge that those who use tests in education (whether we call them psychological tests or not) are going to have to answer one day.

Purposes of Testing

Almost any test can be useful for some function and in some situations but even the best test can have damaging consequences if used inappropriately. This may be avoided if thought is given at an early stage to the purposes of testing and the target group for which the test is intended. Thinking about purpose means thinking about the decisions that are to be based on test scores or, more generally, how the test scores are going to be used. The way in which the test will be put together, the score obtained, and the manner in which scores will be reported depend on what groups are to be tested and what decisions are to be made about them. This cannot be emphasized strongly enough.

The purposes of testing or the kinds of decisions to be made can be categorized in several ways. The following list was proposed by Thorndike:

(a) *Instructional decisions*
Has the individual shown mastery of certain knowledge or skills and readiness to move on to new material?

(b) *Diagnostic decisions*
Where is the individual or the methods of instruction going wrong so that action can be initiated to put it right?

(c) *Selection decisions*
Who is to be admitted or excluded, employed or rejected?

(d) *Placement decisions*
Where can the individual most advantageously be placed? What programme will suit the individual best?

(e) *Guidance decisions*
What can a test score contribute to decisions the individual has to make about his or her future, to help decide, for instance, between a 'person-orientated' job and a 'thing-orientated' job?

(List summarized from Thorndike, 1982, pp. 14–15)

Of these types of decisions (c) stands out as being different. Whereas with the others the object is to help people or to enable them to learn something about themselves — what Sandra Scarr (1981) calls testing *for* people, i.e. testing used in their interests — with *selection* the object is sorting, pure and simple. Nothing of substance is learned about individuals nor do they learn anything about themselves. In a previous Section you read of how the 11+ was defended as a *placement* device: children were to be sent to the schools best able to cultivate their talents. The reality was different, however; the 11+ was always a classic *selection* device and closed far more doors than it ever opened.

Function determines test construction policy. A test that is meant to pick out a small number of candidates for advancement is going to be put together differently from one that is intended to reveal whether an individual has mastered a unit of instruction, or one that is meant to be sensitive to progress made by an individual. Where the aim is to sort, the emphasis is on *discrimination*, which translates into a requirement that the items comprising the test each discriminate as efficiently as possible between those people to be chosen (who ought to get the item correct) and those to be discarded (who ought to get it wrong). Such a prescription would be quite inappropriate for a test of an individual's *capability* in a particular sphere. There the question is not 'Has X scored higher than Y?' but 'Can X do it, can Y do it?' Knowing that X scores higher than Y does not necessarily provide an answer to the second question, whether both of them can do a certain thing.

Norm-referencing and Criterion-referencing

The distinction made in the previous paragraph is that between *norm referencing* and *criterion referencing*. The distinctive characteristic of norm-referenced measurement is that scores are interpreted in terms of how the individual stands with respect to some appropriate larger group. In criterion-referenced measurement, by contrast, scores are interpreted as having some sort of absolute meaning in terms, for instance, of level of performance or amount achieved or degree of mastery; in other words, the criterion-referenced score has some sort of meaning in itself, irrespective of the scores for specified groups. There is a tendency to see norm-referenced tests as a bad thing and criterion-referenced tests as a good thing. This can be assigned to the fact that norm-referencing is identified with selection and criterion-referencing with person-centred testing (though this is only superficially true).

It is necessary to get some perspective on this matter. Some people *want* to know where they, or those for whom they are responsible, stand relative to others, and we should not despise them for it. When working on the project reported in Gipps *et al.* (1983), I encountered headteachers in primary schools who were desperate to know where their school stood, either in relation to neighbouring schools or to the local authority or to the country at large. Norm-referenced test results seemed to them a respectable way of finding out. Criterion-referenced tests would not have satisfied these heads; where are the yardsticks? It is quite likely that such tests were used in the schools on a routine basis (we might hope they were) but the point is that they did not suffice for all purposes.

Fixing on individual learning does call for a criterion-referenced approach to testing and that needs to be encouraged. Yet you should not suppose that criterion-referenced testing is always person-centred while norm-referenced testing is always instrumental and unconcerned with the individual. In recent years there have been court cases in the USA where decisions made on the basis of criterion-referenced tests (minimum competency tests) have been challenged by litigants who have claimed that their civil rights were being violated inasmuch as they were being denied leaving certificates or were not being allowed to leave school because they had not reached a given standard. Remember, too, that while the Stanford-Binet and the Wechsler are certainly norm-referenced — the whole point is to discriminate between 'bright' and 'dull' — that does not mean that individual needs are not discerned and attended to, often as much by what is noticed during the course of testing as by interpretation of score profiles.

My feeling is that too much has been made of the distinction between norm-referenced and criterion-referenced testing (although you need to know what the difference is). You may have noticed that the results of criterion-referenced tests can themselves be given a norm-referenced interpretation. People vary in the time taken to reach the criterion (mastery), the number of criteria met, etc. You can still know your position relative to others in the most impeccably conducted criterion-referenced testing arrangements.

Activity (allow about 10 minutes)

Note down the tests you have taken (or could have taken) over the last few years (for example, driving test, Christmas-time quiz, Open University exam).

How would you classify them using Thorndike's categories (page 133) and the distinction between norm- and criterion-referenced tests?

How do you think the items that made up the test were selected?

Comment

A driving test, which is, of course, a performance test, could lead to an instructional decision (try again or go on to an advanced driving test) and also to a diagnostic decision (practice hill starts or revise the Highway Code), depending on the examiner's comments. It is certainly criterion-referenced, but note that the results could also be interpreted in a norm-referenced way, as in 'He needed four tries, his sister two, but I passed first time'.

Nothing much will hang on the results of a Christmas-time quiz in the newspaper, or so one imagines. Items will be chosen so as to maximize differences on a scale of 'smartness' and once the correct answers are published, scores will be totted up and comparisons made. So it is norm-referenced.

An Open University examination is not intended to create or foster distinctions, much less to reject, and so while norm-referenced interpretation of results will always be possible, you who take the examinations are likely to view them in a criterion-referenced spirit in the sense that your own performance and your evaluation of it will be all you want to know. Likewise, exam questions are likely to be designed, not so much to pick out the 'first-class minds', as to give everyone the chance to show that they have mastered the material in the course. Actually, the correct way to construct a criterion-referenced examination would be to administer a collection of possible questions to students who have *not* yet had the course, as well as to those who have, and choose only those questions that differentiated between these groups. That way you get an examination that is sensitive to learning. The Open University does not follow this practice, nor does anyone else as a matter of routine.

Validity and Reliability

When it comes to evaluating how tests work and how well they serve the purposes assigned to them, there are two characteristics of test scores that have to be studied — *validity* and *reliability*. Validity is more important than reliability but is impossible without it.

Textbooks on psychological measurement frequently state that the validity of a test is the degree to which it measures what it was designed to measure. The suggestion is that the validity of any test can be captured in one index which is good for all time and all places and for all aggregations of people. This is not so; a test cannot be valid in general, it is valid *for a purpose*. Depending on purpose, the validity of an 'A' level examination can be assessed primarily either in terms of its soundness as a test of achievement (syllabus coverage) or its value for predicting suitability for university. Likewise, a test can be both valid and not valid, as for example, an 'A' level examination that predicts university success for women but not for men. Context matters crucially. It is therefore incorrect to speak of the validity of a test. We do better to talk about test *validation*, that is validating the use to which a test is put. Modern thinking places responsibility for the valid use of a test squarely on the person who interprets it. What one has to validate is a proposed interpretation of the test; for any test, some interpretations are reasonably valid and others are not (Cronbach, 1971).

Any attempt at validation depends equally crucially on the reliability of the observations. If these cannot be trusted then a misleading judgment concerning validity is likely to be reached. You and I might agree that the number of empty bottles in the dustbin is a good (valid) measure of the alcohol consumption of a household, but not if I told you that the neighbours were in the habit of sneaking in some of their empties (when there seemed too many for respectability) or that the household sometimes kept back some of its own (for the same reason). The validity of a test is limited by its reliability, and there is no way of getting round that. But it certainly does not follow that a reliable test will necessarily be valid. A test of your ability to recall strings of seven random digits may give the same results time and time again, but it may not be a valid test of your ability to remember the telephone numbers of your friends, just as being able to remember numbers does not necessarily say anything about, say, personal popularity. As with all validation exercises, it is necessary to set down (or be able to set down) a justification of why it is acceptable to draw inferences or even conclusions about particular behaviour from test scores. You also need to provide persuasive evidence that those scores can be trusted for the purpose for which they are being used.

Validity has many aspects and test validation will usually require the investigation of several of them: the important ones are summarized in table 2.

A methodological problem with predictive validity has already been pointed out. Criterion information is seldom available for all people. (That is true for the example in table 2, since not all people will reach full adulthood.)

Table 2   Types of validity

Type	Explanation	Example
Predictive validity	Does the test predict some future performance event?	Height at age 3 predicts full adult height
Face validity	Does the test look as if it is relevant to the performance in question?	A typing test is relevant for secretaries not for firefighters
Content validity	Does the test test those skills required for good performance?	You need to write to be a police officer, but you do not have to be able to write well to be a *good* police officer
Concurrent validity	Does the test give the same result as another test purporting to test the same performance?	Two intelligence tests should produce similar results with the same group of people
Curricular validity	Does the test test the objectives in the curriculum?	You can only test survival skills if the curriculum was designed to teach survival skills
Instructional validity	Does the test test what has been taught?	You can only test Latin if Latin was taught in the school
Construct validity	Does the test correlate with the tests you expect it to correlate with and not with those you would not?	A verbal reasoning test should correlate with a reading test and a vocabulary test, but not with a physical strength test or a typing test.

There is another problem with the criterion, and it applies also to concurrent and construct validity. Like the test scores you are validating, you hope the criterion scores will be reliable and relevant. The trouble comes when you can put less trust in them than the scores you are validating. You know where you stand with an unreliable test (you need a better test); when the *criterion* is unreliable, the test may or may not be valid and there is no way to tell until a better criterion is found (Green, 1981). The same point may apply to the use of other tests for validating (concurrent validity); sometimes even less is known about such tests than about the one currently being validated. Neither of these dangers is sufficiently appreciated.

A clear breakdown in *content validity* occurs when tests of verbal reasoning or such like are used in place of tests based on an analysis of job performance, thus increasing the likelihood that what is being tested is not competence, but intelligence (McClelland, 1973). In recent years, the US courts have been tough on companies that have been sued by rejected applicants or promotion-seekers on the grounds that the tests have not been sufficiently well matched to the jobs concerned. In requiring these companies to show content validity, they have sometimes asked for more than the companies could humanly give and the result has been the withdrawal of the tests.

Content validity does not ensure either *curricular* or *instructional* validity, nor does curricular validity ensure instructional validity. The latter is bound to present difficulties of definition (what is meant by 'taught'?) but it would be relatively easy to show that the test is measuring what the school *never* taught. What price the instructional validity of school examinations when schools and teachers choose what they will teach and what they will leave out from the syllabus?

Construct validity addresses the most important question of all: what is it that is being measured? It starts with an expanded definition of the attribute you are interested in. If done properly, that will suggest the testing operations by which the attribute can be assessed. Appropriate tests are constructed and evidence is collected. The results are interpreted in terms of expectation and with an eye to alternative explanations of why tests do or do not correlate and why low scores occur. Solid negative evidence is more useful than positive evidence, which can never be conclusive. As one's conception of the attribute is clarified, the tests too are modified; there is continuous movement between conceptualization and instrumentation. Any resting place is only a provisional one. Consider a construct such as reading comprehension and think how that process would unfold.

There are those who claim that construct validity is irrelevant where educational testing is concerned. This position has been shaped by the preoccupation with criterion-referenced testing, where mastery of content has been the focus to the exclusion of other considerations. Yet, as Messick (1981) has argued, without evidence of construct validity and relying only on content validity judgments, there is no evidence available to discount plausible rival interpretations of low scores. Such low scores may be indicative not of incompetency or reading deficiency but of low motivation, inattention, anxiety and the like. Then again, what are we to make of constructions such as basic skills, minimum competency and mastery? Is a basic skill one that enables performance in a wide variety of situations at some functional level of environmental complexity? Is it a skill that facilitates later learning in the same area or across areas? And so on. Valid test interpretation is hardly possible without unpacking what the constructs being measured mean, which is why construct validation analysis is imperative in all circumstances. Much bad testing practice can be traced to its neglect.

The Impact of Context

A test score *describes* but it does not *explain* a level of performance. Test performance may be influenced by many factors such as the amount and quality of training, distractions during testing, sensory defects, such as poor eyesight or arthritis, inappropriate language in instructions or in the test questions, problems with reading, motivation and interest, relevance of the task, cultural background of the testee and the tester and how these interact, test-taking strategies, and the way tasks are presented. The fact that so many factors can be listed should not be taken to mean that they are overwhelming in their impact or of equal significance, but it does mean that we should take their existence seriously. The significance of these contextual variables for construct validation was stressed in the previous paragraph.

The Competence-Performance Distinction

It is an obvious question to ask what can be done to alleviate the effect of some at least of these contextual variables (for some will be too deeply embedded to be altered) so that, when tested, individuals can produce more authentic performances. The distinction between *competence* and *performance* may not be familiar to you, but the idea is simple.

Competence is defined as the individual's actual level of cognitive functioning, if performance impediments such as those referred to above are removed or eliminated. In practice one can never eliminate them entirely, so the operational definition of competence is simply the performance under elaborative conditions that maximize the improvement in performance beyond the performance level obtained under standard conditions. Performance is thus the surface expression of competence. It is generally the case that group tests of achievement give little or no opportunity for direct observation of the testee's behaviour or for establishing rapport, gaining cooperation and maintaining interest. Individually administered intelligence tests, on the other hand, allow an opportunity for the tester to bring out the best in the testee, although, of course, this will not necessarily happen. Generally speaking, individual testing is more likely to 'actualize' competence.

The way in which questions are worded can cause performance to falsify competence. To give but one example, two British investigators (Johnstone and Cassels, 1978) found that many low exam marks in science subjects were attributable to failure to understand the language in which the questions were couched. They concluded that changing no more than a single word may bring about a marked improvement. A discussion document on the Assessment of Performance Unit's mathematics testing programme has made a similar observation (Eggleston, 1983). Whether or not many children obtain a correct answer, it says, seems to depend as much on the way the question is asked as on the maths involved. Alternative formulations of questions, the use or non-use of mathematical concepts, the direct or indirect indication of the process involved, are all repeatedly shown to have considerable influence on a pupil's capacity to perform similar mathematical tasks. In general, mathematical performance is higher — often considerably so — when the questions are posed in a direct fashion using non-technical language.

Testing for Instructional Purposes

In the first Section we saw how, in early twentieth century California, testing was used to group children for instruction. In this Section we look at what has happened in Britain when testing has been used for that purpose. Naturally, this involves us in a discussion of streaming and mixed-ability grouping and here I am indebted to a recent critical analysis (Gregory, 1984). We also look at the larger issues inherent in ability grouping: the fairness of grouping arrangements and fairness in the allocation of instructional resources. A brief treatment of individualized learning follows and this Section ends with a consideration of a way in which testing can be individualized, that is to say, can be undertaken when the individual feels ready for it. This departure from conventional examining practice goes under the name of *Graded Testing* in the United Kingdom.

Activity (allow about 5 minutes)

'I'm so far down I might as well be a submarine.' That remark made by a pupil has stuck in my mind and comes back whenever I think of streaming. It illustrates, I think, the difficulty of remembering that streaming is an instructional strategy, or should be, when, as we know, it is also an ideological stamping ground.

Note down your own views on streaming (or mixed-ability grouping).

Streaming Versus Mixed-ability Grouping

Cyril Burt was as influential in this country and in the same sort of way as Lewis Terman was in the USA. He, too, divided the ability distribution into five segments and gave each a label, not dissimilar from Terman's (see table 1). The Hadow Committee (see the Reader, p. 261) had the benefit of Burt's thinking and we find their 1926 report recommending streaming with classes of able, average and backward children. Five years later the 1931 Primary Schools Report reinforced this recommendation and codified it using some very familiar symbols; there should be an A stream for bright children, B for average, and a smaller C stream for the retarded. That set the pattern for thirty years.

Probably the most influential polemic against streaming, the one that certainly conditioned my thoughts for a time, is the late Brian Jackson's book called *Streaming*, published in 1964. Jackson compared ten streamed and ten unstreamed schools. He found that streaming seemed to carry with it the attitude that ability is largely inherited and consequently that there is little one can do for the less able (positions that I have suggested many teachers hold). There was also, Jackson thought, some prejudice against children of below average ability. Unstreamed schools appeared more relaxed, having less drive and competition in academic work and less desk-work than in streamed schools. Jackson also reported that children in A streams tended to be the oldest of their year and of higher social class while the lower streams contained dispropor-tionate numbers of younger and lower social class children. There is every reason to suppose that these findings together with similar evidence from J.W.B. Douglas's large national sample (Douglas, 1964), were instrumental in causing the switch from streaming to mixed-ability grouping in primary schools, and to some degree in secondary schools, which occurred in the later 1960s and which continued through the 1970s.

The great complaint against streaming has been that it reinforced and maintained patterns of social advantage and privilege. It was implicitly expected that abolishing streaming would result in patterns of achievement less correlated with social class. However, that seems not to have happened. Even with the increasing prevalence of mixed-ability teaching, the evidence from research was that children from the lower social classes and larger families had poorer attainments than children from higher social classes and smaller families, both at age 7 and at age 16. As the National Child Development Study has shown, the gap in educational achievement between children of contrasted backgrounds is maintained as the children progress through school. Between 7 and 16 years of age there is relatively little change in the academic position of children; the lowest performers at 7 are by and large the lowest at 16. As an agent for equalizing achievements, mixed-ability grouping and teaching seems not to have worked, whatever other effects it has had.

The last statement is, of course, not the same as saying that mixed-ability grouping produces poorer academic results overall. Indeed, it is consistent with saying that mixed-ability grouping produces better results than streaming, if the better results are achieved by those who are already doing well. Research findings on this issue are extraordinarily inconclusive. As Gregory (1984) notes, many review authors conclude that there is no real difference in the effects on academic progress or social adjustment of streaming and mixed-ability group-ing in primary and secondary schools. And perhaps that is the way it is: mixed-ability grouping has failed to make an impression on inequalities. You should note, however, that many of these studies are methodologically flawed and this will have contributed to the 'no difference' verdict. There are real problems in making the right comparisons. For example, the widely cited Barker Lunn study (1970) had to contend with the fact that only half the teachers in the mixed-ability schools actually supported mixed-ability grouping and of these nearly half were *steaming within* the class for one or more subjects. When to these are added the proportion of the teachers who were against mixed-ability in such schools and also streamed within the school it turned out that 53 per cent of all staff in the mixed-ability schools were streaming within the class for some of the time.

If I have seemed to act briefly as a devil's advocate for streaming I would not want to conceal the pernicious effects associated with it, which are the pernicious effects associated with selection generally; the disillusioned Scottish boys bear witness to those. The crucial error, compounded over two or three generations, has been to regard ability grouping as an essential part of the meritocratic process wherein scarce resources are distributed efficiently for the benefit of all. Given this, all the familiar findings of lowered teacher-expectation, injured self-esteem, stigmatization, hopelessness, alienation and so on, follow. It is often forgotten that ability grouping is supposed to be about the matching of instructional characteristics (such as pace or difficulty level) to the needs and ability level of the student — placement, not selection. If this is true (and I suppose we have to wonder), then there is no reason to treat any group as inherently more desirable than any other, or membership of a group as a scarce benefit to be competed for and awarded on merit. Each student is presumably put in the group that is best for that student. As Strike (1983), on whose thoughtful essay I have drawn, puts it:

> A given classification can be regarded as successful when each student is in the group which is best for that student, not when the most desirable group is occupied by the most deserving students. (Strike, 1983, p. 127)

This is a powerful reminder that the *educational* purposes of ability grouping have to be attended to. And it is because we were so fixated on the ideological aspects of streaming that we replaced it with what Gregory (1984) calls:

> ... probably ... one of the most pervasive scientifically unsupported changes to occur in primary and secondary education in the last thirty years. There were problems with streaming but instead of changing the system of grouping to an unsubstantiated alternative, efforts should have been made to remove some of the undesirable practices and attitudes associated with streaming. (p. 224)

I would not want to disagree with that statement, just as I would not disagree with the general statement that Y is not necessarily to be preferred to X, just because X is unsatisfactory, and especially if X has been misunderstood or incorrectly applied. What do you think?

Activity (allow about 10 minutes)

Mixed-ability teaching implies individualization of instruction, a point that is sometimes overlooked. Gregory concludes that:

> where mixed-ability grouping has been observed in secondary

schools the predominant teaching method found has been whole-class teaching aimed just below the middle of the ability range. This is associated with the most- and least-able not being catered for, resulting in discipline problems for even experienced teachers. (Gregory, 1984, p. 224)

Review your own experience as a teacher or parent or former school student. Can you come to a conclusion on whether, and in what circumstances, mixed-ability teaching is workable?

Consider, also, what is entailed by ability grouping done in the right educational spirit.

We are looking at ability grouping because it is an important application of testing, historically and contemporaneously. (Of course, you don't have to test to place children in ability groups, and many teachers do not, trusting instead to their own judgment, but the issue of whether or not tests should be used is not one I am entering into here.) Gipps *et al.* (1983) report, from their survey of English and Welsh schools, that the main use of test scores in the secondary school is in the formation of teaching groups. They found that about a quarter of the schools used test information to form sets i.e. groups for subjects, another quarter formed mixed-ability groups of roughly equal ability, and an eighth formed broad ability bands, i.e. streams. (There is some overlapping because some schools both banded and set pupils.) Nearly half the schools said that they used the scores, or some components of the scores, to identify children in need of special attention, and place them in remedial groups; shades of Binet.

Group Characteristics Affect Individual Learning

Barr and Dreeben (1983) have made several forthright statements about grouping. Two of the most important are:

(a) The properties of groups (notably the distribution of ability, and to a lesser extent behaviour) affect the characteristics of groups, which then directly influence the design of instruction, which in turn affect individual achievement.

(b) Grouping involves trade-offs between different kinds of instructional arrangements. It is difficult to tell whether instruction is more individualized when a teacher spends thirty minutes working closely with eight children and a reading book or when children are working by themselves at their own pace with very little supervision, waiting for their group's turn with the teacher.

In principle, one might expect group membership to affect individual differences. It could amplify them, dampen them or leave them as they are. It is fair to ask what exactly it is about grouping students of 'similar' abilities which is so advantageous; and what is the expected effect on individual differences.

We know very little about how individual and group characteristics interact. A 1977 study by Webb (see Snow and Yalow in Sternberg, 1982, pp. 558–9) is one of the few to have tackled individual and group characteristics simultaneously. Students were given instruction and then asked to solve mathematical problems, both on their own and working within a small group. The groups were either of mixed ability or of uniformly high, medium or low ability. Performance under all conditions varied as a function of the group composition as well as individual ability. High-ability students did equally well as individuals and in mixed-ability groups, but not as well in uniform high-ability groups. Medium-ability students did best in uniform medium-ability groups and worst in mixed-ability groups. Low-ability students did best in mixed-ability groups and worst in uniform low-ability groups. Observation of what went on within the groups indicated that high-ability students in mixed-ability groups tended to act as teachers, offering explanations to lower-ability students who benefited from them. In the uniform ability groups, those medium-ability students who offered explanations showed excellent performance; those who did not participate in this way performed worse than when learning alone. Webb concluded that *active* group members did better than those who did not participate and that they performed as well or better than in individual learning. The tendency to participate was a function of both individual ability and group composition.

The Effectiveness of Learning in Groups

Barr and Dreeben's point (b) touches on a fundamental question: having formed ability groups, how should teachers allocate their time between and, indeed, within groups? If the principle behind the grouping is to match instruction to the needs of each individual, the question should be answered, but Barr and Dreeben's example casts doubt on how such matching will be achieved, and be seen to be achieved. It is easy to see how the governing criterion could shift by degrees towards 'the greatest learning for the greatest number'. Strike (1983, p. 129) provides an example that makes the point. John and Jim are in the same (middle) ability group but they fight, and their disruptive influence has an adverse effect upon the rest of the group. The teacher decides to put Jim in the top group for reading. John and his group get on better but Jim makes little progress in reading, suffers considerable loss of self-esteem, and loses interest in reading. Jim's progress, it might be said, has been traded for the progress of the middle group, in the interests of maximizing aggregate learning. Clearly, grouping raises difficult questions of equity, which cannot easily be ignored. The matter of how much time should be allocated to different ability groups is a case in point: who should get more time, the top or the bottom group? As you answer this question be aware of the criteria you are using.

Individualized Learning and Testing

Individualized learning is not the same as individual learning. Whereas individualized learning strongly implies the availability of an instructional programme tailored to the individual, individual learning may mean no more than that the individual works on what everyone else does, but alone, or alone within a group. Then we may ask whether materials are tailored to or tasks made appropriate for individuals or not, and whether teaching is tailored to individuals or indeed whether there is any teaching at all.

There now exists a range of programmes, all originating in the USA, designed to adapt instruction to individual differences. There is Computer Assisted Instruction (CAI), Individually Prescribed Instruction (IPI), Individually Guided Education (IGE), Programmed Learning According to Needs (PLAN), mastery learning and the Keller Plan or Keller Personalized System of Instruction (PSI). As Snow and Yalow note (Sternberg, 1982, p. 510), the basic idea behind all these programmes is to accommodate individual differences in pace of learning across an orderly sequence of instructional steps, on the assumption that intellectual differences among students are reflected mainly in differences in learning rate. The emphasis on *pace* is a direct result of the educational implications B.F. Skinner drew from his behavioural theory of learning, notably that correct responses could be shaped with immediate reinforcement or reward. Pacing variation is judged successful if more students reach the immediate criterion, without regard for what faster learners do, or could do, beyond that criterion. This is very much the case with mastery learning, and critics (for example, Messick, 1981) have objected to it on those grounds. What sort of construct is it if we do not know anything about it beyond the criterion?

The question to be asked is whether individualization in the pace of instruction is enough to accommodate intellectual differences with respect to learning. Snow and Yalow (Sternberg, 1982, p. 511) are quite clear on this. Their reading of the evidence to date is that no method of individualization yet invented removes all effects of prior differences in intellectual abilities. To their minds, what is wanted are qualitatively different alternative treatments adapted to intellectual differences. Going faster or slower down the same track isn't going to do it. You can examine this statement from your own experience. It is also at least possible that group-paced individualized systems, of the kind studied by Webb might be more effective than self-paced systems. We have tended to make a holy cow of individualization but it may not necessarily be worth striving for, at least during the early adolescent years.

Graded testing

Varying the pace of instruction may not be sufficient in itself, but it is certainly the case that individuals will want, and should be able, to control the pace at which they are tested. In the UK there is a lobby that wants individuals to be able to choose when they can present themselves for testing (that is, when they are ready to pass), instead of having to take the same tests at the same time and at the same stage of their school or college careers (when they may not be ready to pass). The movement is called *graded assessment*.

Reading (allow about 1 hour)

If you read the article entitled 'Graded assessment' by Andrew Harrison in the *Block 4 Supplementary Readings* you will see that the primary aim of graded testing is the improvement of the individual pupil's learning, in the spirit of Scarr's testing *for* children. Taking the emphasis off sorting and labelling constitutes the break from the psychometric tradition Harrison talks about. That improvement is to be secured by integrating assessment with learning, which Harrison claims is the 'one real novelty' of graded testing. You will have to ask yourself how this is to be done. Evidently, much will depend, as always, on the teacher. The questions I have been raising in this section about organizing and managing instruction will be pertinent, I suspect. It is certainly interesting to speculate on what will happen when graded testing collides with mixed-ability teaching, if it does. Is a teacher to concentrate on getting all or most of the group through the sequence at much the same rate or will there be a propensity to pace pupils differently, since the opportunity to do so would have been effectively underwritten?

Naturally there are technical problems associated with graded testing. One consequence of unreliability is wrongly ascribed failure and it will need to be seen whether failure in a graded testing system is less stigmatizing or traumatizing than it tends to be in conventional assessment systems. Being criterion-referenced in nature there will be a strong temptation to restrict validation of graded tests to content validation. This will be a mistake. Construct validation will have to be attended to if coherent and intellectually respectable statements of what has been attained are to be made. Then there will be the crucial matter of the characteristics of the items comprising the tests. It is not customary to pretest or pilot criterion-referenced tests because, unlike norm-referenced tests, no deliberate attempt is being made to engineer test characteristics, notably the expected distribution of scores. Rather, the policy is to devise the items, based on a (hopefully) one-to-one correspondence with very specific objectives, and then let the scores turn out as they will. The trouble with this policy is that you never quite know the extent to which the test characteristics have confounded the criterion you have set up. If the items are harder or easier than you wanted there will be consequences in terms of the numbers of candidates judged to be passes or fails. That said, these difficulties may well be of the same order of magnitude as those now experienced by examination boards, who invariably have to adjust pass rates when an examination proves too hard or too easy.

Graded testing is just getting off the ground and it is far too early to say whether it will be successful. It is in that uneasy phase, common to all innovations, especially in education, where more is expected of it than it can possibly deliver. Harrison's paper is commendably honest and if he is vague about exactly how learning and assessment are to be integrated, he is in good company. In this unit we have tried to acquaint you with aspects of testing, and to show, in particular, how the use of testing affects the kind of education, and learning opportunities, people receive. The outstanding questions are the perennial questions and they have much more to do with learning than assessment.

References

AMERICAN PSYCHOLOGICAL ASSOCIATION (1974) *Standards for Educational and Psychological Tests*, Washington, American Psychological Association.

BARKER LUNN, J.C. (1970) *Streaming in the Primary School*, Windsor, NFER.

BARR, R. and DREEBEN, R. (1983) *How Schools Work*, Chicago, University of Chicago Press.

BRITISH PSYCHOLOGICAL SOCIETY (1983) 'Psychological tests — a legal definition', *Bulletin of the British Psychological Society*, 36, p. 192.

CHAPMAN, P.D. (1981) 'Schools as sorters: Testing and tracking in California, 1910–1925', *Journal of Social History*, 14, pp. 701–17.

CRONBACH, L.J. (1971) 'Test validation' in THORNDIKE, R.L. (Ed.) *Educational Measurement*, Washington DC, American Council on Education.

DOUGLAS, J.W.B. (1964) *The Home and the School*, London, MacGibbon and Kee.

EGGLESTON, S.J. (1983) *Learning Mathematics: How the Work of the APU Can Help Teachers*, London, Assessment of Performance Unit, DES.

EVANS, B. and WAITES, B. (1981) *IQ and Mental Testing*, London, Macmillan.

EYSENCK, H.J. and KAMIN, L. (1981) *Intelligence: The Battle for the Mind*, London, Macmillan.

FREDERIKSEN, N. (1984) 'The real test bias: Influences of testing on teaching and learning', *American Psychologist*, 39, 3, pp. 193–202.

GARNIER, M.A. and RAFFALOVICH, L.E. (1984) 'The evolution of equality of educational opportunities in France', *Sociology of Education*, 57, 1, pp. 1–11.

GIPPS, C., STEADMAN, S., BLACKSTONE, T. and STIERER, B. (1983) *Testing Children*, London, Heinemann Educational Books.

GRAY, J., McPHERSON, A.F. and RAFFE, D. (1983) *Reconstructions of Secondary Education*, London, Routledge and Kegan Paul.

GREEN, B.F. (1981) 'A primer of testing', *American Psychologist*, 36, 10, pp. 1001–11.

GREGORY, R.P. (1984) 'Streaming, setting and mixed-ability grouping in primary and secondary schools: Some research findings', *Educational Studies*, 10, 3, pp. 209–26.

HILL, C.J. (1972) *Transfer at Eleven*, Windsor, NFER.

HUNT, E.B. and LUNNEBORG, C.E. (1973) 'On intelligence' in SJURSEN, F.H. and BEACH, L.R. (Eds.) *Readings in Psychology*, New York, Holt, Rinehart and Winston.

JACKSON, B. (1964) *Streaming*, London, Routledge and Kegan Paul.

JOHNSTONE, A. and CASSELS, J. (1978) 'What's in a word?', *New Scientist*, 18 May, pp. 432–4.

KANG, H-C. (1983) 'Education and equal opportunity between the wars', *Oxford Review of Education*, 9, 2, pp. 91–108.

McCLELLAND, D.C. (1973) 'Testing for competence rather than for "intelligence"' *American Psychologist*, 28, 1, pp. 1–14.

Messick, S. (1981) 'Constructs and their vicissitudes in educational and psychological measurement' *Psychological Bulletin*, 59, 3, pp. 575–88.

Scarr, S. (1981) 'Testing *for* children: Assessment and the many determinants of intellectual competence', *American Psychologist*, 36, 10, pp. 1159–66.

Sigel, I.E. (1963) 'How intelligence tests limit understanding of intelligence', *Merrill-Palmer Quarterly*, 9, 1, pp. 39–56.

Sternberg, R.J. (Ed.) (1982) *Handbook of Human Intelligence*, Cambridge, Cambridge University Press.

Stott, D.H. (1983) *Issues in the Intelligence Debate*, Windsor, NFER-Nelson.

Strike, K.A. (1983) 'Fairness and ability grouping', *Educational Theory*, 33, 3 and 4, pp. 125–34.

Sutherland, G. (1984) *Ability, Merit and Measurement*, Oxford, Oxford University Press.

Terman, L.M. (1911) 'The Binet-Simon scale for measuring intelligence', *The Psychological Clinic*, 5, pp. 204–5.

Thorndike, R.L. (1982) *Applied Psychometrics*, Boston, MA, Houghton Mifflin.

Vernon, P.E. (Ed.) (1957) *Secondary School Selection: A British Psychological Society Inquiry*, London, Methuen.

Watts, A.F. and Slater, A.F. (1950) *First Interim Report on the Allocation of Primary School Leavers to Courses of Secondary Education*, Windsor, NFER.

Wood, R. (1986) 'The agenda for educational measurement' in Nuttall, D.L. (Ed.) *Assessing Educational Achievement*, Lewes, Falmer Press.

Paper 12: Sex-linked Discrimination in Educational Selection

A little known aspect of selection at 11 + is the apparent discrimination against one sex or the other which occurs as a result of the local authority refusing to apply the same criterion of acceptability to both sexes. Instead, the sexes are treated separately and different criteria or cut-off points are applied. Thus a girl might have a higher score than the cut-off for boys yet fail to gain a place. It is the incidence of cases like this which have led to complaints being brought against authorities acting in this way. There was a case brought against Avon in the late 1970s and another was reported to the Ombudsman in 1983. (I suspect this is the case discussed by Wilby, 1983.) The Equal Opportunities Commission (EOC) ruled in 1979 that Avon was contravening the 1975 Sex Discrimination Act by using separate lists and quotas and instructed the authority to cease the practice. The outcome of the case considered by the Ombudsman is not yet known. This is bound to be a sensitive area with parents and the programme which follows aims to explore the matter further and to use it to open up the related and more general issue of how to provide equal opportunity to achieve, regardless of gender.

(What follows is a conversation between a Bryan Magee-like interlocuter and a fairly omniscient expert.)

A: What exactly were the grounds for the Commission taking the view it did?

B: We don't really know but I imagine that someone would have argued that gender is either an irrelevant category in this situation or is no more obviously relevant than any other, for example, parental income. This sort of reasoning is, of course, at the heart of the Act. It follows that a fair selection procedure ought to be used regardless of the consequences for either gender. Let the chips fall where they may, if you like. But I stress that I'm only guessing at what the Commission had in mind.

A: All the same, it sounds as if you might be right. What about the other side now? What arguments would an authority like Avon have used to defend separate lists and quotas?

B: At its most basic, I think the argument would have been that there is no

149

reason why noticeably more of one sex than the other should be admitted to grammar school. A more sophisticated version would be that there is no reason to expect differences in the capacity to profit from grammar school education. Thus the fact of girls' superior test results at 11 — which does tend to be the rule — should not be taken to mean an intrinsically greater capacity among girls to benefit from grammar school places.

A: You mean that the reason for girls getting higher test scores could be that they mature earlier than boys in the skills needed to do well at these tests but that this early promise does not translate itself into anything more than boys — in the generality — are capable of, at age 16 or 18?

B: Yes, in which case you might as well refer to boys as late maturing. There is, in fact, as I expect you know, evidence in the form of 'A' level grades that boys overtake girls in the end although we have to be careful about that kind of data insofar as the two gender groups have been whittled away in different amounts by the time they take 'A' levels.

A: I suppose a cynic might see it as a plot by (local authority) males to protect males.

B: Perhaps, but what I think these authorities are really saying, although they might not put it in these words, is that there are so many imponderables in the situation that the proper way to act is to treat the sexes as having equal potential and adjust the cut-off scores to secure either equalization of numbers or the appropriate proportions. To say this is quite consistent with Goldstein's insistence that there is no real justification for selecting equal numbers of boys and girls (Goldstein, 1986). Or with his contention that authorities had might as well adjust for factors other than sex differences, notably class. Not wishing to open the Pandora's Box which is multiple adjustments, I believe the LEAs operate according to a sort of principle of indifference, although I doubt if they think about it in those terms.

A: Isn't that an argument which should appeal to the EOC?

B: Well, the Act does say that there is such a thing as *indirect* discrimination when a condition or requirement, not justifiable regardless of sex, means that a smaller proportion of one sex than the other could comply with the requirement. The EOC did agonize over what this clause might mean in the case of Avon. If boys do underachieve relative to girls for reasons which are largely out of their control, is it indirect discrimination *not* to weight the tests or adjust the cut-offs in their favour? The EOC recommended otherwise but had it bought this argument it would have been engaging in what is usually called *reverse* discrimination, which in effect is what Avon was doing. Whether the EOC has found itself prescribing reverse discrimination in any other settings, I wouldn't know.

A: What struck me when you talked of 'imponderables' and having to act in ignorance, is how you can predict what anyone will do later on at school, never mind their sex or whether they will profit from a grammar school education, whatever that means. How is it we can put our money on one lot and not on others?

B: You are asking why select at 11 and, as we all know, many local authorities came to the conclusion some time ago that selection at that age was prejudicial to the development of a large number of children and abandoned it. But some remain unconvinced or allow selection to continue in pockets within their boundaries. Their case rests on being able to pick those who will profit from a grammar school education — which presumably means doing well there, getting lots of 'O' levels and then 'A' levels and so on. That is where the tests come in. They have been told that these tests will predict academic performance at age 16.

A: Just predict, or predict well?

B: Predict well, but I know what you're driving at. The way the term is often used (in common parlance) carries with it the connotation 'well'. And that is often a source of difficulty.

A: What would it mean to predict well?

B: It would presumably mean that most students who were given grammar school places went on to get lots of 'O' levels. But we know that doesn't happen, sometimes for reasons the grammar schools themselves connive at. In Paper 11 Wood has an illustration of how those who were supposed to profit were divided into four streams on day 1 of grammar school according to 11 + test scores. That was second-order selection, if you like, and it immediately reduced the chances of form 1D profiting. No, in practice good prediction means that individuals appear in much the same rank order on academic achievement at age 16, say, as they did at age 11 and, of course, streaming them at 11 does tend to bring about that result.

A: So the prediction of where people will end up relative to each other can be good but can say nothing or next to nothing about the *absolute* levels of achievement those at the top of the final rank order reach.

B: That's correct, and it's a point not well understood. A correlation, which is the customary way of quantifying predictive power, says nothing about *levels* of performance.

A: Would I be right in thinking that the predictive power of 11 + tests could be different for boys and girls?

B: It certainly could and probably usually is. That follows from characterizing girls as earlier maturers or boys as later maturers. Boys' performance at 11 will be less of a good guide to performance at 16 than is the case for girls. It would be good to check this out on some recent data.

A: Whatever direction the differences are in, and whatever the reasons, surely a test which predicts differently for boys and girls is suspect?

B: Perhaps, but that is going to be true of most tests or measures of performance. 'A' levels predict degree class differently and we don't really understand why. Incidentally, it is interesting that as far as I know nobody thinks of drawing up separate lists of males and females when it comes to selecting people for university. I suppose it is thought — if anyone does think about it — that these people have done their maturing and are on an equal footing.

A: I want to ask whether we want good prediction anyway. When the local authority says that it is not prepared to read into the fact that a girl scores higher than a boy on a test at 11 a greater capacity on the part of that girl to benefit from a grammar school place, I want to drop the gender distinction and broaden the issue to include everyone. If good prediction means a fixity in relative standings over time, then poor prediction must presumably mean that there are surprises, with some people catching up and others dropping back. Both positions imply a view of what education is for. I would have thought the latter view was more congenial, in which case shouldn't we be in the business of acting so as to *smash* good prediction (Glaser's word, Glaser, 1977) in the interests of allowing everyone to develop?

B: There is certainly an unpalatable truth there which some people would have difficulty accepting. I come back though to the point I made earlier. You can have good prediction yet fail in your objectives because, judged by examination grades, an unacceptably large number of students are failing to profit from a grammar school education. I think it was Roy Hattersley who said that the grammar schools of the 1950s actually did a rather poor job in terms of producing first-rate minds. Or, at least, lots of 'A' level passes. I know my 1950 grammar school was timid about entering people for Oxbridge. Not the same thing, I know, but indicative.

A: But when you say, 'profit from grammar school education' doesn't it rather depend upon *what* sort of school, large or small, for instance, or, if we are talking about gender differences, whether boys and girls go to single-sex schools or mixed? I am thinking of all those assertions that girls fare better academically when boys are removed from the scene.

B: It's certainly true that the architects of selection at 11+ — the Spens Committee, for example (see Paper 11) — do not seem to have had in mind anything beyond grammar school education, pure and simple. If it were to be found — and I don't think we have the evidence although I know it is rapidly becoming conventional wisdom — that girls in girls-only schools fared so much better than boys in boys-only schools — leaving aside whether they are grammar or not — then I think there would be some searching questions. It would mean, for instance, that you could select more girls than boys at 11 because you would know that they would get on better. But what would the EOC say about that?

A: It seems to me that allocation of children to institutions according to sex must come close to contravening the Act. After all, we wouldn't dare organize schools by ethnic group although we often do it by neighbourhood.

B: I think you're right but you have to ask yourself what the proponents of single-sex schooling would claim to be doing by their actions. They would say that if girls suffer from being in mixed schools they are being denied *equal opportunity to achieve* and it is necessary to rectify that state of affairs.

A: But isn't that just one manifestation of a general problem, and that is how to do the best for everyone, which I take to be the nearest we can get to providing equal opportunity to achieve? I am thinking of the organizational moves schools make routinely — banding, streaming, setting and so forth — which they presumably believe are directed at that problem.

B: You have gone to the heart of the matter. How do we organize learning to bring out the best in each individual? Section 4 of the Unit (paper 00) takes up this theme. A statement like 'Learning in a group may be more effective for some individuals than individual learning' has enormous implications, and the anecdote in the next paragraph about John and Jim, where Jim's progress is traded in the interests of maximizing aggregate learning, is poignant, to say the least. You see I happen to think that the problems involved in the organization of effective learning take precedence over the question of whether boys and girls should be treated differently.

References

GLASER, R. (1977) *Adaptive Education: Individual Diversity and Learning*, New York, Holt, Rinehart and Winston.

GOLDSTEIN, H. (1986) 'Sex bias and test norms in educational selection', *Research Intelligence* May, pp. 2–4.

WILBY, P. (1983) 'Threat to single sex schools', *Sunday Times*, 20 November.

Paper 13: Observations on Criterion-referenced Assessment*

The observations serve as background which I draw on when answering the questions (put by SSABSA). They contain some home truths about criterion-referencing or as another writer has put it, 'shattered icons'.[1] I stick my neck out in places but I think that is what is wanted. The recent McGaw report makes only a passing reference to criterion-referencing (need for research etc.) and, in that respect, is most disappointing.[2]

1   There is a good deal of ballyhoo surrounding criterion-referenced assessment and a lot of tripe has been written and talked about it. To give but one example, it was argued, quite seriously, by two educational philosophers, that norm-referencing constituted a violation of students' civil rights inasmuch as students were ranked publicly, and might therefore feel humiliated. Under criterion-referencing this would not happen.[3] The timing of these philosophers' statement was unfortunate for them because before long in the USA, and especially Florida, the courts were hearing a succession of cases in which litigants claimed that their civil rights had been denied as a result of taking minimum competency tests built on the most impeccable criterion-referenced principles. They had been refused leaving certificates, compelled to stay on at school, and so on. This was one of the silliest examples of praising criterion-referencing by damning norm-referencing.

2   The interest in criterion-referenced assessment comes about because of dissatisfaction with norm-referenced assessment, which is understandable enough. A bald grade says nothing about a person's strengths and weaknesses and only encourages global judgments which are liable to be overly damning or praising. But norm-referenced assessments do serve a function — selection — and, if they

*An edited version of a paper prepared for the Senior Secondary Assessment Board of South Australia (SSABSA), August 1984.

did not, they would presumably soon be discarded. Inertia, alone, cannot be held responsible for their continuing use. (Notice, I say nothing about the validity, reliability and appropriateness of norm-referenced assessments for selection purposes: those should be subject to constant monitoring and, knowing what we know, there is no reason to be sanguine about any one of them.)

3   The objection to norm-referenced assessments is that only those who will be selected benefit from them. For the rest, the case for criterion-referencing is overwhelmingly strong, and to say that, in principle, the selected will benefit too, in no way weakens the case. But they and the others will benefit because the assessment is serving another function — providing information about achievements — and this is the point to get straight. Both norm-referenced and criterion-referenced assessments have appropriate functions, and both categories of assessment are useful. Criterion-referenced assessment ought to have the greater utility, both in terms of numbers affected and the value of the information it can potentially deliver, and this is the source of its appeal. Nevertheless, the two categories of assessment do coexist and may well have to go on doing so, as in Queensland where a tertiary entrance score is being maintained alongside the system of criterion-referenced assessments which the authorities there are putting in place. Some will see this as a surrender to conservative forces but it really is inevitable given the present state-of-the-art in criterion-referencing. That is why nothing is gained by glorifying criterion-referencing and reviling norm-referencing.

4   Often when a call is made to replace X with Y, it is conveniently forgotten that X has usually been the subject of much discussion and reflection over the years, whatever its shortcomings now appear to be, and that Y is untried and unexamined and, quite conceivably, is floated on a tide of euphoric expectation which is quite unrealistic. Sometimes it is better to patch up X and spend more time developing Y. That analysis does not correspond exactly to what we are dealing with here because, as I have argued, the first order of business should not be to replace immediately norm-referencing with criterion-referencing *across the board*. Yet there are elements in common. Norm-referencing could stand more serious investigation; criterion-referencing is certainly in an embryonic state, and I stick to that statement although there are Americans who would tell you otherwise. The power of criterion-referencing to induce, in some minds, a kind of cargo cult mentality, I have already alluded to.

5   It has been said, 'if you scratch a criterion-referenced interpretation, you will very likely find a norm-referenced set of assumptions underneath'.[4] I take that to mean that a norm-referenced interpretation can nearly always be placed upon a criterion-referenced interpretation, simply by admitting comparisons. This is usually because the

criterion-referenced information is not sufficiently satisfying and also, it must be admitted, because the need among humans to make comparisons seems to be deeply rooted. The example of a pure criterion-referenced test which is always being given, is the driving test. But suppose you ask people 'How many times did you take the test before you passed?' then the answers will be given a norm-referenced interpretation. Granted, such a question is against the spirit of criterion-referencing, but it happens. Those who see criterion-referencing as a means of blunting competitive striving will be disillusioned.

6 Switching to criterion-referencing does not make measurement problems any easier, if anything it makes them more difficult. Test construction procedures become more exacting, precisely because the measurement is more closely targeted to stated criteria than was true before, and also, importantly, because the results are going to be made public and will therefore, in principle and perhaps also in practice soon, be subject to the sort of scrutiny which might eventuate in a court case. If you claim to be measuring 'the ability to express ideas and communicate effectively through language to a variety of audiences, for a variety of purposes, in a variety of mediums'[5] it may just happen that someone (an aggrieved party) will ask you to demonstrate how a student rated low fails to evince that ability, or enough of it. Naturally, this would be a tough assignment and none of us would be too eager to climb into the witness box, but I see that a Freedom of Information Act is on its way (in South Australia). Perhaps it is best to draw the conclusion that the more haphazard and less defensible practices associated with norm-referenced testing will have to go. There is a parallel with multiple-choice and free-response testing. The former technique takes more stick because the assumptions underpinning its operation are more clearly exposed to view, above all the quality and drift of the examiners' thinking, which are nicely concealed in essay questions. Not that I advocate multiple-choice exclusively for criterion-referenced testing. The choice of techniques must be informed by a consideration of what kind of questioning will best permit a more or less unequivocal inference that the skill or ability or competence under examination is present, to a sufficient degree, or is not. Actually, that has always been the aim of measurement but it has been lost sight of in the general preoccupation with reliability over validity. Aggregating collections of items may do something for reliability but, logically, can do nothing for validity if some of these items are defective. The single item or question matters, and that is what has been lost sight of.

7 There is a belief abroad that the only validity which matters in criterion-referenced assessment is content validity, the extent to which the test mirrors faithfully, or constitutes a proper sample of, the

domain or universe of content students were supposed to master. Doubtless the main reason is the close connection between criterion-referencing and minimum competency and mastery learning programmes, where it has seemed that all that was meant to be learned was content, or small teachable (and disposable) bits of knowledge. In a domain-referenced test the overall score has absolute meaning (criterion-referenced meaning) in the sense of indicating what proportion of some defined domain of content the examinee has mastered.[6] The question being answered about the examinee's achievement is in terms of 'How many', which is precisely the answer norm-referenced examinations give. This would come as a sore disappointment to the criterion-referencing enthusiast, who was hoping for an answer in terms of 'How well'. In fact, most norm-referenced examinations operate a rough and ready version of the domain-referenced model in which content is matched to a set of behavioral objectives to create a rather imprecisely defined domain and sampling is carried out according to the examiners' notional view of how the content and these objectives (which they may not believe in) ought to be represented in the examination. It could certainly not be called probability sampling, which is what the domain-referenced model requires. In fact it has more in common with the idiosyncratic methods of question selection used by Binet at the turn of the century when he compiled the first intelligence test.

8 I make these points not to draw attention to flaws in prevailing examination methodology, which is easy to do, but to suggest that the movement for criterion-referencing will go astray if it becomes wedded to a view of achievement restricted to mastery of content. I do not think the users of certificates and students and their teachers want to see achievement reported in terms of estimated proportion of content mastered domain by domain (and there would have to be many domains, too many to deal with in one three-hour examination) or, what comes to the same thing, inventories of fragments of achievement (those 'teachable' bits of knowledge). Either way, the enterprise would sink under its own weight, and examples can be found in the USA. The Queensland Board of Secondary Education makes sure that all its subject syllabuses spell out process, skill and content objectives (and also affective objectives). Without commenting on the quality of these objectives, it would seem, at least it would in my view, that the process and skill objectives should have precedence, in that attempts should be made to assimilate the content objectives into them. That is not to say that content and process must be separated; indeed the argument is made later that it is simply not possible, and would not be desirable if it were possible, to engage in processes of enquiry without bringing to bear the relevant knowledge structures, which are a good deal more than constellations of bits of

content. It is certainly interesting that the Queensland scheme, which refers explicitly to competency-based assessment, should show, through some of the wording of its criteria for exit assessments, signs of reaching towards a synthesis of process, skill, content and affective objectives. The problem there is that objectives in all categories are specified for each unit or sub-division of a syllabus, which makes the job of drawing out one judgment at the end very difficult or, to put it more bluntly, next to impossible, given the within-individual variation which is bound to be present. That is especially the case when criteria are worded like this:

> Limited Achievement
> The student should demonstrate some ability to recall formulae and definitions, and should recall and apply learned procedures in routine situations.[7]

Not much process there, and not much of anything else, either. In seeking compression of information, the goal must be something more comprehensive and meaningful to all who are going to read these reports. If process objectives are going to be given precedence then it would make sense to try and follow such objectives through all the units of the course.

9 The conceptualization of achievement hinted at in the last paragraph is one that deserves to be taken seriously. It can be put like this. The nature and power of a student's organized structure of knowledge is crucial to significant educational achievement because it either facilitates or hinders what he or she can do in a subject area. But what a person can do also embraces broad cognitive skills or abilities that are applied to the subject matter in order to interpret, remember, visualize, transform, evaluate and so on. These broad cognitive abilities — comprehension, memory, reasoning fluency, judgment, restructuring and others — interact continually with knowledge (techniques) to produce what we call achievement, or more generally competence (*not* competency). Since this conceptualization is developmental in character, it follows that beginning and advanced learners in a field will differ not only in the amount of knowledge accumulated and the complexity of its structure, but also in the uses and complexity of ability structures.

10 It also follows that what we are calling competence — the whole bundle — is, for a long time and perhaps always, insecurely established and fragile in nature. That should warn us against expecting too much from youngsters but contrary instances are not too hard to find:

> Process objectives refer to the cognitive processes to be

developed in relation to the discipline. In mathematics, these are such higher-order processes as the following: interpreting and analyzing information, mathematical models and results; abstracting, idealizing and formulating mathematical models for relatively new stratims; discovering new relationships, deducing new abstractions in existing models and testing their validity by logical inference; applying a repertoire of mathematical behaviour in other disciplines or areas or in solving unrehearsed problems.[9]

Perhaps one is being unfair. If these objectives were read as ultimate objectives of the kind that a trained adult mathematician would be expected to meet, and acted upon in that spirit, then there would be no demur. But, too often I fear, such objectives are seen as realizable by age 16 or 18, and by most students at that.

11　It is agreed that in criterion-referenced assessment schemes, criteria should be couched in terms of emerging competences peculiar to the subject. (The possibility of generalization and transfer across subjects can be dealt with later.) For the sake of argument let us say that the sort of statements Queensland calls process objectives. These offer the best approximation to a working model of competence in a subject, pending a more parsimonious and insightful reformulation which will have to wait on the results of research and controlled experience. The measurement task is to construct achievement tests that capture functional dimensions of developing competence (which, as just noted, can be taken to be process objectives for the time being), and are sensitive to different states in the acquisition of competence.[10]

Along with the promise of more information about people, criterion-referencing offers liberation from 'grading on the curve'. Some of those running norm-referenced examinations, for example, the British GCE boards, have stoutly denied that they follow fixed percentage formulas but it seems clear that they act within certain constraints which prevent them varying percentages by too great a margin. And no one should be surprised at this, since they do not claim to be in the business of criterion-referencing; the most they say is that examiners' judgments of the overall quality of candidates is taken into account. That said, there is need, in a fully criterion-referenced system of grading, say along Queensland lines, ranging from Very High Achievement to Very Limited Achievement, to be watchful that the allocation of students to grades does not, by an insidious creeping process, end up with the same sort of result as norm-referenced systems. Loose exit criteria combined with difficulty in rendering consistent, or just making sense of, many diverse ratings of achievement (such as teachers in Queensland must experience) will tend to produce conservative grading strategies which will deny grade A to all but a few and concentrate students in the middle grades, just as happens now. Not, of course, that such an outcome would not be possible under criterion-referencing, even though the instructional ideology associated with criterion-referencing viz. mastery learning, would indicate otherwise.

The Questions

What are the implications for SSABSA in moving away from norm-referencing of assessment towards a system of criterion-referencing (or various adaptations of this)?

(i) *What subject areas are amenable to this or other related models and which present special problems?*
No subject areas are ruled out a priori from criterion-referenced treatment. Given a commitment to competence-based assessment the only reason why a subject would be ruled out would be if the analysis of competence proved impossible or if the measurement requirement suggested by the analysis could not be met. Neither sounds probable although that is not to play down the difficulties. However, inasmuch as it has proved possible to produce lists of process objectives in a number of areas and also to identify skills which teaching in a particular subject seeks to produce and enhance[11], there is no call to be pessimistic. The more searching problems are likely to come with assessment itself. There will be subject-specific problems when it comes to deciding on appropriate measurement techniques, especially given that some subjects have been in the habit of using a technique such as multiple-choice which, for the purposes of ascertaining competence, now appears unsatisfactory. It seems likely that school assessment will have to take more of the brunt of assessment than has been the case hitherto, if not in weighting terms then in terms of exploiting the extra opportunities it offers (beyond external examinations) for pinning down students' states of competence.

(ii) *Can it be reported in a form which allows easy interpretation by 'users' of the scale?*
Depends what you mean by 'easy'. For some users anything you can think of will be difficult or will be resisted. The British CSE boards have been bedevilled by users who would have nothing to do with any grades below 1. These were not difficult to interpret, just unpalatable with GCE around. Do you think that the sort of thing Queensland produces[12] is easy to interpret? Perhaps the word is not

easy, but informative. The way one user might respond has just been discussed. Where employers are concerned, who is to say? In the first place, it is legitimate to ask whether schools are or should be in the business of doing employers' work for them, that is, involved in complicity in the process of selection for jobs. Leaving that aside, there is evidence around[13] that many companies are more interested in the qualities of individuals, such as 'common sense', 'conduct' and 'punctuality'. If this were so, then perhaps assessments should be tailored in this direction with more being made of the so-called affective objectives. At this stage, the only answer can be to develop a code of reporting which you can live with and see what 'users' make of it in the local situation.

(iii) *Can it be reported on a point or graded scale?*

Queensland uses a graded scale without attaching letters or numbers although it is obvious how the grades would be quantified. There is little to choose between points and letters. Points give slightly more encouragement to quantify; letters are perhaps more stigmatizing, looked at historically. It would be good if a reasonably neutral shorthand could be found for encapsulating states of competence.

(iv) *What kind of expertise is required of curriculum writers, examiners and moderators, and teachers in such a system?*

If a competence-based view of the curriculum is taken, where process objectives are superordinate, the task for curriculum writers is to devise sequences of learning experiences which will be conducive to the development and exercise of the identified competences. Whereas before the need to treat the structure of knowledge in a subject might have been uppermost in a curriculum writer's mind, to that will have to be added the questions What develops? and What should develop? It will be no good stating process, skill and content objectives, as Queensland does, if the requirement to put across content is still heavily signalled in the syllabus. The process objectives cannot be left to look after themselves. To reiterate the position sketched in earlier, it is the existing cognitive structure, developing through instruction and experience, which is seen as the critical factor affecting the possibility of meaningful learning and retention. At the outset of secondary education, and for a long time afterwards, this structure is unstable, incomplete and disordered, but given developmentally sensitive programs, systematic instruction, diagnosis and remediation, it can be expected to become more stable, ordered and complete. Ultimately, in the case of the expert, the cognitive structure is so well established as a result of years of learning practice and application — automatized, as it were — that we are able to infer competence from consistent, correct task performance. The reality, however, where schools are concerned, is that subjects are not studied long enough, or in ways which would lead to structures deep or stable enough for us to expect the type of consistent performance on significant tasks which enables any supportable inference about competence to be made. That is the point made earlier about expecting too much from students. Measurement will inevitably deal with states of immature competence.

Allegiance to a model of competence where subject-specific knowledge (including techniques) and general cognitive skills *drive* each other along, suggests the need for formative assessment programs in schools directed towards diagnosing deficiencies in knowledge structure and knowledge (technique) use, and also deficiencies in general cognitive skills. Students will vary according to the attention they need on one or other front. That should not be read as meaning that content and process should again be separated; the whole point is that knowledge and abilities need to be married, in the right proportions, for competence to develop properly and, more importantly, endure.[14]

It might seem superfluous but let the point be made: examiners and moderators and teachers need to be able to demonstrate the competence they seek to find (and, in the case of teachers, develop) in students. They have to be experts. Moreover, they all need, as assessors, the ability to see through to the student's present state of competence. For examiners, this means setting questions which will permit more or less unequivocal inference that competence is present (in some immature state); for teachers the burden is heavier because they have the job — they certainly have the opportunity — of getting to the bottom of where students are, in terms of developed competence. This is why school assessment must assume more importance; a three-hour examination cannot do the job on its own. The examination will give a certain impression of competence; only the teacher, by continual observation and interrogation, can confirm that impression.

(v) *Is it reliable, comparable between subjects in the same year, same subjects in different years?*
Reliability is the responsibility of test constructors. It will depend entirely on how well they do. However, an orientation towards competence i.e. How well? rather than How many? should sharpen up test construction practices insofar as more attention ought to be given to single sources of evidence, whether they be multiple-choice items, essay questions or behavioural descriptions in rating scales.

Comparability between subjects is always a vexatious issue and it will seem more so in a criterion-referenced system, since there is no reason to expect that sets of criteria across subjects will be commensurable. (That they might turn out to be so is another matter.) Perhaps there will be limited correspondence in cognate subjects. It is fair to ask whether concern for comparability is not a product of norm-referenced thinking. In this connection, the McGaw Committee has something interesting to say. After describing the rationale for scaling — to adjust results which have been competitively allocated after being normatively established — it goes on:

> We believe scaling cannot be abandoned unless a thorough-going adoption of criterion-referenced assessment becomes feasible ... (p. 42)

(vi) *Is a system of 'profiling' students workable? Can it be used for tertiary selection?*

The Queensland exit assessment does not come in the form of a profile. There is one terminal judgment which is arrived at by collapsing a good deal of information. The difficulties inherent in this procedure have already been mentioned. A profile which allowed of reports on several dimensions of competence would therefore be attractive. Profiling is really just the reporting arm of criterion-referenced assessment. The state of the art on profiling presents a mixed picture.[15] That profiles can be produced is undeniable. Whether they have the utility in practice their proponents claim for them, is another matter. The reported indifference of employers to elaborated descriptions of academic achievement can be cited. Perhaps two points can be made about profiles. The first has already been made.

1 The more information you report, the more vulnerable you are to being held accountable for the fidelity of that information. This is likely to be a greater concern in future.

2 There is an unspoken assumption that to provide more information about people, as criterion-referencing does, is bound to be a good thing. That assumption should be looked at from time to time. It is conceivable that extra information can cause more harm than good inasmuch as it may fix a person in other peoples' eyes for longer than a single score or grade might do. As more information is generated, some of it is bound to be untrustworthy, but it will not always be clear which it is. It is those unknown effects which might prove injurious to some students' prospects or life chances.

> Having made those points, they should not be taken as an argument for the continued use of single scores or grades.

(vii) *What can written exams validly assess? What kinds of objectives and curriculum are not well assessed by examinations?*

The McGaw Committee has a discussion of this question and I have borrowed what it has to say (p. 40).

At present, final results in subjects are based, to varying extents, on external examinations and school assessments. Both sources of data have strengths and weaknesses. A view that the weaknesses of external examinations outweigh their strengths led to their abolition in Queensland more than a decade ago. This is not a view we share. We see the weaknesses of external examinations to be that they

- can cover only a limited part of the course syllabus within the three hours available at the end of a course:
- can capture only a small sample of a student's performance, even on the topics tested, within the three hours;
- can be biased against students who do not perform well under the unique pressure of an examination or who are not well on the day or whose examinations are concentrated in a limited period;
- may encourage a concentration in teaching on those aspects of a course which are most readily assessed by an external examination; and
- may encourage didactic teaching and rote learning.

In contrast to these, we see the strengths of external examinations to be that they

- provide an objective assessment of a student's performance without consideration of the student's personal relations with teachers or of the school attended; and
- define common standards of performance required for adequate completion of a syllabus.

Some might have expected to see more strengths mentioned. I, myself, would have sympathy with the view that the first strength might well be cancelled out by the third weakness. The list of situational factors which impede an examinee producing a best performance is long and has to be taken seriously. The second weakness is pertinent to points made earlier in this paper. As already noted, the syllabus or domain-sampling paradigm has been dominant and it has been expediency caused by extreme time pressures which, as much as anything, has kept it going. A switch to a competence-based paradigm would not cure this problem; if anything time would have to be even more preciously used. Thus, the urgent need to exploit school assessment more vigorously.

The McGaw Committee saw this too. This is what it had to say on school assessments (pp. 40–1).

The supplementation of external examinations which we propose is a more systematic use of school assessments. We see the strengths of school-based assessments to be that they

- can be used on a substantial sample of student performance, over time and over the full range of the syllabus requirements; and
- in addition, can assess aspects of a course not accessible to external examination.

We recognize, however, that school assessments can have serious deficiencies too. We see these to be that the assessments

- can be biased for or against a student by the relationship between teacher and student;
- can, in some cases, take undue account of early performance in a course and, relatively, too little of the level a student finally reaches;
- can change the relationship between teacher and student by casting the teacher in the role of judge instead of that of supporter in the preparation for external assessment; and
- can be undertaken with variable criteria from school to school.

Again, only two strengths are offered but these seem to me to be a good deal weightier than the two for external examinations. Of the weaknesses, the first and third are essentially the same and the second can be taken care of by specifying when assessments should be made. One weakness which is not mentioned is that poor teachers will make poor assessors. (Good teachers should make good assessors but it may not happen without training.)

There is also the matter of harmonizing external and internal assessments. While norm-referencing persists, the problem seems relatively straightforward (albeit there is scaling) but with criterion-referencing it takes the form of making compatible the information sought and extracted by examiners and that provided by teachers. It will be necessary to have a clear view on the extent to which school assessment is supplementing external examinations on the one hand, and complementing them on the other.

Notes

1 SHAYCROFT, M.F. (1979) *Handbook of Criterion-referenced Testing*, New York, Garland STPM Press, p. 102.
2 McGAW, B. *et al.*, (1984) *Assessment in the Upper Secondary School in Western Australia*, Perth, Ministry of Education.
3 See WOOD, R. (1976) 'A critical note on Harvey's "Some thoughts on norm-referenced and criterion-referenced measures"', *Research in Education*, 15, pp. 69–72.

4 ANGOFF, W.H. (1974). 'Criterion-referencing, norm-referencing, and the SAT', *College Board Review*, 92, pp. 2–5.

5 Queensland Board of Secondary School Studies draft senior syllabus in English, March 1981, p. 2.

6 Definition from SHAYCROFT, M.F. (1979) *op. cit.*, p. 102. This type of measurement is most suitable when the area to be measured is a domain that can be clearly defined, and from which a probability sample can be drawn. Typically, rules are specified for generating items to comprise the domain. To give a trivial example, but one which domain-referencing advocates have not really been able to go much beyond, a rule might be set up to generate exhaustively all addition sums involving two three-digit numbers. The resulting domain (sometimes called a universe) would then be sampled according to a formal sampling rule. Evidently, the intention is to remove from achievement testing operations all influence of human idiosyncracy. The limitations of such an ambition will be obvious.

7 Queensland Board of Secondary School Studies draft senior syllabus in mathematics, July 1983, p. 34.

8 MESSICK, S. (1984) 'The psychology of education measurement', *Journal of Educational Measurement*, 21, 3, pp. 215–38.

9 Queensland Board of Secondary School Studies draft senior syllabus in mathematics, p. 34.

10 More on this conceptualization of competence and on the measurement task involved, can be found in WOOD, R. and POWER, C.N. (1986) 'Aspects of the competence-performance distinction: Educational, psychological and measurement issues', *Journal of Curriculum Studies* (in press) and in this volume.

11 For instance, Wyatt, writing in the context of secondary school biology writes,

> We want to know about each student:
> how much he knows;
> how well he can communicate, both orally and in writing;
> how well he can reason from and about biological data and ideas;
> how well he can make relevant observations from biological material;
> how accurate and precise he is in both word and deed;
> how well he can use the literature and books;
> how well he can design experiments;
> how well he can handle apparatus and improvise or make his own;
> how far he can be trusted with biological material;
> how skilled he is with mathematical, statistical and graphic manipulation
> of data. (WYATT, H.V. (1973) 'Examining examined', *Journal of Biological Education*, 7, pp. 11–17.

12 To add to the description of Limited Achievement for Mathematics, here is the description of Sound Achievement for Accounting:

> The student has demonstrated understanding of the basic concepts of control procedures and accounting procedures pertaining to sole traders, partnerships, companies and clubs as detailed in the Senior Accounting Syllabus. In addition he/she can apply this knowledge for the most part in accounting records. (Queensland Board of Secondary School Studies draft senior syllabus for Accounting, August 1982, p. 36).

13 See references in STEVENSON, M. (1983) 'Pupil profiles — an alternative to conventional examinations?', *British Journal of Educational Studies*, 31, pp. 102–16.

14 Glaser suggests that rather than switch between general and specific, the possibility ought to be looked at of teaching specific knowledge in interactive,

interrogative ways so that general skills are exercised in the course of acquiring subject-related knowledge. This strategy would be a natural counterpart to the school assessment procedure I am advocating. GLASER, R. (1984). 'Education and thinking: The role of knowledge', *American Psychologist*, 39, pp. 93–104.

Paper 14: Verbal Test D — A Review[*]

Test Content

This test is published and distributed by NFER-Nelson Ltd. All the manual has to say about the rationale behind the test is that is it is meant to 'measure those aspects of intelligent behaviour relevant to a verbally biased education; thus most items dealt with words; some, however, deal with numbers' (p. 2). The reader will immediately wonder, 'Why do *some* deal with numbers; *how* do they deal with numbers; what does *some* amount to, and why that many? In fact, 'some' means thirteen out of eighty-four items (but not one in the last twenty); of these, eight are pure sums while the other five are items of the 'missing number in a series' type. These last might (*might*) be justified on the grounds that the test also contains items of the 'missing letter in a series' type but it is a mystery why the eight sums are there. If the test had been called an intelligence test one might have let the matter go but it is called a verbal test and that must mean something. The only other reference in the manual to what the test is supposed to be about is on p. 3 where it says that the test is meant to provide a 'general measure of scholastic ability'. So that must be what it is, if you know what that is.

Of the test content dealing with words, the tasks set are the staples of intelligence tests, antonyms/synonyms, missing words/letters, word swaps, codes using letters and numbers (but as symbols only). The distribution of items across these types is not even. There is a powerful smell of 11 + about this test. Evidently the items do tap intelligent behaviour — which items do not? — but one would be hard pressed to *describe* what performance on the test means, or does not mean.

A few items are written in such a way as to give cause for concern. In items 21 and 53 the word 'series' should have been used instead of 'order', which has no meaning as it stands. Item 14 may be out-of-date in the sense that through

---

[*]Reprinted from *Tests in Education*, Levy, P. and Goldstein, H. (Eds.), Academic Press, 1984.

eating Chinese food children are becoming accustomed to linking sweet and sour, rather than juxtaposing them (even if the contrast in taste is intended). Two other answers seem just as sound. Item 33 calls for a very subtle discrimination which verges on trickery. Again two other answers seem just as acceptable. Curiously one item (58) is considered so potentially obscure that the author has taken the trouble, in a footnote to the marking key, to show the marker how the correct answer is arrived at.

Purpose

According to the manual (p. 3):

> Scores yielded by Verbal Tests have been found to correlate highly with criteria for academic success and can therefore be used by class teachers as a guide in:
>
> (1) giving an estimate of the expected degree of success should any particular pupil follow an academic course of study;
> (2) streaming or banding;
> (3) vocational and educational guidance.

It is therefore seen as an all-purpose test. However, since the test is intended for pupils aged 10–12 years, it is hard to imagine how it could ever be used for vocational guidance, and the absence of a profile feature probably makes it inadequate for educational guidence, even if one were happier about the content. As for the test's predictive value, the Validity section of this review has some comments to make. Here, perhaps it is sufficient to note the unpleasant whiff of determinism about the first purpose, although goodness knows this is a common enough claim by test makers. To imply that a prediction *for a particular individual* is likely to be at all accurate is, of course, misleading.

Item Preparation

Two hundred and seven items were administered in three drafts of sixty-nine items each to groups of between 100 and 169 pupils considered to be representative of the 9.06–11.00 year-old population. A second draft of eighty-nine items was administered to two further groups and the item analysis repeated, resulting in the final form of eighty-four items. Items were arranged in order of difficulty to form a rectangular distribution so that a rank-ordering of pupils would be obtained with approximately equal precision over all parts of the range, and the reliability of discrimination would be maximized. That is what the manual says.

Now the matter of producing tests with particular distributional forms is a difficult business, especially where the rectangular distribution is concerned (Scott, 1972), but it is certain that success in achieving a targetted distribution depends crucially on the intercorrelation of the items. It is generally agreed (see, for example, Henrysson, 1971) that where item intercorrelations are low (of the order of 0.10), as they generally are with achievement tests, maximum discrimination is most likely to be achieved by choosing items which are all at, or around, the 50 per cent difficulty level. As the average intercorrelation rises, and particularly when it exceeds 0.33, it becomes necessary to spread the item difficulties over the range to avoid the middle of the distribution thinning out too much.

Just what the appropriate prescription should have been in this case is impossible to say, with authority, from the data provided. Probably the intercorrelations are closer to 0.33 than to 0.10. Even so, it may be that Stanley (1971) is right when he argues that 'for most ability, aptitude and achievement tests in many situations it will be best if all items are of equal (and middle) difficulty. Such a test is likely to be better than other-difficulty tests of the same content for discriminating among all except 1 or 2 per cent of the examinees in each test, unless the group is exceptionally heterogeneous'. Scott (1972) says essentially the same thing. For this test, which wants to serve so many purposes, that was probably the right advice. But it is understandable that the test maker should have distributed his item difficulties uniformly. Doubtless he was following his intuition. Beware of intuition in this area.

What does the data provided in the manual actually tell us? They tell us that the standardization sample, mean age 11 years 0.21 months, had a mean raw score of 37.75 and a standard deviation of 20.99. So the sample was not rectangularly distributed; there is evidence of flattening but also of downward skew. Perhaps the number items pulled down the intercorrelations. All the same it looks to be at least as close to a rectangular distribution as to a normal distribution (a rectangular distribution would have had a standard deviation of 24; with a normal distribution the figure would have been more like 14), so that the transformation to a normal distribution requires a fairly considerable stretching of the raw score distribution.

Sex Differences

The manual takes the trouble to point out (p. 2) that 'care was taken in writing the items (and in the subsequent analysis) to avoid the inclusion of those that might favour one sex more than the other'. This policy does not meet with my approval. The absurdity of selecting items just because they show no sex differences was pointed out long ago by Lorge (1952). He took the view, which I share, that genuine differences should be allowed to reveal themselves, the important thing being to have a convincing rationale for including items in a test. That is what this test does not have and the policy on sex differences only increases the impression of arbitrariness. It also plants doubt in the mind of the reader concerning the credibility of what *has* found its way into the test.

If the object of such a policy is to produce identical score distributions for boys and girls, or at least, approximately the same means, then it did not succeed in this case because girls out-scored boys, on average, to the tune of 4.26 raw score points or 3.08 standard score points. This must be the result of small margins at the item level accumulating to produce a significant difference. Separate conversion tables for the sexes are provided even though the manual points out that this was not strictly necessary because the difference is constant over age. So, presumably, what has been produced is a test where the girls are not as superior as they would have been but are still superior. It would have been interesting to look at an item analysis for each sex, especially for the number items.

Administration

The administration of this test is straightforward and the manual provides instructions which are clear and uncluttered. There are no unusual features. Answers are written in pencil, sometimes by underlining and sometimes by supplying words, letters or numbers. Erasers are banned and the instructions say nothing about changing answers although the marking principles which follow do anticipate that answers will be changed. The total working time, including the time required for the practice items (of which there are nine), is approximately 45–50 minutes, with 40 minutes exactly for the test. The manual provides no evidence on whether this degree of speededness (eighty-four items in 40 minutes) is reasonable for all age-groups of the target population (10–12 years), although one would have said it was not particularly severe.

Standardization

The test was standardized in the spring term of 1976, on a sample of 10,345 children (5223 boys and 5122 girls). Authorities and schools were selected at random, the manual notes, in an attempt to obtain a sample which is representative of the national population. No further details are given about any attention paid to LEA and school size so the authority of the sample rests on its size, which is more than adequate.

The raw scores have been standardized to have a mean of 100 and a standard deviation of 15 and, of course, are constrained to follow a normal distribution. Adjustments for age, on a monthly basis, have been incorporated into the conversion tables. This may seem a thoroughly conventional thing to do but there are hidden assumptions which need exposing. The conversion method used is by Lawley (1950). In defence of his method, he offers the following: 'Errors of estimation arising from the construction of the conversion table are in most cases negligible compared with the errors of measurement of any mental test, however good' (p. 86). Let us turn Lawley's argument on its head and see what happens. If conversions were available at each raw score for 10:06 and 11:06 only, which I suppose we would call 10+ and 11+ following other usage, for example AH2/AH3, then the maximum 'error' incurred by taking the 10+

figure for 10:00 or the 11 + figure for 11:00 or 12:00 is consistently 2 or 3 points, and most often 2, standardized score points that is. That margin is strictly comparable with the standard error of measurement, given in the manual as 2.7 raw score points (at age 11) which, in standardized score terms, would be about two points. I do not say that the effects of the error of measurement and the 'error' of reading will cancel out but since the first is more powerful than the second, as Lawley said, it will still be dominant even if the errors operate in different directions.

Lawley felt obliged to defend his method because he had to rest it on several questionable assumptions, of which his assumption concerning the nature of increase in 'intelligence' over time (strictly linear throughout the age span) is the most dubious. Also, by using the cross-sectional method of adjusting for age, which was customary then and now (and in any case was forced on him by the method of data collection),he was unable to take into account *seasonal* effects, which can be detected by measuring individuals over a given period (for example one year: see Goldstein and Fogelman, 1974, for more on the distinction between cross-sectional and longitudinal age standardizations). Lawley, as I say, was not to blame for that, nor did he make exaggerated claims for his method. He simply said it was workable. And, anyway, why quibble when all we are talking about is distributing 2 or 3 points across 6 months? I believe there is every reason to quibble. The point about monthly calibrations is that they give an impression of accuracy which is almost always spurious. That impression extends to the whole test and can easily be instrumental in persuading the potential user to choose the test, especially when it is thought that audiences 'back home' will be even more impressed with the accuracy of the test. It would have been better in this case to report conversions for 10:06 and 11:06 and 12 years exactly and invite the user to interpolate or better still, provide separate tables for 10 + and 11 +, as other test manuals do. As a matter of fact, these particular tables could not have been compiled without some interpolation *and* extrapolation; interpolation because Lawley's method requires it, extrapolation because data collection was restricted to the range 10:04–11:05, necessitating extrapolation over nearly half of the range! One has to conclude that, on their own, neither the data nor the method support such elaborate conversion tables, and certainly not together.

Scoring

The scoring is straightforward with the usual provisos such as where the pupil has changed an answer, credit is to be given if it is clear that the final intention was correct. Where appropriate, phonetic or otherwise recognizable spelling of words is accepted. As noted before, there are no part scores.

Reliability

The manual reports that the reliability coefficient was calculated 'from an answer pattern drawn up from a sample of 400 scripts from the standardization sample'. The value was found to be 0.97 (by KR-20). The language used here is rather curious, 'answer pattern', 'drawn up', and it seems a pity that only 4 per cent of the sample should have been utilized. With such a large sample there ought to have been an opportunity to run a test-retest exercise, if not other checks on reliability. We are not told how heterogeneous the 4 per cent sample was in terms of the age-range tested. Naturally, that affects the size of the reliability estimate. Although the manual is no doubt trying to he helpful, it is debatable whether the following sentence on its own actually helps the reader who is not quite on terms with educational measurement theory: 'The Kuder-Richardson formula is accepted for comparison of tests, being associated with (although distinct from) the test-retest correlation' (p. 3). Let us not beat about the bush. High values of KR-20 are so common that after a time the experienced reader ceases to pay any attention to them. What is wanted is a purchase on those aspects of reliability-stability and dependability of scores — concerning which KR-20, being a measure of internal consistency, is dumb. It is likely that the practice of reporting reliabilities will decline in favour of the kind of information about an instrument which generalizability studies can provide (see Thorndike, 1982).

Validity

The validity section of the manual is disappointing, to put it mildly. This is the seventh impression of the manual, printed in 1979, the test is in its 21st impression and has been sold since 1970, yet all the manual can offer is one correlation ($r = 0.90$) between the test and 'an NFER closed verbal test (12A)' on a group of 100, yes 100, pupils! Other than that, it harks back to studies carried out in the 11+ era or pre-comprehensive school era referring, in an allusive way, to 'evidence on the predictive value of verbal tests for success in future academic courses'. This is pretty pathetic. Now that it is conventional wisdom that the validity of a test varies according to the purpose to which it is put, it is quite improper for a manual to propose, as this one does, several very different purposes, from streaming to guidance, without offering supportive data against which the user can evaluate these claims.

Interpretation

The interpretation section is the most useful in the manual because it is full of the sort of cautions and qualifications the user needs to be made aware of, or reminded of. There is also a short bibliography of mental measurement texts which, like the term mental measurement, could do with up-dating. But what, one wonders, is the likely effect of laying down this good advice alongside a poor test? Will it not persuade users to overcome any qualms they might have about the content of the test and the absence of back-up data, and lull them into thinking that as long as they observe the warnings they will come to no harm? Or else be sufficiently impressed by the manual's candour to swallow their doubts? I fear so. The point is that these warnings are necessary enough for a good test; for a poor test they cease to be relevant, because they no longer protect.

Test Use

Verbal Test D was used by Child and Croucher (1977) in their investigation of the relationship between divergent thinking and ability (intelligence) in the upper ranges of ability. They describe the test as a 'standardized test of intelligence' but say nothing about it other than that the range of scores runs from 70 upwards. Nothing is said about reliability; perhaps they thought that, being a published test, everyone would think the reliability OK. For their divergent thinking tests, however, which were modifications of other tests, they did report reliability estimates (test-retest) and these were 0.45, 0.44 and 0.42. Now these are *lousy* responsibilities, albeit over the period of a year, but they do not appear to have concerned the authors one bit. They press on regardless. The cavalier attitude to test desiderata shown by these authors is typical, I would say. The analysis in the remainder of the paper proceeds as if the various measures were impeccable, whereas from what we know of Verbal Test D and what is said about the divergent thinking tests the likelihood of divining anything trustworthy concerning the relationship between 'divergent thinking' and 'ability' from these tests is negligible.

General Evaluation

If a test is meant to be an intelligence test it should be labelled as such. Why shelter behind the code 'Verbal' except to avoid accusations of peddling 11+ tests? It is sad that Vernon, of all people, should hail the replacement of 'intelligence' by other labels as a smart idea. 'There is likely to be much less criticism by educationists and parents of instruments called Verbal or Non-Verbal Reasoning Tests — that is the name which Moray House adopted many years ago' (Vernon, 1979, p. 19). Vernon is hinting at what Guterman (1979) comes straight out with. 'If we were to eschew the term "intelligence" and instead use "scholastic aptitude" for IQ tests, such a finding would arouse less resistance and there could be a more enlightened discussion about the education of disadvantaged children' (p. 164). But is anyone so naive as to believe this? I suggest that Gillham (1975) is nearer the truth when he writes,

'What does seem likely to happen is that the old ideas will be given new names, will not be presented in the form of "intelligence" tests and will not have their results expressed as single figure IQ scores; and yet will continue to fulfil traditional functions — the presumed measurement of "underlying abilities" or "latent traits", and predictions based on these' (p. 435). One thing is clear. To call a test 'Verbal' when it contains eight sums is to debase the meaning of language. What we have here is a test with a preponderance of verbal items, as have most intelligence tests, chosen so that sex differences will not show up, except that they do.

Since the test is in its twenty-first impression it must have sold well. With the booklet comprising seven pages and the manual eleven pages, and no fancy marking keys, and no part scores to worry about, the test is cheap, uncomplicated and easy to administer. There is no denying the selling power of that constellation of characteristics. However, the discerning user who is prepared to pay a little more will avoid this test, preferring instead tests which are founded on principles, educational or psychological, and which offer data bearing on how they might serve different measurement purposes, or even a single purpose.

If it is the case that some users are liable to be swayed in their choice of test by the norms provided, or rather by the provision of month by month figures, then they should realize that neither the data collected during standardization nor the method of conversion used, warrant the elaborate month by month conversions of which the tables consist.

Pupils could consider themselves unfortunate were they to be streamed or banded or even given guidance on the basis of the results of this test.

References

CHILD, D. and CROUCHER, A. (1977) 'Divergent thinking and ability: Is there a threshold?', *Educational Studies*, 3, pp. 101–10.

GILLHAM, W.E.C. (1975) 'Intelligence: The persistent myth', *New Behaviour*, 1, pp. 433–5.

GOLDSTEIN, H. and FOGELMAN, K. (1974) 'Age standardization and season effects in mental testing', *British Journal of Educational Psychology* 44, pp. 109–15.

GUTERMAN, S.S. (1979), 'IQ tests in research on social stratification; The cross-validity of the tests as measures of scholastic aptitude', *Sociology of Education*, 52, pp. 163–73.

HENRYSSON, S. (1971). in THORNDIKE, R.L. (Ed.) *Educational Measurement 'Gathering, analyzing and using data on test items'*, (2nd edn). Washington DC, American Council on Education.

LAWLEY, D.N. (1950). 'A method of standardizing group tests', *British Journal of Psychology* (*Statistical Section*), 3, pp. 86–9.

LORGE, I. (1952). 'Difference or bias in tests of intelligence', in ANASTASI, A. (Ed.) (1966) *Testing Problems in Perspective* (A. Anastasi, ed.). Washington DC, American *Testing Problems in Perspective* Washington DC, American Council on Education.

SCOTT, W.A. (1972). 'The distribution of test scores', *Educational and Psychological Measurement*, 32, pp. 725–35.

STANLEY, J.C. (1971). 'Reliability', in THORNDIKE, R.L. (Ed.) *Educational Measurement* (2nd edn). Washington DC, American Council on Education.
THORNDIKE, R.L. (1982). *Applied Psychometrics*. Boston MA, Houghton Mifflin Inc.
VERNON, P.E. (1979). *Intelligence Testing 1928–1978: What Next?*. Edinburgh, Scottish Council for Research in Education.

Paper 15: Belated Homage to Cronbach and Gleser[*]

Cronbach and Gleser's *Psychological Tests and Personnel Decisions* first appeared in 1957 and was republished in 1965 in an augmented form with the inclusion of papers by others bearing on the book's themes. I was going to observe that it is a book more talked about than read but even that is going too far. It is neither talked about nor read. It's Ghiselli this and Schmidt and Hunter that but hardly ever Cronbach and Gleser. Where did Schmidt and Hunter get their ideas from? You've guessed. I am glad of this opportunity to pay my respects to Cronbach and Gleser but especially to Lee Cronbach who I believe has contributed more to psychometrics than anyone else.

Cronbach has always been a theoretician, in the best sense, and Cronbach and Gleser comes across like a manifesto. It is modern because, although you know Schmidt and Hunter have made their mark, the ideas in Cronbach and Gleser's *Essentials of Psychological Testing* are still fresh. It should be read, both as a counterpoint to Schmidt and Hunter's somewhat relentless and harrying style, and as a necessary statement of first principles; necessary because it would be sanguine to suppose that the decision-theory approach to testing has arrived.

Cronbach and Gleser set out their stall on page 1 of the book.

> Our society continually confronts people with decisions for which they have inadequate information. It is for this reason that psychological and educational tests exist ... It is therefore desirable that a theory of test construction and use considers how tests can best serve in making decisions. Little of present test theory, however, takes this view. Instead the test is conceived as a measuring instrument, and test theory is directed primarily toward the study of accuracy of measurement on a continuous scale. Hull voiced a principle that has been the root of nearly all work on test theory. The ultimate purpose of using aptitude tests is to estimate or forecast aptitudes from test scores. *It is*

[*]Reprinted from *Guidance and Assessment Review*, 2, 1, February 1986, pp. 2–3.

this view we propose to abandon (my emphasis). We acknowledge the usefulness of accurate estimation — but maintain that the *ultimate* purpose of any personnel testing is to arrive at qualitative decisions . . . Recommendations regarding the design, selection and interpretation of a test must take into account the characteristics of the decisions for which the test will be used, since the test which is maximally effective for one decision will not necessarily be the most effective elsewhere.

So, tests should not be studied for their intrinsic properties, measurement always takes place in a context and there is no such thing as *the* validity of a test.

Now turn to the common or garden test manual. There you will see mention of *the* reliability or *the* standard error of measurement, also suggestions as to the various uses to which the test can be put but without any supporting data against which the interested party can evaluate the claims. Why do so many test manuals have a desiccated air about them? Because they lack data from real applications. The follow-up has not been done. It is a requirement of the decision-theory approach that these data be made available. Otherwise tests will continue to be presented like exhibits in museums with fixed parameters and yellowing labels, rather than as dynamic aids to decision making.

There is, in my experience, widespread ignorance of the decision-theory approach and where it is known there is resistance to it. There were test theory brahmins who found the utilitarian aspect distasteful, especially having to introduce filthy lucre into equations. The systematizers wanted to elevate psychological measurement to the status of physical measurement so that measurements would be independent of context and purpose. That is the appeal of the Rasch model. Cronbach and Gleser hardly had a chance to take root before the Rasch model came along and up-staged it. And, of course, the relativist ethos of one clashed head-on with the absolutist ethos of the other. Now that people are saying, 'O.K., so Rasch doesn't fit as well as we might like, but will it do for this purpose, or for what purpose will it do?', the possibility of a reconciliation between Rasch and decision-theory opens up.

The statistician George Box once said that all models are wrong, but some are useful. It is an amusing dictum but what does it mean? If you know a model to be flawed, dare you trust it at all? The answer must be that it depends on the loss associated with the worst thing that can happen should the model be wrong for that particular application. If that loss, and other expected losses contingent on other less calamitous events are tolerable when weighed against the usefulness of the model, then it is possible to proceed. My point is this: allegiance to the decision-theoretic paradigm carries with it an obligation to come up with a number of estimates, none of them easy. I notice Peter Herriot jibbing at putting a financial tag on job performance or lack of it (Herriot, 1985). If the objection to quantifying job performance is deep-seated then it would be interesting to have a defence of this position which took into account that no hiring procedure is costless and which demonstrated how an alternative testing paradigm which ignores costs (presumably time-honoured practice) will produce superior results in some global utility sense.

Before Cronbach and Gleser came along conventional wisdom was — perhaps still is — that a high validity coefficient (correlation of predictor with criterion) was necessary to obtain substantial benefit from testing. It was not recognized that the value of a test varies with the particular decision for which it is to be used. Credit for this insight goes to Taylor and Russell (1939) — note how early the year is. Their claim that 'very considerable improvement in selection efficiency may be obtained with small coefficients' must have seemed counterintuitive to many, but they provided tables to substantiate their point and it makes sense. If you are choosing 1 in 100 you need all the help you can get. It was Taylor and Russell's work, and that of Brogden, which Cronbach and Gleser drew on to produce their key result. Given an estimate of the validity of the selection method, the ratio of applicants to vacancies (the selection ratio), which had crucially been ignored, and the value, in money terms, of variations in job performance, it is possible to calculate the increase in productivity which will result from choosing a certain proportion of applicants.

Cronbach and Gleser's other great contribution was to draw attention to what they called the *fidelity-bandwidth dilemma*. In essence they saw test users faced with a choice between a 'narrow-band' test, which gives high validity but only with one or perhaps two criteria, with a 'broad-band' test, which gives only fair but potentially useful correlations with a number of criteria. It's a version of the fox and hedgehog fable. The fox knows one thing supremely well; the hedgehog several things passably well. The hedgehog fares better.

What does the 'dilemma' mean in practice? For any decision problem, say Cronbach and Gleser (p. 144), there is an optimum bandwidth. Bandwidth is purchased at the price of lower fidelity or dependability. Two important wideband procedures are the interview and the projective technique. Cronbach and Gleser ask themselves the question we all ask ourselves: why, given such poor validity evidence, does the interview retain its popularity? Their answer? 'The virtue of the interview is that it can turn in any of hundreds of directions, following leads in a way that the structured narrowband procedure cannot'. Of course, it is precisely this elasticity which worries people; this from Tenopyr (1981, p. 1123). 'At best, it (the interview) introduces randomness to the selection process; at worst it colours selection decisions with conscious or unconscious biases.'

Tenopyr was comparing interview with test supposing one had to be preferred to the other. Cronbach and Gleser were not. Rather they were saying that though any one fact or judgment from a wideband procedure is unreliable, the procedure as a whole contributes more in some circumstances than a narrowband procedure. The wideband procedure, they say, can perhaps improve every decision that is to be made. But it is best to make the wideband instrument the first stage in a sequential procedure, to arrive at reversible rather than terminal decisions. A low validity is acceptable if the cost of separating the true leads from the false is tolerable.

Cronbach and Gleser may have overstated their case on this occasion, not in respect of the last sentiment, which is sound, but in respect of the gains which can be got by capitalizing on the wideband procedure, on what is, in the case of the interview, serendipity by any other name. Evidently, there is a tension between fairness and making the best decision from time to time. Equally evidently, legislation against adverse impact, or any procedure which is not palpably evenhanded, would outlaw or at least neutralize the advantages of wideband procedures.

Cronbach and Gleser weren't to know that legislation would drive testing towards narrowband procedures. They wrote their book in innocent pre-legislation times. In all other respects, the book was ahead of its time and remains so, above all in its insistence that a view of tests and testing conditioned by a costless, decisionless world is false and unproductive. 'Generalizations decay,' wrote Lee Cronbach once, and if true the sentiment must apply to my claim that he is top of the psychometrician's league. I've a feeling, though, that it will be a while yet before he is overtaken.

References

CRONBACH, L.J. and GLESER, G.C. (1965). *Psychological Tests and Personnel Decisions.* Urbana. IL, University of Illinois Press.

HERRIOT, P. (1985) *Guidance and Assessment Review*, 2, 8.

TAYLOR, H.C. and RUSSELL, J.T. (1939). 'The relationship of validity coefficients to the practical effectiveness of tests in selection', *Journal of Applied Psychology*, 23, pp. 565–78.

TENOPYR, M.L. (1981).'The realities of employment testing', *American Psychologist*, 36, pp. 1120–7.

Paper 16: Achievement Tests*

Evidence of Achievement

It seems barely conceivable that the subject of achievement (attainment) testing can be discussed without considering the nature of educational achievement, but that has often happened, above all in the mass of analytical work which has aped psychometrics in regarding achievement as interchangeable with (latent) ability, itself never adequately defined (see *Abilities and Aptitudes*). It is extraordinary that so little attention has been given to what constitutes evidence of achievement or to the kinds of evidence that can be collected and reported. The philosopher's warning that achieving understanding does not necessarily result in a person's doing or saying anything of any kind, seems largely to have been ignored. What *has* been discussed — incessantly — is the manipulation of item responses and aggregations of responses in an effort to make quantitative statements concerning achievement. Whether surface data ever deserve much trust is a permanent issue. Here, there is certainly doubt, enough to bring to mind some remarks of Sir Joseph Stamp on governments' attachment to statistics. 'They collect them, add them, raise them to the Nth power, take the cube root and prepare wonderful diagrams. But you must never forget that every one of these figures comes in the first instance from the village watchman, who just puts down what he pleases.' It is not that children are as capricious as this but rather that an item response results from an encounter between a child and an item, and it is items — single items — which give cause for worry. The single item used in traditional achievement testing constitutes an uncontrolled, ambiguous measure that can only in rare instances be shown to be related directly to the learning outcome of interest (Gagné, 1970). Who will say that Gagné has been proved wrong?

Doubtless the results are being observed of an overelaborated division of

---

*Reprinted from *International Encyclopedia of Education: Research and Studies*, Pergamon Press, 1985.

labor. When someone argues that the kind of tests used are inconsistent with, and in many cases irrelevant to, the realities of teaching; that teachers do not focus on goals and outcomes; that they do not evaluate in terms of general assessments of achieved outcomes; that they attend instead to variations in students' activities; that they think about content covered (Shulman, 1978), who is in a position to judge whether that person is right? Certainly not the testers.

Test Construction

The story since the early 1960s is of testers conceptualizing achievement so as to make their own work coherent and manageable but without reference to what teachers habitually do. It was testers who decided that achievement testing was in such a mess that a new system was necessary to tidy things up. Unfortunately, or perhaps fortunately, the apparatus was delivered with the paint still wet, with bits missing, bits without instructions, and bits that wouldn't work. Item universes were unworkable and had to be modified to item domains. Item domains themselves proved hard to define exhaustively, and some material seemed intractable; in fact it was and is hard to get beyond arithmetic computation. Random sampling of tasks was quickly extended to stratified random sampling yet if the necessary stratification is built in, the result is tests which differ little from what expert opinion would have produced (Wood, 1976). Opting for stratification introduces complications into the estimation of mastery; plain proportion correct will not do. Even that apparently straightforward estimation problem has been the cause of much agonizing and what many would regard as futile excursions into betabinomial distribution theory and the like, mathematizing for its own sake. Above all, and crucially, there is the matter of how items get written in the first place. The fixation with subjectivity has led to outlandish developments whose utility even their most enthusiastic perpetrators, who write of a 'science of item writing', have felt obliged to summarize in a formula which will surprise no one, viz. 'the rigor and precision of item-writing specifications are inversely related to their practicability'. The proposed compromise solution, whereby some items are created by domain specification and others by 'more subjective methods', seems neither fish nor fowl.

Doctrinaire treatment of item writing and test construction is counterproductive. A reading of what is still the best contribution to this area (Anderson, 1972) will bear that out. The question posed there, 'Which of the innumerable things said to students should they be tested on?' is as valid as ever, regardless of theologies. A table of specifications can help but it is no more than a reasonable intermediate step in test construction. It is not a systematic solution to the problem of which questions to ask, any more than a ledger sheet is a system of accounting. Nor are behavioral objectives wholly determining. When asked why an item was included in a test, it is no answer to point to an objective, for that only leads to a further question, 'How and why was that objective chosen?'. Even if objectives possessed overriding authority, they are rarely sufficient to generate test items without some slippage occurring between item and objective, for which item format is as often as not responsible. If a student fails to answer items correctly when presented in one format, but could answer them correctly if they were presented in another format — and this happens often enough to be taken seriously — then the inference that the student cannot divide is invalid. Achieving the objective is a necessary condition for getting a large proportion of the related items correct, but it is not a sufficient condition (Linn, 1980).

Evidently the validity of a proposed interpretation of achievement test scores rests ultimately on the quality of inference available at the item level. The need to worry about single items seems obvious enough but it has frequently been ignored or else dismissed as fussiness. It has become conventional wisdom that the single item doesn't matter because items come in congregations and weakness in one will be compensated by the others, but if one item can be treated in cavalier fashion why not all items and what, then, of the test?

The issue, as always, is how to construct questions so as to assuredly require whatever it is the questionmaker claims to be measuring. It is a pity that a serious attack on the problem made some time ago has not been followed up (Gagné, 1970). Gagné's desiderata of distinctiveness and distortion-free measurement are broadly analogous to validity and reliability but, unlike other writers, he goes on to suggest how distinctiveness, in particular, can be achieved. His argument against the single item (or even collections of them) is that a correct answer seldom constitutes unequivocal proof that, for instance, knowledge of a concept has been demonstrated rather than knowledge of a concept dependent on knowledge (not asked for or given) of a principle. To deal with this objection he draws on experimental psychology for techniques of control which will enable alternative inferences to be ruled out. Items need to be formulated in two or even more stages. The first stage filters out ignorance and succeeding stages allow the necessary differentiations to be made, all of which the single item is presently being asked to do.

If this methodology for item writing has been rejected as too finicky and time-consuming for routine application that is understandable, but it is no comfort that the alternatives are palpably less rigorous and certainly less capable of delivering a sound inference. The care and nourishment of the single item remains on the agenda.

There is plenty else besides. 'Educational researchers do not seem to be following anyone's advice about test construction' (Anderson, 1972). The remark was provoked by a survey of the literature which had shown that investigators were sadly remiss in not providing adequate information about why some questions were asked rather than others, about why they thought their tests were measuring, say, comprehension and not something else, about how tests were developed, about the formats used, about technical desiderata and so on and so forth ('In most cases it would be impossible for an independent investigator to construct an equivalent test based on what was reported'). Would a survey now produce the same result? Probably, but at least a reading of the past suggests a message for the future. Doctrinal squabbles are unimportant beside the need for good practice, which starts with disclosure. Better to be doing the wrong thing with full disclosure than to be doing the wrong thing with little or no disclosure.

It is interesting that Gagné should have thought that once the 'What' question was dealt with satisfactorily, the 'How much' question would prove straightforward. It is difficult to share this optimism. Psychometric tests are now offering a choice between two models of estimation — domain sampling or domain mastery and latent trait — but one of them, latent trait, may not be suitable at all for estimating achievement and the other rests on a mechanical and pedagogically uninspiring conceptualization. Both pose unavoidable questions concerning the representation of reality which adherence to one or other of these models commits the user to.

Latent Trait Models

When latent trait models were coming into vogue and ability, aptitude, and achievement were treated as interchangeable, it was widely supposed that these models would provide the most efficient and coherent means of estimating extent of achievement. Now that there is great sensitivity to what is characteristic of achievement (Thorndike (1982) assigns the measurement of achievement to domain-mastery theory and the measurement of aptitudes, attitudes, interests, and temperaments to latent trait theory, although he warns of 'a certain amount of ambiguity in practice'), the relevance of latent trait models is being challenged. Of Thorndike's four conditions that data ought to meet for the assumptions undergirding the Rasch model to be plausible the third — item responses must be generated — is enough to rule out many achievement tests, but it is the fourth — that items should reflect general growth in some attribute rather than specific instruction so that focused instruction can be expected to radically shift the relative difficulty of items involving a topic that had just been taught — which is conclusive, or ought to be, especially as it might actually be desirable or even routine to engage in focused instruction. But is anyone paying attention? Too many people who fit item response data to the Rasch model, especially under the flag of robustness, are too pleased at the 'fit' to bother about asking too closely what it means, or what use can be made of it, or how long it might last, bearing in mind that item response theory is a static theory which gives only a 'snapshot' of the relationship between item performance and achievement at a particular point in time and space. This is true even when the trouble is taken to point out all the reasons why the Rasch model should not work.

Integration with Domain-referenced Approaches

Given the doubts about the appropriateness of latent trait models for representing achievement, which are barely assuaged by moving to three-parameter models, it may be asked whether there is point in even discussing the possibility of integrating the two systems. Integration would not remove the doubts and might even obscure them. At the manipulative level there is no question that integration is possible. Generalizability theory can work equally well or poorly with latent trait estimates, which are after all just transformations of raw scores (Wood, 1976). Not so at the interpretational level. For integration to happen here the latent trait must link the test scores to the behavior domain in a way that permits a statement, not so much about the numerical value of an examinee's latent-ability parameter, as about the *behavior* that the particular numerical value represents, not 'How much' but 'What'. There is no point pretending that this linkage is other than problematical but that is as much a comment on the uninterpretability of latent traits as anything else.

A more promising channel for articulation is through construct validity evidence for which lies in response consistency. Now response consistency is precisely what latent trait models deal in; in fact, 'fit' can be read as minimum evidence for construct validity. The difficulty here is that domain mastery supportors have been reluctant to admit that construct validity has any place in their system (Messick, 1981).

Any effort at integration will have to negotiate one important difference and that is in how items are regarded. In one system the single item hardly matters since it is exchangeable with every other, at least within a stratum; in the other, the single item is a measuring instrument in its own right. It is because latent trait theory is item oriented, and so can be readily tailored to different curricula, that some believe that it is the proper psychometric foundation for a dynamic achievement testing system, or even a descriptive system. Current developments (Bock and Mislevy, 1981) would seem to bear this out. But the strictures made earlier about the unsuitability of achievement data for these models, including the dangers of obsolete and therefore distorting calibration data, will continue to apply, however well-behaved data turn out to be. The point is that they may cease to be so, for very good educational and societal reasons.

Learning Outcomes

The emphasis on total congruence between objectives, instruction, and measurement was no doubt necessary to draw attention to degenerate tendencies in thinking about achievement and the use to which measures were put. The persistent classification of achievement testing as a branch of psychometrics has led to undue stress being placed on the prediction of performance at the expense of what ought always to have had precedence — the measurement of learning outcomes. When prediction is paramount it is likely to make little difference whether a distinction can be drawn between the learning of, say, a concept, and the learning of a principle; the individual who knows more is going to exhibit faster learning and a better ultimate performance, regardless of what the particular components of his or her capability are (Gagné, 1970). Why bother, therefore, with meticulous measurement at the item level?

But, as often happens in education, the antidote turns out to be at least as problematic as the disease. A recent conceptualization of educational attainment as a mastery of knowledge or abilities which it was intended that one should master, which disavows totally the relevance of psychology, and which seeks to abandon measurement altogether (McIntyre and Brown, 1978), can only be described as impoverished, if not regressive. Measurement-driven instruction has nothing richer to offer, only a primitive output-input model founded on crude behaviorism. The danger that people will think that such vulgarities say all there is to be said about achievement seems all too real. That achievement might stretch beyond what instruction seems to permit through, for instance, independent study, has no place in this world view. The possibility of learners achieving objectives and passing tests but being alienated from the subject matter as a result of the instruction and the prevailing ethos surrounding achievement, is likewise ignored. Nor is there any acknowledgment that achievement builds on achievement in a so far unexplained fashion, that knowledge accumulates synergistically as connections are made and unassimilated material is suddenly assimilated. Rather the image is of chunks of achievement lying about with no means of putting them together. No doubt this is why it is not always appreciated that the achievement of fixed common goals may be attained by individuals only at the cost of differential achievement of other goals (Messick, 1981), which may not be in their best interests.

Reconceptualizing Achievement

Much of what is being identified here as unsatisfactory can be traced to the habit of reducing achievement to one-dimensional terms when what is wanted is a stereoscopic view. It starts with some way of thinking — let's not call it a model — of how achievement accumulates, into which all the elements mentioned so far can be fitted — the connections, the aftermath of mastery, the changes that take place as skills and knowledge develop. It goes on to seek better definition of achievement in its conventional cognitive sense. Evidently, group testing places a ceiling on performance, mastery learning tests likewise; it is not known what else people might be capable of. It may be necessary to run unconventional 'open' achievement testing alongside conventional 'closed' testing to satisfy curiosity about what people can do, to add to what they are supposed to be able to do as a result of instruction — not only what people can do unaided but also what they *might* be able to do with sympathetic help cf. Vygotsky's exciting notion of the 'zone of next development' and associated concepts (Glaser, 1981). Exposing learners to instruction in advance of development so as to draw them up, implies tests to assess levels of learning that might possibly be attained. Note the heresy of having tests go beyond instruction, and the implications for question writing.

Achievement needs to be understood within the context in which it occurs, the school or college. This means paying attention to noncognitive states conveniently regarded as extraneous but which affect and are affected by achievement, or lack of it. A strong plea for taking motivation and self-esteem explicitly into account has been made recently (Scarr, 1981). It is very much in line with the view that tests should be treated as only one part of an assessment procedure and work should be done on ways of helping teachers better use the other observations which they so frequently employ in the classroom (Shulman, 1978). Testers do a disservice by ignoring complexities in favor of their own procrustean creations.

References

ANDERSON, R.C. (1972) 'How to construct achievement tests to assess comprehension', *Rev. Educ. Res.* 42, pp. 145–70.

BOCK, R.D. and MISLEVY, R.J. (1981) 'An item response curve model for matrix-sampling data: The California grade-three assessment', *New Direct. Meas.* 10, pp. 65–90.

GAGNÉ, R.M. (1970) 'Instructional variables and learning outcomes', in WITTROCK, M.C. and WILEY, D.E. (eds.) *The Evaluation of Instruction: Issues and Problems.* New York, Holt, Rinehart and Winston.

GLASER, R. (1981) 'The future of testing: A research agenda for cognitive psychology and psychometrics', *American Psychologist*, 36, pp. 923–36.

LINN, R.L. (1980) 'Issues of validity for criterion-referenced measure', *Appl. Psychol. Meas*, 4, pp. 547–61.

MCINTYRE, D.I. and BROWN, S. (1978) 'The conceptualisation of attainment' *Brit. Educ. Res. J.* 4(2), pp. 41–50.

MESSICK, S. (1981) 'Constructs and their vicissitudes in educational and psychological measurement', *Psychol. Bulletin*, 89, pp. 575–88.

SCARR, S. (1981) 'Testing *for* children: Assessment and the many determinants of intellectual competence'. *American Psychologist*, 36, pp. 1159–66.

SHULMAN, L.S. (1978) 'Test design: A view from practice', *Eval. Comment*, 6, 4, pp. 9–10.

THORNDIKE, R.L. (1982) *Applied Psychometrics*, Boston, MA, Houghton Mifflin.

WOOD, R. (1976) 'Trait measurement and item banks.' in de GRUITJER, D.N., and VAN DER KAMP, L. TH J. (Eds.) *Advances in Psychological and Educational Measurement*, New York, Wiley, and in this volume.

VII Under-achievement, Aptitude and Standards

Comments

I have linked these papers together because I was working on them at the same time. Working on several papers simultaneously is a pleasure. Sir Richard Burton's biographer recounts how Burton used a separate table for every book and when tired of one moved on to another. On one occasion, a visitor counted eleven such tables, covered with manuscripts and writing materials (Brodie, 1971, pp. 339–40). That way of working appeals to me too.

The under-achievement paper has strange origins. One day in December 1982, while I was at Flinders University on a brief visit, I bumped into John McLeod of the University of Saskatchewan who was there on sabbatical leave. I was with Colin Power who afterwards showed me McLeod's paper (see paper 17) in which he described 'regression-referenced underachievement identification'. This exercised me considerably and I was still bothered by it when, later the same day, I came across Yule's paper in the Flinders Library. Another example, I suppose, of what has been called the 'library angel' phenomenon. With the discovery of Kirby's papers a little later, I had something to get my teeth into.

With reactive papers like that you run the risk of appearing self-righteous because you seem to be administering a wigging. Certainly, Yule was having none of it; indeed, as often happens, it pushed him the other way for when he rejoindered he claimed to have 'dispelled' doubts. That told me he had not paid any attention to, or had failed to grasp, the rules of model-fitting, which categorically deny the possibility of doing anything so final as 'dispelling'. There was no offer of surrebuttal from the journal but the exchange stayed on my mind and in the end I discharged it by writing the paper 'As long as it gets me from A to B etc' which is reproduced as paper 18.

To my mind under-achievement should be regarded as a particular competence state, stunted if you like, but capable of regeneration (see paper 22). We might look at what achievement can actually be produced, and under what conditions. I warm to the suggestion in some German work

(Ludwig, 1981) that achievement problems should be treated regardless of their association with intelligence 'deficits.' As for over-achievement, I read in a newspaper article once (*Guardian Weekly*, 12 June 1983) that Mrs. Thatcher is an over-achiever, one sign being that she lacks the innate resource to carry out with ease and grace the normal duties of her high office. Does that make Lord Home an under-achiever? Clinical usage can be just as daft.

The aptitude paper came out of my inaugural lecture at the University of the West Indies (Wood, 1982), in which I tried to reflect on what various conceptualizations of aptitude and achievement and their relationships, meant for a country like Jamaica. Ed Brandon, a philosopher colleague at UNI, picked up some of the things I was saying and we decided to talk about aptitude, and to see what a philosopher and psychologist might come up with. Our cogitations resulted in a paper 'Is there a concept of aptitude worth having?' which the BPS Bulletin did not want. We decided tacitly to go our separate ways and in the end both of us produced papers, quite independently. A little of the material is common to both so it is a kind of collaboration. Mine is reproduced here; the reference for Ed's is Brandon (1985). I'm not sure that either of us has yet nailed down aptitude. There were ideas in our original paper which we abandoned. I saw aptitude as peculiarly distributed, (cf. Heyns on skill distributions in Section II) with a discontinuity at the upper end. Does it make any sense to talk of a 'little' aptitude?

Attribution of aptitude retrospectively is commonplace. Jacques Barzun's biography of Berlioz is shot through with it, 'The beginning of Berlioz' musical vocation was his discovery of an old flageolet in a bureau drawer ... Berlioz's inclination, it is clear, was marked even before he left for the seminary' (Barzun, 1956, p. 26). Sometimes aptitude is bestowed, taken away and bestowed again, for example, Winston Churchill. The vulgar error at the root of these infelicities is the notion of aptitude as entelechy — or mind 'stuff'.

The idea of a 'talent search' is an interesting one, but I insist that the question has to be, 'Talent for what?' The paradox is that you can only get an answer to the question by putting the individual through schooling.

In this respect Snow (1986) is right to call education an aptitude-development programme, and to insist that the educational improvements of most importance are those that make education adaptive to aptitude differences at the start of instruction and promotive of aptitude development through and beyond it, from which, of course, the extremely skewed and long-tailed distribution predicted by Heyns would follow.

Note 39 of the aptitude paper deals with lotteries. Missing is an important Dutch reference (Hofstee, 1980). I hope to write about lotteries at some time in the future.

The 'standards' paper could have been in a section of its own, along with the two companion papers referenced there, but there was not enough space. Having left the Evaluation of Testing in Schools project to go to Jamaica I felt I had not had my say about the APU and standards, and Colin felt he still had something left in his locker after doing the evaluation of ASSP. The paper was finalized in mid-1984 and reviewing it I see no reason to add or subtract, although I grant that the reference to Mondale's proposed fund for excellence seems awfully dated. The national standards scene has gone quiet. The APU is in (animated?) suspension; National Assessment is under new management; ASSP stays dead.

'The trouble with standards in education is that they can be made to look good or bad, depending on the yardstick'. Thus John Rae (1986). This is the measurement point we were at pains to make in all three papers. Rae thinks that in a competitive world the most realistic yardstick is the standard achieved by the school children of other industrialized countries, and offers Japan as *the* yardstick. He may be right but there still needs to be found the connecting rod which will convert grave and contrite realization of Japanese superiority into improvement of achievement among young Britons. That is the fallacy of all national assessment programmes — believing that individuals, whether teachers, parents or students, will think that the results apply to *them*.

Standards rhetoric is permeated by an unsophisticated view of human behaviour. Macro-events will produce appropriate micro-reactions. Rae, quite rightly, rejects the notion that educational reforms like GCSE will raise standards. Why? Where is the compelling causal narrative connecting the two? Rae is most plausible when he argues that the GCSE will depress standards still further (because teacher assessment — see Section II — leaves too much room for the incompetence or eccentricity of teachers to undermine the intentions of the planners).

The perception is now (writing in May 1986) that in Britain standards have fallen markedly since, say, 1979 (which just happens to be the year the Conservatives came to power on the back of their manifesto — we shall promote higher standards of achievement etc). Falling standards happens to be short-hand for 'Schools are in a mess'. As so often before, the word 'standards' has been hijacked to describe, and therefore explain away, an educational predicament.

References

BARZUN, J. (1956) *Berlioz and his Century*. New York, Meridian Books.

BRANDON, E.P. (1985) 'Aptitude analyzed', *Educational Philosophy and Theory*, 17, pp. 13–18.

BRODIE, F.M. (1971) *The Devil Drives*, Harmondsworth, Penguin Books.

HOFSTEE, W.K.B. (1980) 'Policies of educational selection and grading: The case for compromise models', in *Proceedings of the 1980 International Symposium of Educational Testing*, Antwerp.

LUDWIG, S. (1981). 'Are the concepts of over- and under-achievement outdated?', *Psychologie in Erzeihung und Unterricht*, 25, pp. 282–92 (Psychological Abstracts).

RAE, J. (1986) 'This 16-plus fails to make the grade', *The Mail on Sunday*, 25 May, p. 8.

SNOW, R.E. (1986) 'Individual differences and the design of educational programs', *American Psychologist*, 41, pp. 1029–39.

WOOD, R. (1982) 'Aptitude and achievement', *Caribbean Journal of Education*, 9, pp. 79–123.

Paper 17: Doubts About 'Underachievement', Particularly as Operationalized by Yule, Lansdown and Urbanowicz*

A paper by Yule, Lansdown and Urbanowicz (1982) purports to be about predicting educational attainment but is really about under-achievement, operationalized in a certain mechanical way. This paper, and one in the same genre by McLeod (1982), are challenged on several grounds which need to be convincingly rebutted for the operationalization to have any value. It is worrying, too, that if the paper is to be judged for what it purports to be, the prediction equations it offers are quite indifferent, the n is too small to be useful, and WISC-R is a poorer predictor of some measures of achievement than are other measures of achievement. Finally it is suggested that the relationship between measured intelligence and achievement is far from being straightforward, as a recent court case illustrates.

The article by Yule *et al.* (1982) is disturbing on several counts. It purports, through its title and synopsis, to be about predicting educational attainment from IQ but, as the opening sentence makes clear and the synopsis does not, it is really about underachievement, operationalized as the discrepancy between predicted and observed attainment.

I had always supposed that when the object was to predict it was the quality of prediction which mattered, not the so-called unexplained variation, although the obligation is always there to try and explain how that might arise. To make capital out of what *cannot* be explained by giving it a label, in this case underachievement or overachievement, is certainly unusual, but undoubtedly powerful. The stronger the prediction, the better the predictive validity of the instrument; the weaker the prediction the more can be made of under- and overachievement. The only snag is that underachievers, by not fitting the model, thereby fail to demonstrate the relationship between intelligence and achievement, on which everything depends.

*Reprinted from *British Journal of Clinical Psychology* (1984), 23, pp. 231–2.

Yule *et al.* proceed on the premise that the variation in attainment 'explained' by WISC-R is wholly contained within the total variation in attainment, which is the standard linear regression model assumption. This may or may not be so but it is a simple matter to show that by assuming measurement error in the independent variable (WISC-R), as one should, a source of variation is introduced or made explicit, which has nothing to do with attainment. It therefore cannot be attributed to under- and overachievement. Had the appropriate 'error-in-variables' model been used (see, for instance, Goldstein, 1979), all this would have been clear, for the authors would have been obliged to state a model and expose their assumptions.

The usual consequence of taking error into account is to correct downwards. If that were to be done in this case, already indifferent prediction equations would look even more so, besides which the *n* is so small (167) as to make them practically useless, if not misleading, for practical purposes. The judgment 'indifferent' comes from a reading of table 3, out of which two thoughts occur: (i) except for mathematics, the WISC-R is not a particularly good predictor of achievement; (ii) it is a poorer predictor of some measures of achievement than are other measures of achievement. Thus spelling is a better predictor of comprehension and accuracy in reading than WISC-R and is not far behind for mathematics. Mathematics is a better predictor of reading accuracy than the WISC-R and only slightly inferior on comprehension. Age, which is plugged into the regression equations along with WISC-R, works for reading but not at all for spelling and mathematics, which is odd. Is there a simple explanation?

If the task was to choose a predictive instrument for reading on the basis of the information presented in table 3, I, for one, would choose the Vernon spelling and mathematics tests ahead of the WISC-R. But, of course, to do that would be to eliminate the concept of under- and overachievement. The only reason for allowing WISC-R to make such demands on our attention must be that IQ is accorded primacy. Underachievement, in this formulation, is merely part of old-fashioned IQ testing paraphernalia. McLeod actually uses the term 'educational quotient'.

Other questions trouble me:

(a) How and why can an individual at the same time score 120 on an IQ test and 90 on an achievement test? Is it even plausible? Maybe it happens because of a fluke or as an extreme expression of natural covariation. Why look beyond these explanations, especially when there is no mention in any of these articles of repeated measures to see if a discrepancy of the same order turns up again or if it shows up with *another* IQ test and *another* attainment test?

(b) How can someone who scores 120 on an IQ test or even 100 be thought to have 'severe spelling mathematics problems' (Yule *et al.*, 1982, p. 45), or even a learning disability (McLeod, 1982, p. 231)? One is reminded of Heim's (1982) crack at two colleagues that if they could produce a few borderline defectives (her word) who speak four languages she was sure that she would not be the only psychologist who would be interested to meet them.

(c) It would seem to be α consequence of 'regression-referenced under-achievement identification', as McLeod terms it, that the 60–60, 70–70, even the 80–85 or 85–90 performers will be overlooked completely. They are performing according to prediction (expectation), so forget about them. But as Pikulski (1975) observes, the use of intelligence tests which are reading-dependent would naturally bring about this outcome, and that, of course, is an association which can work both ways.

(d) It is noteworthy that Yule and his colleagues are silent on the subject of 'overachievement'. Perhaps it is too embarrassing to unpack the concept. As I try to imagine what clinical value it could possibly have, there come to mind recent exchanges in the BPS *Bulletin* over a certain court case (see Heim, 1982; Tunstall *et al.*, 1982a and 1982b). This is because the defendant X in that case appears, in one view, to be an overachiever, for his life achievements were far in excess of what his measured IQ (80–90) suggested he was capable of. Thus Heim's crack. I say 'appears' because not the least interesting aspect of those exchanges was the effort, by both sides, to reconcile the IQ and achievement estimates (the latter not measured — an important point), Tunstall *et al.* by trying to devalue the achievements, and Heim by alleging that the IQ scores were faked. No one was happy about leaving the discrepancy intact, thus denying, as it were, the possibility of under- or overachievement in favour of a position where achievements serve as *collateral* information in the assessment of intelligence. 'The question of life-style and achievements is crucial and is not usually omitted when a psychologist is endeavouring to assess level of intelligence' (Heim, 1982, p. 332). Note the reversal: achievement is used to arrive at intelligence, although not predictively. Overachievement remains to be explained.

Yule *et al.* declare that underachievement is an 'attractive' concept. Why is it attractive? Its aetiology, as usually described, is anything but attractive. Perhaps it is attractive because it seems to encapsulate neatly everything that is meant by 'could do better'. Or is it attractive because the chosen operationalization makes no great mathematical demands? It is certainly attractive that 'statistically speaking, "overachievement" is observed as frequently as underachievement in any population' (Yule *et al.*, 1982, p. 43). What is to be made of this statement? It is in the same league as the old howler that 50 per cent of candidates lie below the median. It certainly has nothing to do with the complications and contradictions of life brought up in that court case. The formulation of underachievement favoured by Yule and McLeod should be questioned on conceptual and methodological grounds. Regrettably, it may already be routinized.

References

GOLDSTEIN, H. (1979). 'Some models for analysing longitudinal data on educational attainment', *Journal of the Royal Statistical Society, Series A*, 143, pp. 407–22.

HEIM, A. (1982). 'Professional issues arising from psychological evidence presented in court: A reply', *Bulletin of The British Psychological Society*, 35, pp. 332–3.

MCLEOD, J. (1982). 'Administrative screening of students for language learning disabilities at school and pre-school levels', *Annals of Dyslexia*, 32, pp. 231–46.

PIKULSKI, J.J. (1975). 'Assessing information about intelligence and reading', *The Reading Teacher*, 29, pp. 157–63.

TUNSTALL, O., GUDJONSSON, G., EYSENCK, H. and HAWARD, L. (1982a). 'Professional issues arising from psychological evidence presented in court', *Bulletin of The British Psychological Society*, 35, pp. 329–31.

TUNSTALL, O., GUDJONSSON, G., EYSENCK, H. and HAWARD, L. (1982b). 'Professional issues arising from psychological evidence presented in court. A reply to Dr. Heim', *Bulletin of The British Psychological Society*, 35, p. 333.

YULE, W., LANSDOWN, R. and URBANOWICZ, M.A. (1982). 'Predicting educational attainment from WISC-R in a primary school sample', *British Journal of Clinical Psychology*, 21, pp. 43–6.

Paper 18: As Long As It Gets Me From A to B: Psychologists and Statistics

How much statistics should psychologists who use statistics in their published work know? Given that a statistical analysis by a psychologist can always be made more sophisticated by an experienced statistician — and perhaps also more veridical — how much ignorance ought the psychologist to be permitted? What harm is done by psychologists who do not realize the limits of their statistical competence? How much of what psychologists claim rests on a purely statistical argument? Is it too much to expect that a psychologist will take the trouble to master his or her favourite methodology? These questions were brought to the fore, in my mind at least, by an exchange I had in print on the subject of 'underachievement' (Wood, 1984; Yule, 1984).

Basically, I took Yule and his colleagues to task for failing to appreciate the consequences of applying a simple linear regression model to certain data. Bear in mind that I am not a professional statistician. If my objections are well-founded a statistician could certainly have been harder on Yule.

No one wants to have their fun spoiled by statisticians and methodologists stomping all over their work. In that respect Yule is unlucky. He himself has managed to publish essentially similar papers (see the references in Yule *et al.*, 1982) without attracting published rebuttals. As we all know, there are relativities operating in all sorts of ways. What will get by in one journal is picked up in another. What passes muster in a journal at one time fails later. What will get by in one field will be stopped in another. Quite where psychology stands in this respect compared to, say, medicine, I do not know, but it is an issue which would bear scrutiny. I doubt if the respective hardnesses of the data have much to do with it.

In Yule *et al.*, (1982) the ostensible purpose was to present data supporting the claim that IQ is a good predictor of achievement but the hidden (actually not so hidden) purpose was to present a method for detecting underachievement. Those who do not achieve as well as predicted by IQ are defined as underachievers. Now to want to pursue good prediction *and* underachiever detection simultaneously is to pursue strictly conflicting objectives. This is because:

as prediction improves, the proportion of individuals classified as underachievers falls, as it logically must as prediction weakens, model fit worsens and more observations become indicative of underachievement. If some other model could be found for which the observations fitted better, then fewer would be outliers, as logic again dictates. The model could even be one which posits explicitly that IQ will consistently 'over-predict' achievement, perhaps because schooling has been interrupted, or whatever. The old saw about weeds being flowers out of place conveys exactly the appropriate way to think about 'discrepant' observations.

That does not exhaust the possibilities. Any sample can always be regarded as having been drawn from a mixture of populations, in this case a mixture of 'normals', who conform to the imperative that IQ and achievement should correlate strongly, and a 'deviant' group who do not conform. But this is too easy. Name two (or more) populations you are interested in and call the sample you have a mixture. The same thing can happen when statisticians top and tail data ('edit' is the polite term) to suit their models. Evidently statistics is vulnerable right here to ideological muscle.

I make no apologies for introducing ideology. To go no further than the Yule *et al.* paper, it was the decision to stand on the primacy of IQ, with all its attendant ideological baggage, which shaped the outcome of the analysis. Just as with height and weight, it would have been perfectly possible to swap dependent and independent variables and have achievement predict intelligence, in which case 'underachievement' would have become 'overintelligence'. Or else the IQ and achievement measures could simply have been regarded as fraternal measures, like spatial and perceptual, concerning which no one thinks to attribute any significance to the discrepancy or even think to calculate it. Why invoke IQ at all? It is at least as plausible to regard underachievement as a function of resources applied to the individual.

The Yule-Wood exchange says something about how ideology infiltrates analysis. It also, and this is what I am concerned with here, illustrates a way psychologists behave with data, in particular how situations arise where, to do the chosen statistical analysis properly, they are bound to be tugged beyond the limits of their knowledge and understanding. By stopping short and presumably operating within the limits of their competence, they produce results which are at best dubious and at worst misleading.

Can statistics change lives? We don't know but there is the famous case where the statistician (Aitkin) set to work on the empirical type (Bennett) and caused that worthy to make a U-turn, in a paper which he actually co-authored (Aitkin, Bennett and Hesketh, 1981)! Whether the revised results were more veridical is impossible to say but it is likely that they were. I hesitate to be categorical because of doubts about the quality of the data and therefore fears of garbage in, garbage out. It would be a Pyrrhic victory if sound statistical technique were to be prized above all else (Goldstein, 1984).

Deciding what statistical competence can reasonably be expected from empirical psychologists is a bit like deciding what civility can reasonably be expected from the police. In practice, the responsibility for spotting the duds falls on journal editors and referees. The problem for them is that there are too many papers which appear to be using statistics only glancingly but which in fact rely almost wholly on them for their impact. Unfortunately, it is a version of statistical practice which is degraded and routinized — what Ravetz (1971), writing about science, called 'vulgarized' knowledge. That ought to make these papers easy to spot but it doesn't seem to work that way. In this country, at least, a certain way of doing statistics in empirical work has been legitimated and too many have been co-opted to leave many whistleblowers.

The paper by Macintosh (1986) illustrates very well the sort of statistical treatment which not only gets by but, because the readership is habituated, actually seems felicitous. Here is a senior experimental psychologist intervening in magisterial fashion to knock a few psychometricians' heads together. The paper contains some elegant argument and undoubtedly makes some telling blows. If, that is, you accept the way Macintosh uses statistics. On page 5 of his paper he asks us to believe that a correlation of 0.60 is 'very much the same' as a correlation of 0.73. This we might be prepared to do if we didn't know that the figure of 0.73 was based on a sample of upwards of 7500 while the 0.60 was based on less than 100. Macintosh then notices that, for blacks, IQ 'over-predicts' achievement and concludes from this that IQ is not biased against blacks in the sense that it systematically underestimates the achievement of which they are capable. Others in the U.S have drawn the same conclusion. What, though, if both IQ *and* achievement measures are biased? Certainly if one is biased the other is likely to be given that both rely heavily on the same modalities. Over-dependence on reading, expressed in too-wordy items, is one way in which both measures could be biased. Pushing the argument on, the fact that the correlation between a biased predictor and a biased criterion is 'much the same' as the correlation between an unbiased predictor and an unbiased criterion is neither here nor there.

The Macintosh paper is typical of a whole genre. It is treating big questions and wants to make big points but in order to do so must pass everything through the filter of a statistical model which almost certainly cannot stand the load placed upon it. Slatkin, writing about mathematical models in evolutionary theory, called this an *hourglass* effect;

> First, a problem of real evolutionary importance is presented and discussed. Second, a model or class of models, which are very special and restrictive in their assumptions, is introduced. That is the point at which the mathematics takes over ... finally, the results from the narrow models are expanded into conclusions of grand importance with respect to the problem originally posed. (Slatkin, 1980)

Coombs (1983, p. 79), commenting on the hourglass effect, suggests that mathematical models are especially vulnerable to such criticism because of the visibility and precision of the assumptions; 'when they are misused it is readily detected'. First, though, the assumptions have to be laid out, something Macintosh and Yule quite failed to do. Even the humble correlation derives from a statistical model and its appropriate application cannot be taken for granted (Wood, 1986).

I am sure no one is suggesting that statisticians should be the arbiters of solutions, that analyses should be referred to them for ratification and validation. In the debate over whether schools have an effect, the impression grew that statisticians were being ceded this kind of power. But this would hardly be a healthy development; besides statisticians would not want it. What I think does go against the grain is when psychologists, or anyone else, use statistics opportunistically,to get from A to B without understanding what they are doing. To extend the car simile, too many psychologists drive jalopies which should not be on the road.

References

AITKIN, M., BENNETT, S.N. and HESKETH, J. (1981) 'Teaching styles and pupil progress: A reanalysis', *British Journal of Educational Psychology*, 51, pp. 170–86.

COOMBS, C.H. (1983) *Psychology and Mathematics*. Ann Arbor, MI, University of Michigan Press.

GOLDSTEIN, H. (1984) 'Statistics in the social sciences: some personal views', *Journal of the Royal Statistical Society*, A, 147, pp. 260–7.

MACINTOSH, N. (1986) 'A biology of intelligence?', *British Journal of Psychology*, pp. 1–21.

RAVETZ, J.R. (1971). *Scientific Knowledge and its Social Problems*. Oxford, Oxford University Press.

SLATKIN, M. (1980) 'Altruism in theory', *Science*, 210 pp. 633–4.

WOOD, R. (1984). 'Doubts about "underachievement", particularly as operationalized by Yule, Lansdown and Urbanowicz', *British Journal of Clinical Psychology*, 23 pp. 231–2 and in this volume.

WOOD, R. (1986) 'Think before you square correlations — or do anything with them', *British Journal of Educational Research*, 12 pp. 249–55.

YULE, W. (1984) 'The operationalising of "under-achievement" — doubts dispelled', *British Journal of Clinical Psychology*, 23, pp. 233–4.

YULE, W., LANSDOWN, R. and URBANOWICZ, M.A. (1982) 'Predicting educational attainment from WISC-R in a primary school sample', *British Journal of Clinical Psychology*, 21, pp. 43–6.

Paper 19: Aptitude Testing Is Not an Engine for Equalizing Educational Opportunity*

Abstract

A recent article on education in China succeeded in giving a fresh tweak to the arguments concerning whether aptitude or achievement testing is more likely to promote equality of educational opportunity. In *The Diploma Disease* Ronald Dore expounded the view that aptitude testing is to be preferred for selection purposes on the grounds that it gives more weight to 'innate potential' (his term) than does achievement testing which produces results more affected by quality of schooling, an influence which is all too variable, especially in emerging countries. Although shot through with considerable ambivalence, Dore's view could still be instrumental in persuading educational and political authorities in those countries that aptitude testing will do what he says it will do — 'make for greater equality of educational opportunity and be more effective in mobilizing all available talent'. And even if these authorities have never set eyes on Dore's book, there is sufficient evidence that some of them are acting as if they had taken Dore's view on board for it to be worth re-opening the question. It is argued here that Dore's position cannot be supported.

Dore Says Several Things About Aptitude Tests But Only One Sticks

Ronald Dore makes several statements about aptitudes tests in *The Diploma Disease* and they do not all hang together. The argument here is that the statement which makes most impact occurs in the middle of the book while the ones which are apt to be overlooked or simply not reached appear in the last section called 'Afterthoughts' (it could have been 'Second thoughts').[1] When Dore says that aptitude tests are to be preferred for selection purposes over

*Reprinted from *British Journal of Educational Studies*, (1986) XXXIV, 1, February, pp. 26–37.

achievement tests because they give more weight to 'innate potential' (his term) and are less susceptible to quality of schooling, people pay attention. But if they read on they will find him noting that a survey of the use of aptitude tests for job selection finds most of its examples in places where it is an almost exclusively white expatriate group which does the testing and blacks who are 'culled' by the process.[2] Perhaps Dore is now out of date; that usage could be regarded as a concomitant of colonial rule. Read that way, his first statement is left stronger. But can it be substantiated? That is what this paper is concerned with.

The Case of China

Julia Kwong has examined the arguments concerning whether aptitude or achievement testing is more likely to promote equality of educational opportunity, as they are working themselves out in China.[3] Since Ronald Dore also writes about China, and says things which bear on those arguments, it is a useful way of motivating the discussion to compare the two writers' views.

The first point to note is that they were there at different times. Dore looks at China while Mao was alive and sees it moving to take what he calls 'natural selection' out of the schools. He thinks it fitting that the nation which invented examinations should also be the first to abandon them.[4] Kwong, who visited China in 1981, finds the public examinations system back in place and observes that while it 'is not the root of the social inequities, it certainly reflects, maintains and even exaggerates them'.[5] Presumably, if Dore had been in China when Kwong was, he would not have written what he did. What is revealing, however, is the reason *he* gives for aptitude tests being unacceptable in China. 'One possible method of avoiding favouritism — the overt use of IQ or aptitude tests — is almost certainly ruled out. The very ideology of egalitarian group activity would forbid a system which utilized, drew attention to — even admitted to exist — significant differences of innate ability between individuals'.[6] Compare that with Kwong, 'Aptitude tests and, especially, IQ tests in the west have been shown to favour children from the middle class partly because these tests are not based on a clearly defined corpus of knowledge from which students are to be examined . . .'.[7] Dore sees aptitude testing as fair, Kwong reports that the Chinese only see it as unfair. Where they agree is in finding achievement testing prejudiced in favour of the well to do, and also, on the 'cooling out' function of achievement tests.[8] Kwong's report is much more pessimistic than Dore's. It is possible to read into Kwong, but not into Dore, the conclusion that *any* form of testing can be co-opted and utilized by the privileged in *any* country.

Achievement tests are meant to be fairer than aptitude tests because all syllabuses are published so that everyone has a chance to learn the rules of the game, rather than guess at them as in the case of aptitude tests. But such a gesture cannot neutralize the effect of the extra-willing (intellectual-cadre) family. Rather the reverse; it gives it more to work on so that, indeed, as Kwong remarks, existing differences (which would have existed given aptitude tests) are exaggerated.[9] Dore prefers to believe that one kind of test — the aptitude test — is beyond the influence, or largely so, of the intellectual/cadre family. He sees aptitude test performance as largely resistant to the effects of schooling; *school-proofed* as it were. But that, as he well knows, is precisely what the Chinese will not tolerate.

Aptitude and Achievement and Some Prevailing Myths

School-proofing is necessary for Dore because schooling, especially in poorer countries, varies so much in provision and quality. Dore wants to tap the genotype without the phenotype getting in the way or not getting in the way much. Happily that is a futile project. Even if he could remove the phenotypic element due to schooling, there would still be left that due to upbringing with all the variation present there, and the scope for unequal treatment, not least in learning possibilities. If we ask what is involved in school-proofing, we find that tasks must be chosen which are not susceptible to influence by what has been learned (or not) at school. That eliminates reading, writing and calculation — at least — and leaves non-verbal and perceptual tasks as falling beyond the school's influence and thus offering a direct channel, as it were, to the genotype. But is this really so? First, there is the assumption that anything which is not achievement is aptitude and is therefore under control of the genotype. This can only hold in the extreme circumstances where the individual has had no experience i.e. immediately post-birth. It has long since ceased to hold by the time the child starts school. Then there is the assumption that non-verbal and perceptual and suchlike 'pure' tasks could not be influenced by schooling and do not need to be learned. Superficially, this assumption appears to hold for abstract perceptual tasks of the kind found in Raven's Matrices and in spatial visualization tasks. Formally, it could probably be demonstrated that at no time during schooling is a child ever taught to solve perceptual puzzles as such (unless being coached for an aptitude test), but it could probably also be demonstrated that at various times, sometimes more or less continuously, the kind of thinking which will facilitate that kind of problem-solving is encouraged via other sorts of exercises.[10]

Finally, even if we could accept that these tasks qualify as appropriate tasks for an aptitude test and supply evidence of innate potential, what would it be potential *for* and would it be of any use in society? When Vernon observed that it would hardly be desirable to fill Jamaican schools with brilliant but barely literate children, the appropriate reaction was 'Brilliant at *what*?'[11]

Attempts to Define Aptitude

Operationalizing aptitude by exclusion with reference to 'school-proofing' will not produce a coherent, grounded conceptualization. Nor will ad hoc complaints that aptitude tests are deficient in this or that respect. When Maehr and Nicholls protest that, in failing to include measures of 'social competency', traditional aptitude tests discriminate against women,[12] the question is not whether they are right but, first, what was the aptitude these traditional aptitude tests were measuring and, secondly, what would it become if measures of social competency were to be incorporated?

It has been suggested that 'attempts to describe the nature of an aptitude demand subtle and penetrating psychological research and analysis'.[13] Having seen the conceptual dog's dinner which is aptitude it is hard to see what empirical work will do. Things are bad when a risible definition like the following is allowed into an important handbook:

> The term *aptitude* signifies some present state of a human being that is propadeutic to some future achievement, whether that achievement is defined as the attainment of heaven, good citizenship, socialization, vocational or marital satisfaction, higher education or greater intelligence.[14]

Monty Python would have had fun with that. What do others have to offer? Jensen is happy to equate aptitude with intelligence but then has to invoke 'special aptitudes' to cater for Mozart and athletes.[15] Some of those opposed to monolithic g would want to replace it with many *specific* aptitudes. Here it seems to me that Wiseman's judgment[16] still stands and that there is as yet no firm empirical evidence for the existence of manifold specific aptitudes.[17]

J.B. Carroll has toiled for years attempting to characterize aptitude, usually in the context of foreign language learning: 'aptitude is the time needed to master a task under optimal conditions'; 'language learning aptitude is some characteristic of an individual which controls, at a given point in time, the rate of progress that he will make subsequently in learning a foreign language'; 'a present capability symptomatic of future performance, given motivation and opportunity'.[18] The notion that aptitude might have something to do with rate of progress surfaces again in Jensen; 'differences in aptitude are inferred when individuals with roughly equal or equivalent experience, opportunity and motivation to acquire some particular knowledge or skills, show marked differences in their rates of acquisition and levels of performance after a given amount of exposure'.[19] In other words, call the residual component of performance you can't explain, aptitude.

Then there are those, notably Anastasi, who want to get rid of the concept of aptitude altogether, or if we must have it, call it 'developed abilities'. 'If a benevolent wizard were to give me the power to eliminate four words from the tester's vocabulary I would choose "intelligence", "aptitudes", "abilities" and "achievement". Then if a malevolent wizard were suddenly to appear and demand that I take back one word, I would choose to retain "abilities".[20] Odd wizards to be sure, not obviously benevolent or malevolent; funny too that a psychologist should rely on wizards to rid her of unwanted concepts.

Conceptual Distinctions, Yes; Operational Distinctions, No

Michael Scriven does not want to get rid of aptitude and achievement; he can see a clear conceptual distinction between the two (which I think we can even if we are fuzzy about aptitude), but cannot see the way to constructing distinctive measures.[21] Putting daylight between aptitude and achievement measures is indeed the problem; in practice, in the academic context, the similarities far outweigh the differences and the results reflect this.[22] Both require reading, writing, calculation and such school-fostered skills, and although perceptual tasks and suchlike appear in aptitude tests they are definitely not school-proofed by design. Is there then a difference? We might say that achievement tests are sensitive to recent learning while aptitude tests are sensitive to cumulative learning but, of course, that recent learning will be heavily conditioned by the quality of past learning, and so forth.[23]

The difference between aptitude (or ability) measures and achievement measures has too often been taken for granted, and not only by Ronald Dore. Researchers will use ability (aptitude) measures to 'control' for pre-existing differences in propensity between groups prior to treatment yet, on analysis, these measures turn out to be as influenced by schooling as the achievement measures they use as outcomes, or rather it cannot be demonstrated satisfactorily that they are not.[24] Another way of making the point is to say that, were researchers who are doing this kind of work to be offered these wild or 'native' measures (the perceptual puzzles and so forth), it is highly likely that they would turn them down as inappropriate. As has been said,[25] the further one tries to get away from tests that are culturally conditioned, the less accurate they become as predictors of future educability.

Do scholastic aptitude tests like the Scholastic Aptitude Test (SAT) actually succeed in placing applicants for college education from secondary schools of varying quality on a more equal footing than achievement tests do? Do race and SES affect conventional achievement scores as strongly as they affect SAT scores? The available data are too thin to permit any firm conclusions but, from what there are, it has been argued[26] that SAT scores appear to be just as dependent on home environment and school quality as scores on conventional achievement tests, and that conventional achievement tests predict success in college and adult life just as well[27] as the SAT or other 'aptitude' tests do; '. . . for those concerned with equality of opportunity the choice between so-called aptitude tests and conventional achievement tests is a toss-up'. It will have to be faced that aspirations based on a textbook conception of aptitude have not translated into practice. Those like Dore and his colleagues,[28] who base policies on this conception, will have to ask whether they can go on doing so.

Equality of Educational Opportunity

We all recognize that equality of educational opportunity is a slippery customer. Is it:

(a) equal life chances,
(b) open competition for scarce opportunities,
(c) equal cultivation of different capacities,
(d) independence of educational attainment from social origins?[29] or something else?

Aptitude testing has nothing to say to (a) for, if it is to be construed literally, as Flew does in berating Barrow, it means that everyone must have the opportunity to do the same thing, and so there is no need for testing of any kind. (b) looks a more promising application but why[30] should something acquired *accidentally* i.e. ability, intelligence, aptitude, talent be used as a basis for allocating reward? This, of course, is Rawls' 'talent equals luck' formula.[31] Dore is fully alive to it[32]; in fact, he seems to settle for the action advocated by Rawls, which is to compensate (financially) to equalize, but does so without any great conviction. It is not necessary to argue the point here. It is more germane to ask whether an educational policy-maker in a developing country would pay any attention to it at all. A person who is convinced of the virtues of aptitude testing is unlikely to be deterred by being told that talent equals luck. It is an argument for an advanced liberal society, and Dore is pessimistic that it will be taken seriously there. The cutting edge of the policy expressed in (c) was the 11 + examination; an aptitude test, we would have to say, the aptitude being the ability to profit from grammar school education. (It could have been the aptitude to profit from technical or secondary modern education but authorities like Hadow and Spens were reticent on that subject.) Just how to construct an aptitude test to discern different capacities (for what exactly?) is a mystery, let alone how to cultivate them equally, even supposing they could be discerned. But that has not put others off. The case of Jamaica comes to mind. There is a plan to rescue Jamaican secondary education which is in a sad state. One of the recommendations is to divide students into three streams post age 14 (grade 9), the basis of selection to be aptitude tests or, as the UNESCO report says elsewhere, a national orientation examination.[33] Nothing is said about these tests; readers are assumed to know what is entailed so commonplace and well understood is the term 'aptitude' thought to be. The UNESCO people had probably read Dore. It is unlikely that they would have reflected on the deep confusion surrounding the concept.

The trifurcation idea was taken up more or less immediately by the

Jamaican Minister of Education; it seems to have been one of the first points she grasped although, interestingly, it comes out a little differently. 'An in-house aptitude and achievement test would be set by the Ministry of Education to streamline students into academic, technical and vocational areas'.[34] Note the belt-and-braces approach to the two kinds of test, surely symptomatic of a mind which does not understand the differences or similarities. As far as this technocratic politician is concerned, the construction of these tests is a routine matter. It is a throwback to the early years of the century in California when aptitude testing was assimilated into the prevailing doctrine of efficiency in education.[35]

The formulation of equal educational opportunity in (d) would seem to be close to Dore's heart. The trouble is that it is not coming to pass, at least not in France, where the Garnier and Raffalovitch data come from, nor, it appears, in China. For that to happen, aptitude would have to be distributed independently of social origin, and then converted into achievement without disturbing that null relationship, or else initially positive correlations between aptitude and social origin would have to be cancelled out by determined teaching practices which would need to be extraordinarily well directed, as well as being successful.

It has been noted how daunting are the tasks that await a thoroughgoing proponent of equal opportunity.[36] Having ensured that schools give the same advantages to everyone, he must then set about equalizing homes and parents. Nor are his troubles over, for the differences in genetic endowment remain to be neutralized. If one believes, as Dore does, that aptitude tests tap directly into the genotype, then it cannot follow that aptitude testing will make for greater equality of educational opportunity (Dore's original claim); in fact, the reverse would seem to be true. The only way it can appear to promote that objective, as Dore himself makes clear, is in a perverse way by making inequality so apparent, through the aptitude testing machinery and accompanying ideology, that the introduction of the companion and consequent measure, compensate-to-equalize, is made to seem imperative. But that hardly corresponds to equal opportunity.

Aptitude Tests to Mobilize Talent

Dore's views notwithstanding, there are no grounds for thinking that aptitude tests, as conventionally conceived and constructed, will be any more effective in social engineering than achievement tests. There is a touching belief — and Dore seems to share it — that if only the effort were to be made, aptitude tests could identify and flush out the hidden talent which is out there in the bush or the boondocks or the barrios waiting to be discovered. For Third and Fourth world countries this is an exceedingly powerful idea, but it exerts fascination in the USA too.[37] Nor need the idea be dismissed. The proposition that some talent is being overlooked is universally true, above all in developing countries.

Again, though, it depends what you mean by talent. Whatever you define it to be, if you select at an early age that talent still has to be schooled and converted into achievement, and if it was not a talent that would respond well to schooling, then what was the point of the exercise? If you are trying to locate those who will have occupational success, become leaders in society, etc, a similar point applies. Schooling comes first and there is no necessary connection between school success and life success.[38] A colleague has suggested to me that it does not do to take aptitude tests too seriously, nor to worry too much about what they might be measuring. He sees them as a device for allocating opportunities, whether school or work, but keeping the two separate, and to the extent that they measure something which is not particularly functional in society, the fairer they become; in other words, the more trivial the tasks, the more the test approximates to a random selector.[39]

Conclusion

The purpose of this paper was to establish that the account of aptitude testing represented in *The Diploma Disease* will not do. Aptitude testing does not possess the hygienic properties Dore claims. It will not neutralize privilege or the effects of varying quality of secondary schooling. Despite the qualifications, caveats and ultimately plain ambivalence, Dore's account offers too much of an encouragement to the educational policy-maker in poorer countries, who is already likely to be predisposed in favour of aptitude testing as an efficient solution to admittedly serious selection problems. Which is not to say that achievement tests come out of the analysis any better; it is just that they do not have the same ideological freight riding on them.

Acknowledgement

I would like to thank Ed Brandon for spending time discussing aptitude with me. A small amount of material has been taken from our unpublished paper, 'Is there a concept of aptitude worth having?'

References

1 DORE, R. (1976) *The Diploma Disease*, London, Unwin Educational. The 'middle of the book' refers to pp. 155–7.
2 *Ibid.*, p. 193.
3 KWONG, J. (1983) 'Is everyone equal before a system of grades: Social background and opportunities in China?', *British Journal of Sociology*, 34, pp. 93–108.
4 DORE, R. (1976) *op. cit.*, p. 168.
5 *Ibid*, p. 107.

6 *Ibid.*, p. 174.

7 *Ibid.*, p. 106.

8 'Achievement tests "cool out" the failure more gradually; hopes have time to adjust to prospects; few people can approach their fourth shot at "O" level maths with the same expectations as the first' (DORE, p. 193); 'through its reputation of judging ability impartially on the individual's performances the examination system helps the disadvantaged to be reconciled to their fate' (KWONG, p. 106).

9 Given a mother like Maxine Hong Kingston's (see *The Woman Warrior*, London, Picador, 1981), that is not hard to believe at all.

10 A recent exchange brings this point out well. Researchers A and B produced evidence to support their views that the non-verbal abilities measured by tests called the Visualisation in Three Dimensions Test and the Mosaic Comparisons Test may very well be addressed by school curricular materials and objectives and took researchers C and D to task for offering these tests are measures of 'school-free' ability. In reply, C and D conceded that there is no such thing as a mental skill that is *completely* independent of school — nor of home, community or genetics. They claimed further that they were seeking 'relatively school-free' measures and accused A and B of transforming this objective into 'necessarily school-free', which they rejected as a straw man. (*Educational Researcher*, 11, 4, 1982, pp. 24–6).

11 VERNON, P.E. (1960) *Selection for Secondary Education in Jamaica*, London, University of London Institute of Education.

12 MAEHR, M.L. and NICHOLLS, J.G. (1980) 'Culture and achievement motivation: A second look'. in WARREN, N. (Ed.), *Studies in Cross-Cultural Psychology*, Vol. 2, New York, Academic Press.

13 CARROLL, J.B. (1981) 'Twenty-five years of research on foreign language aptitude'. in DILLER, K.C. (Ed.), *Individual Differences and Universals in Language Learning Aptitude* Rowley, MA, Newbury House Publishers Inc., p. 87.

14 SNOW, R.E. and YALOW, E. (1982) 'Education and intelligence', in STERNBERG, R.J. (Ed.), *Handbook of Human Intelligence*, New York, Cambridge University Press.

15 JENSEN, A.R. (1980) *Bias in Mental Testing*, New York, Free Press, p.239.

16 'In the twenties and thirties, some psychologists believed that it would prove possible to identify and isolate many separate "aptitudes" which would be of the greatest help in vocational guidance and selection. This hope has proved a vain one.' (WISEMAN, S. (1900) 'Introduction'. in WISEMAN, S. (Ed.), *Intelligence and Ability*, Harmondsworth, Penguin Books Ltd, p. 14).

17 A referee suggested that specific aptitudes speak to the question of what is it aptitude *for* and indicated that I might have given more attention to the relevant research literature as surveyed, for instance, by Benjamin Bloom in his book *Human Characteristics in School Learning* (1976). The referee also noted — and I agree — that had I done so it would not have altered the nature of my argument. Claims for specific aptitudes are founded either on some form of factor analysis (which produces results which are fundamentally flawed because of arbitrariness — the indeterminacy problem) or on what amounts to pointing and naming (wishful thinking). Lauren Resnick's proposal for treating aptitudes as learning skills which can then be taught, is interesting but it does represent a shift of ground. (RESNICK, L.B. (1981) 'Instructional psychology'. in ROSENZWEIG, M.R. and PORTER, L.W. (Eds.), *Annual Review of Psychology*, 32, pp. 690–1.)

18 Respectively, CARROLL, J.B. (1963) 'A model of school learning', *Teachers College Record*, 64, pp. 723–33; CARROLL, J.B. (1974) 'Fitting a model of school learning to aptitude and achievement data over grade levels' in GREEN, D.R. (Ed.), *The Aptitude-Achievement Distinction*, Monterey, CA, CTB/McGraw-Hill; CARROLL, *op. cit.*

19 JENSEN, A.R. (1980) *op. cit.*, p. 240.

20 ANASTASI, A. (1980) 'Abilities and the measurement of achievement.' *New*

Directions for Testing and Measurement, 5, pp. 1–9.

21 SCRIVEN, M. (1980) *Evaluation Thesaurus*, Port Reyes, CA, Edger press.

22 A recent survey of the effect of coaching before the test (KULIK, J.A., KULIK, C.C. and BANGERT, R.L. (1984) 'Effects of practice on aptitude and achievement test scores', *American Educational Research Journal*, 21, pp. 435–48) did not even bother to distinguish between aptitude and achievement tests, other than in the title. The effects were judged to be the same.

23 Humphreys has a nifty argument which says that since no test can possibly be a pure measure of genotype, the practice of attaching the label 'aptitude' should cease. By the same line of reasoning, the label 'achievement', in as much as it connotes a strongly environmental contribution to phenotypic variance, should likewise be proscribed. All psychological tests, he avers, measure current performance levels which are phenotypic characteristics. Back to 'developed abilities'. (HUMPHREYS, L.G. (1978) 'Relevance of genotype and its environmental counterpart to the theory, interpretation and nomenclature of ability measures', *Intelligence*, 2, pp. 181–93).

24 A good example is the paper by COLEMAN, J.S., HOFFER, T. and KILGORE, S. (1982) 'Achievement and segregation in secondary schools', *Sociology of Education*, 55, pp. 162–82. These workers were criticized for failing to control adequately but turned (p. 165) and accused their critics of too easily assuming that vocabulary, for instance, qualifies as an ability measure. As they see it, and one has to agree, researchers have an obligation to back up their choices of ability and achievement measures with an empirical demonstration; not at all easy, as perhaps will be apparent by now.

25 VERNON, P.E. (1960) *op. cit.*

26 By JENCKS, C. and CROUSE, J. (1982) 'Should we relabel the SAT . . . or replace it?', *Phi Delta Kappan*, 63, pp. 659–63. It turns out that they are of the same mind as Humphreys (note 23) where labelling is concerned.

27 Or poorly, which is more the truth. A quantitative synthesis of thirty-five studies of the association between academic and occupational performance (*American Educational Research Journal*, 21, pp. 311–21, 1984) concluded that 'the overall variance accounted for makes academic grades or test scores nearly useless in predicting occupational effectiveness and satisfaction'.

28 Writing of selection for jobs in Mexico, three of Dore's colleagues at the Institute of Development Studies (BROOKE, N., OXENHAM, J. and LITTLE, A. (1978) *Qualifications and Employment in Mexico*, IDS Research Report) maintain that 'a battery of aptitude tests which, at least in principle, are not related to either level of education or social class, would have the effect of offering access to high level positions to those who do not at present form part of the same social class as the employers' (p. 76). The weakening clause 'at least in principle' seems to indicate that the writers are not too confident that their suggestion will work out in practice.

29 (a) is taken from Barrow by Flew and used by him to pummel Barrow (FLEW, A. (1983) 'Review of R. Barrow *Injustice, Inequality and Ethics*', *British Journal of Educational Studies*, 31, pp. 159–60); (b) is offered by Flew as an alternative to (a); (c) was favoured by those inter-war education reports chaired by Hadow and Spens; (d) appears in GARNIER, M.A. and RAFFALOVITCH, L.E. (1984), 'The evolution of equality of educational opportunities in France', *Sociology of Education*, 57, pp. 1–11. These writers want to put everyone else right; 'equality of educational opportunities more correctly refers to the independence of a child's educational attainment from social origins'. It might be thought from their title that France has made progress towards this end. It has not.

30 To echo KARIER, C.J. (1976) 'Testing for order and control in the corporate liberal state', in DALE, R. *et al.*, (Eds.) *Schooling and Capitalism*, London, Routledge and Kegan Paul.

31 RAWLS, J. (1971) *A Theory of Justice*, Cambridge, MA, Harvard University Press.
32 DORE, R. (1976) *op. cit.*, p. 196.
33 'Depending on the results of this examination, students would be oriented either towards academic education in the high schools, or towards further education in grades 10 and 11 of the proposed secondary schools (the latter offering general educational courses, and prevocational skill training courses), or towards juniors' technician training in the proposed specialized technical, agricultural and commercial schools' (UNESCO, (1983) *Jamaica: Development of Secondary Education*, Report EFM/119, UNESCO, Paris, p. 23).
34 *Daily Gleaner*, 18 May 1983.
35 See CHAPMAN, P.D. (1981) 'Schools as sorters: Testing and tracking in California', *Journal of Social History*, 14, pp. 701–17.
36 SINGER, P. (1979) *Practical Ethics*, London, Cambridge University Press, p. 35.
37 A US senator has estimated, or someone else has estimated for him, that the nation has 2.5m gifted children, of all classes and races, of whom half have never been discovered (*New York Times*, 14 November 1983). This prompted the sour rejoinder that 'there is no evidence that precocious children as a group go on to contribute more to society than those whose talents emerge later' (HACKER, A. (1984) *The New York Review*, 12 April).
38 Rather there seems to be a marked disjunction (see note 27). Even if this were a result which held only in developed countries, that would be no reason to be sanguine about the possibility of life success being doled out at an early age in lesser developed countries.
39 As it happens, Dore is attracted to random selection and has much of interest to say on the subject. His modified lottery (first choose your target group and then select randomly on a 1 in x basis from that group) has been studied seriously in Holland, where apparently students were willing to back it. No one knows what motivation and commitment students selected by lottery will exhibit. South Korea has been using lotteries to select students for middle and high school education since 1969. There have been signs that the system is under pressure. *Korea Newsreview* (5 January 1980 pp. 21–2) reported that the system 'is contributing to the downgrading of the quality of high school students. Teachers are also suffering from increased workloads'. In 1982 the same journal was saying 'Equalization resulted in "mediocrity" in high schools. Another demerit is that some students get bored in class while others are heavy laden (sic)'. This piece added that the current policy, stressing 'universalism' over 'elitism' will continue, more or less as conceived, but that to make up for the drawbacks in an otherwise 'ideal' system, separate schooling for the gifted is being tried (*Korea Newsreview*, 20 February 1982, p. 20). In fact, a special class for gifted students had been in operation for one year (*Korean Newsreview*, 1 May 1982, p. 21). I doubt if this turn of events needs any commentary from me.

Paper 20: Have National Assessments Made Us Any Wiser About 'Standards'?*

Introduction

'Standards' is one of the most abused words in education and it is reasonable to expect national assessment programmes to contribute substantially to the elucidation of what is meant by this term which is so freighted with different, often contradictory meanings. No one is closer to solving the problem; so one would expect clarification to be necessary for the job to be done well (or at all), particularly in the light of the circumstances in which these programmes were set up. The Australian programme (Australian Studies in Student Performance or ASSP) was set up directly as a result of concern voiced over 'standards'; the United Kingdom programme (run by the Assessment of Performance Unit or APU) was quickly adapted to meet the 'standards' issue even though the original explanation given for introducing it was quite different; while the oldest programme, the US National Assessment of Educational Progress (NAEP), although established before the 'standards' issue took off in earnest, was unable to avoid being drawn into it.

So it would appear that we are justified in looking to the three national assessment programmes for guidance on the meaning of 'standards' both in the definitional and the reporting sense: if by *that* is meant standards, then *this* is what we have to say. This seems a minimal requirement, calling for an intellectual effort from somewhere within the programmes which need not be attached to any ongoing data collection, analysis or interpretation.

In pursuing this theme we are fortunate in having to hand recent evaluations of all three programmes (Power *et al.*, 1982; Wirtz and Lapointe, 1982; Gipps and Goldstein, 1983). Although one of us (Power) was the chief evaluator of ASSP, and the other for a time chief evaluator of the APU, we do not rely on these evaluations for authority; and if we have strictures for the one in which neither of us was involved, it is because that evaluation has actually confused the issue concerning 'standards'.

---

*Reprinted from *Comparative Education* (1984), 20, 3, pp. 307–21.

The APU Has Shilly-shallied Over 'Standards'

A historical account of the programmes is available in another paper (Power and Wood, 1984). For our purposes here it is convenient to start with an account of how the United Kingdom programme, the APU, has dealt with the matter of 'standards'. Nothing, we feel, better illustrates the looseness with which the term has been used and, more generally, the prevarications and trimmings which are apt to result when impetuous positions on standards are taken up, or else when technical problems prove insuperable or emerging political stances dictate soft-pedalling and low-profile entrenchments. In this connection it is necessary to know that the APU is an arm of the Government, being under the direct control of the Secretary of State for Education and Science. That is not true of NAEP which is federally controlled only at several removes (and then only technically) or of ASSP which, although it owed its being to the then Commonwealth Minister of Education, was in practice under the undisputed control of the State Administrators, themselves antipathetic to the wishes of the Commonwealth Government.

The manner in which the APU almost immediately converted itself from a task-force charged with identifying underachievement and assisting with the amelioration of disadvantage into a monitoring body concerned with 'standards' is related in the APU evaluation. It had always intended to do so; this was merely a public acknowledgement. The circumstances were, of course, propitious since the accountability swell was running strongly in 1975 and the charges of declining 'standards' made by the Black Paper people back in 1969 still lay on the table. By the time the APU issued its first publicity material in 1976 the dominant theme was 'standards' and you had to look very hard to find any mention of underachievement. Here is what that first leaflet had to say:

> Everyone wants to raise educational standards. But how do we know what the educational standards are? How can we monitor progress? (Gipps and Goldstein, p. 15)

One statement and two questions, and the language is already loose. Is 'standards' being used to mean 'present levels of achievement'? It would appear so, but then why not say that, and leave out the troublesome word? Or is 'standards' being used to mean 'desired' or 'looked-for' levels of achievement? In other words, is the usage descriptive? There should be no doubts about this. Standards are prescriptive, even if common-language usage — standard of living, for example — wants to make them descriptive.

Doubts about the nature of that usage were cleared up in the same pamphlet.

> The first task of the APU is to identify and define standards of performance pupils might be expected to achieve through their work at school.

So the intentions are (or were) to be prescriptive. The statement could hardly be clearer. Yet a year elapses, and what do we find in the next publicity material?

> Procedures, actual tests and the conditions in which they (tests) are used vary widely; it is neither possible to compare the results nor to put them together to give a national picture of performance.
> Thus, at present, there are few national facts and figures available on which to base significant statements about standards in schools. We need such information not only to describe the current position but also to record changes as they occur.

The emphasis is back again on the descriptive — 'national picture', 'current position', etc.

These days (1984) the APU — or rather the Department of Education and Science (DES) — is going to some lengths to interpret and present the data, when in the beginning it was content to let them speak for themselves. It is now producing score cards which attempt to encapsulate the results, for example, DES (1983). But it refuses to be prescriptive; it is merely the gatherer and bearer of information and it is for others to argue over what that information means. And please don't kill the messenger! 'The aim is not to pronounce on whether standards revealed by the survey are higher or lower than they should be' (APU 1st Language Report, 1981).

Another message has come through: don't expect any help on the clarification of 'standards' because it's a bit more complicated than we thought. Here is the present chairman of the APU Consultative Committee (the Committee of the 'great and the good' which watches over the APU) writing in 1982. After claiming that the APU has helped to defuse the public argument (over the performance of schools, if it ever was a public argument) and that is all that could reasonably be expected so far, he cites three examples, of which this is the first:

> First, it (the APU) has shown how complex is the concept of 'standards', that simplistic slogan of the mid-seventies. In fact, it is some years now since we heard the word standards used *tout court*. (Dancy, 1982)

This is audacious stuff, but only to those of us who have followed the APU. We recognize the propensity and capacity to rewrite its own history, and the absence of any collective memory. As it happens, no one has used the word 'standards' more simplistically than the APU.

The only way it has shown how complex is the concept is through its own muddled thinking. The analysis which would have shown how complex the concept is — an attempt to unpack it — has not been forthcoming. And as to whether the word has been used *tout court* over the past few years — just look at the quotation from the first language report mentioned above or at this parliamentary reply from the APU's master, the former Secretary of State for Education and Science, Sir Keith Joseph, which begins, 'The Government's policies for education in schools are directed towards improving the standards attained by pupils' (Hansard, 1982). This, of course, is about as informative as saying that the Government's policy is to raise productivity or to reduce infant deaths, as the APU recognized in its first publicity material. We are left no wiser about standards, but we note that the word continues to be used when the more precise phrase 'present levels of achievement' is available, although that phrase is not without its problems, as we shall see. Presumably, politicians are unwilling to relinquish a word which is so useful in mobilizing emotion, in calling forth what *The Times* (12 April 1983) called 'the tribal cry of "Standards"'. It is instructive here to recall the 1979 Conservative Party Manifesto, which has this to say about standards and the APU:

> We shall promote higher standards of achievement in basic skills. The APU will set national standards. ... (cited in Gipps and Goldstein, p. 9)

What was that reference to simplistic slogans of the mid-seventies? The APU has, in fact, settled for a relativist formulation of standards with little descriptive content tied, quite arbitrarily, to the baseline of the first year it tested. In an appendix to the APU evaluation, Rosen (1982), writing about the language performance testing programme, complains bitterly that the whole (standards) debate has not been about what children can do with language but about whether they are getting better or worse at doing it. There are two parts to this complaint. Not only is he chiding the APU for failing to grasp the evaluative nettle (is what children can do with language satisfactory?) but he is also doubting whether the APU, because of its measurement policy, is able, anyway, to describe adequately what that is. Howson (1978), writing in the context of mathematics, echoes him on the first part. How was it, he asks, that the APU could ignore the evaluative aspect when a report from its own Ministry — *The Attainment of the School Leaver* (HMSO, 1979) — has pointed out that 'The major question ... was not so much whether the standards are rising or falling, but rather whether the standards of school-leavers are appropriate'? We are not surprised; it is clear that the APU sees itself as a data generator and nothing else. Judgments about what is adequate or appropriate can be left to others, on the basis of whatever information the APU cares to publish. That is worrying enough, but the second part of Rosen's charge is actually more serious. If national assessments cannot be trusted to represent accurately present levels of achievement (that is, cannot properly discharge the descriptive task chosen for them), then the whole exercise seems pointless. We shall take this question up later when we show how reported levels of achievement and measurement policy are wholly interdependent.

NAEP Tried to Keep 'Standards' at Arms Length but Failed

Where the APU has used 'standards' indiscriminately, its more mature counterpart in the USA has been altogether more circumspect in its use of the word. We refer to the era which has just ended with the handing over of the contract to the Educational Testing Service. Under the Education Commission of the United States NAEP did not make promises which it could not or would not deliver. A typical statement by NAEP of its own purposes was this:

> The primary goal of National Assessment is to report on the current education status of young Americans and to monitor any changes in achievement over time. (NAEP, 1980, p. 6)

Notice that while we might not like 'status' it is certainly better than 'standards'.

Here are NAEP views on standards, and the setting of them, as expressed in 1980. Even this short exegesis far surpasses anything the APU has attempted.

> NAEP understands that setting performance standards would enhance the utility of the data for some audiences. This would enable NAEP to provide literacy rates that could be used by policy makers, comparative information on subject areas that could be used by curriculum decision makers to know which areas need the most attention, guidelines for proficiency levels that could be used by states and local districts, and so on. However, such a procedure is technically difficult, politically volatile and fairly expensive. As many states and local districts have found, setting defensible criteria for required performance levels is a very difficult task. To make such statements for the nation, and have them be both equitable and meaningful, could well be impossible. (*Ibid*, p. 40)

As to what is meant by 'equitable', NAEP explains: Are reading educators requiring an equitable level of performance as compared with mathematics educators? Furthermore, should these standards be 'equal' or is reading in some sense 'more important' than mathematics? And so on. It says much for the integrity of the old NAEP that it was willing to put up these objections, especially when its future was under a cloud.

Now that the contract has gone elsewhere, it might be said to have been the victim of its own candour and scruples. Certainly, it was hesitant, for the reasons given above, to do what the evaluators asked of it, to take a more aggressive role in promoting higher standards of education across the country. Wirtz and Lapointe's assessment of NAEP was in terms of its 'potential role in developing higher and more effective educational standards' (Wirtz and Lapointe, 1982, p. x). It was, in fact, asked to be prescriptive concerning standards in future, and much play was made by the evaluators (for example, p. 24) of the importance of the 'quality' concept (then a new buzz-word in US educational circles) versus the comparison concept of standards (p. 24).

> The critical question, too rarely asked by the users of educational standards, is how good they are — not just for making comparisons but in terms of education's purposes. . . . This is increasingly important as

emphasis is moved beyond 'what is being taught' to 'what should be taught'. (p. 28)

There is no quarrel with these sentiments. What does concern us, and where we would have felt for the old NAEP had it had to act on the evaluators' chief recommendations (which it had decided against, anyway, see NAEP, 1982), is the impenetrable character of Wirtz and Lapointe's own thinking on educational standards. They introduce confusion immediately by defining an 'educational standard' as being the measuring instrument or process used to determine the level of students' educational achievement (p. 5). A 'better' educational standard is one that measures and reports more accurately on what are rationally determined, in constructing the standard, to be the critical elements of desired student achievement.

But a standard can also be made 'higher', either by improving the educational objectives on which it is based, or by raising scores or grades that are required for 'passing' and for being considered superior or excellent.

Has everyone followed that? A 'standard' — not 'standards' — can be 'better' or 'higher' or, we suppose, 'poorer' or 'lower'. A 'standard' is at once an instrument and a normative statement. Elsewhere (p. 9) Wirtz and Lapointe imply that standards cannot be defined separately from the instrument, but without explaining why this is so. Whenever they mention standards, Wirtz and Lapointe seem to have combined two senses of 'standard' — the instrument and the normative proposal — without admitting to the 'technical difficulties' of the former and the 'political volatility' of the latter recognized by NAEP in the passage quoted earlier. They also manage (p. 5) to equate 'higher educational standards' with 'raising educational standards', which are not necessarily the same thing at all (for an extended critique of Wirtz and Lapointe see Wood and Power, 1984). It is hard not to feel sympathy with the old NAEP. Now the new NAEP, under Lapointe, has a fine opportunity to do some clarifying right at the start. It is not just necessary, it is imperative.

ASSP Was All About 'Standards'

In Australia, as in the United States and Britain, the issue of 'standards' became, in the mid-1970s, a central concern in public debates about education. The publication in 1975 of the first national survey of literacy and numeracy conducted by the ACER (Australian Council for Educational Research) became a focal point and trigger for the debate. That survey was not designed as a national assessment, but it was used as one by the media and politicians and served as the blue-print for the programme created in the fall-out from the survey. For almost immediately the then Commonwealth Minister began to press for the establishment of a national system for monitoring 'standards' in basic skill areas. The end result was that ACER was commissioned in 1979 to undertake further national studies of the performance of Australian students, to be done on an annual basis beginning in 1980.

The 1980 study, which became known as ASSP, was meant 'to provide national data on aspects of student performance in basic skills'. It has not been repeated, so that unlike APU (annual since 1977) and certainly NAEP (annual since 1969), ASSP was a one-shot exercise, or two-shot if 1975 is included. Incidentally, an eminent Australian educationist felt able to say, on the basis of this one comparison, that 'there has been no decline in standards of perform-ance in any significant area over five years but that there have been improvements at a number of specific points' (quoted in Power *et al.*, 1982, p. 96). The poverty of relativism and its propensity to mislead could hardly be better illustrated.

What did ASSP, or rather ACER, mean by standards? Like its counterpart in Britain, it refused to be drawn. It saw its job as information-gathering, and when the time came found it neither 'necessary nor desirable' to make judgments as to whether the performances reported were satisfactory or not (*ibid.*, p. 95). The reticence is disappointing but at least ASSP has spared us the APU's self-serving rhetoric. What elucidation there has been has come from the evaluation. Standards, it is clear, has been used in a descriptive sense, although with strong prescriptive overtones, undoubtedly due to the explicit frame of reference — literacy and numeracy. The ASSP evaluation actually talks of a 'standard' having been planted, that standard being ASSP (*op. cit.*, p. 116). From now on, the implication is, change can be measured against this standard; all statements will be relative. It could hardly have been otherwise. ACER's attempts to define literacy and numeracy were no more successful than anyone else's, as the evaluation makes plain (pp. 55–6). They would not have stood up as prescriptions. It is anyway not just a matter of agreeing on wording. Messick (1981) has pointed out how little effort has been made to subject 'literacy' and 'numeracy' to the demands of construct validation.

There arises the awkward question: if the benchmark is suspect, is there any virtue in measuring trends from it? It is a commonplace that all standards are products of time and space, socially-produced artifacts. They compete, as Feyerabend (1981, p. 159) says. But to take this as approval of the relativist position would be quite wrong. It is prescriptions, thought valid at the time, which shift. These are not be confused with changes in trends measured from a dubious non-prescriptive baseline, for which no respectable defence seems available.

Relativist Concepts of Standards Are Futile

It was NAEP which pointed out that attempts to make absolute statements about standards have generally been abandoned in favour of relative state-ments; which means in effect that the previous level, or some agreed upon baseline which might be a weighted composite of several 'readings', serves as the 'standards'. This, we have seen, is what all three programmes opted for. Worries about this position have already been aired, but there are more. There are statistical and psychometric anxieties, and above all, concern about the veridicality of a national assessment *at any point of time*.

Consider ASSP, the 'standard' that was planted. Viewed as such, it turns out to be a rather unsatisfactory standard, thanks to the minimum competency philosophy which determined the test construction policy. Given tests containing many items with facilities in the region of 80 per cent the results were bound to be uninformative, and of limited value in terms of serving as a yardstick against which progress might be gauged. Had the policy been one of setting a high standard initially (shall we say by including items of 30 per cent facility?) the impact on the populace of the inevitably poorer results would have been harsh rather than soothing; but more would have been learned. To give a topical example, if the present emphasis in the USA on 'quality' and 'excellence' (another new buzz-word and, apparently, the stage beyond 'standards') means anything, and NAEP adapts its test construction policy accordingly, the US population may have to brace itself against the possibility of shock when progress towards 'excellence' is checked out. The APU's test construction policy (as we infer it) of choosing items to produce average scores in the region of 50 per cent now begins to look quite canny. Not only is there headroom to register improvement but even if improvement does not occur assessments will tend to convey the impression, through the middle-of-the-road performances, that things are just about where they should be. Quite clever opinion management, really, although perhaps not intended.

Behind this observation on the APU's standard-setting policy, if it can be called that, is a larger point which tends to be forgotten once the mind is constrained to run along relative standards lines. As the quotation from NAEP of its own objectives makes clear, NAEP, and the other programmes, do purport to portray the educational state of the nation *as well as* record trends over time (report on 'status' and 'monitor change'). And if they do not actually purport to do so the public, or sections of it, will do it anyway. So, in a real sense, national assessments are interpreted *absolutely* as well as relatively. It is, therefore, not good enough to use the argument which says that any one assessment in itself does not matter, because the public will not necessarily agree to avert its gaze and wait until it is told that enough data have accumulated.

It follows that the veridicality of each and every national assessment matters very much indeed; and here we want to reassert some points we have made elsewhere. We start with the observation that the public will generally believe any results of educational measurement put before it. This is not because it is necessarily gullible, but because it has no reason to disbelieve such results and, more importantly, except for a few of its members, has no means at its disposal, technical or otherwise, to enable it to dispute, or to even understand them. Naturally this is a serious matter, and it places great responsibility on those who produce and publish measures of educational performance.

Now we have seen that test construction policies affect directly the results of national assessments. Set easy tests and you get 'good news'; set middling tests and you get 'OK — could be worse'; set difficult tests and you get consternation. To a large extent, you get out what you put in. Obvious, as we said; facts of life for test constructors. But if you are a lay onlooker would you not find such arbitrariness somewhat disturbing? Would you not hold the implicit belief that when NAEP says it is reporting 'current educational status' and APU says it is going to 'describe the current position', there is only one 'status' and only one 'position'? Or, for that matter, one set of 'standards' and one 'present level of achievement', all of which will be taken to be interchangeable? It must come as a shock to be told this is not the case, but it is easily demonstrated. When ASSP reported on 'standards' in Australia, it was clearly not reporting on the present levels of achievement of all students in the nation, because the items focused only on one arbitrary level of achievement. Assessing the minimum level precludes a detailed mapping of what is being achieved at other levels and in other areas by the majority of children (who clearly are superior in terms of the minimum 'standard' employed). A national assessment powered by 'quality' or 'excellence' ideology would be quite different. It would presumably set tasks which correspond to the limits of people's capacity — when they start to fail — and results would be very different.

'Present levels of achievement' does have more than one meaning in practice; hence it is vital to spell out which is being used and why and how it will affect the results; otherwise which is a school or teacher or individual to believe? The possibility of confusion by different indicators is nicely illustrated by Farr and Olshavsky (1980). The Scholastic Aptitude Test (SAT) score decline in the USA had been taken to mean that assaults on basic literacy (sic) ought to be stepped up; but Farr and Olshavsky pointed out that if you took NAEP percentages — an altogether better test of basic literacy — the message was utterly different. If a state or school system wants to improve literacy levels, it does not seem that greater emphasis is needed on lower-level reading achievement. What is needed is increased emphasis on higher-level reading/ thinking skills. (Rosen, 1982, would want to add 'and speaking and listening skills', and so would we.)

The picture of national performance produced depends crucially on the difficulty of the items or, more generally, on the tasks employed; these in turn hinge on technical matters like item format, effect of instructions and so forth. Linn (1980) has a good demonstration of this. Nor is there any necessary one-to-one relationship between the complexity of a concept or object and the difficulty of an item which will reproduce the complexity of one in the other. As Burton (1978, p. 267) observes: 'Items can be written about a passage from Kant that 90 per cent of people can pass, and items can be written about an Ann Landers answer that few could pass'. It is the same problem which bothered Frank Womer, ex-director of NAEP, when looking at the state of Michigan's testing programme: in defining minimums, what is the appropriate level of difficulty? If school districts do poorly on minimal competency tests, does that mean that they are failing to meet minimum objectives? Not necessarily so, says Womer. Either the minimum objectives are not really minimums at all; or the test items were badly written, and turned out to be too hard. 'Womer isn't sure which, and he thinks the results are puzzling' (Murphy and Colen, 1974, p. 70).

Testing and Standards: A Complicated Relationship

Any attempt to assess national educational performance must reckon with the instrument getting in the way, to the extent that ultimately the results and the characteristics of the instrument which produces them are totally confounded. We wonder if this has been sufficiently realized by those who run the programmes. But then the relationship between testing and standards, of which this is a crucial feature, has seldom benefitted from clear analysis. That is why we think it necessary to deal with two propositions which have found favour in some quarters in recent years. The first is that testing can maintain or secure standards; the second is that testing can raise standards.

Testing to Maintain Standards

This from *The Times Educational Supplement*: 'Standards could be maintained by a test at the end of each year, he said' (15 October 1982). The speaker was Rhodes Boyson, Black Paper man and later junior Minister of Education in the UK. It is a fine example of hyperrationalization, defined by Wise (1978, p. 598) as that which obtains when efforts to rationalize persist in ignorance of the relationship between means and ends. Not only was Boyson guilty of this (we do not think he could possibly explain why testing *necessarily* maintains standards) but he managed to fuse the two completely — the means is the end.

Here, too, is an affirmation of something else he obviously believed, that 'standards' and what tests (any test?) measure are coterminous. Nothings else at school matters, or at least matters enough to be subject to 'standards'. It also helps to maintain how the APU, as claimed by Dancy (and it seems to be true) has succeeded in defusing (diffusing?) or dampening the public argument over 'standards'. The most important fact about the APU is that it is testing regularly, thereby showing concern over 'standards'. Moreover, depending on what you are prepared to believe, it is actually maintaining or protecting or securing 'standards' by the tests it gives, or even — and this is the ultimate view — by the act of testing itself. That is what has comforted, mollified, defused, diffused or dampened. No matter that a means-ends articulation in the context of national assessment, where children and teachers are not expected to prepare for the tests, is simply not plausible. Likewise, the belief that the act of testing will secure standards borders on the magical; but people hold it, or appear to by their behaviour. Wood and Gipps (1982, p. 52) write of school governors and local education councillors who lost interest in testing programmes, which in some cases they had demanded in the teeth of the 'standards' debate, once these had been established.

It is as though it was the act of setting up the testing programme that satisfied. Standards have been taken care of, and so we can forget about them. As Wise says, 'Policy makers may believe it is sufficient to cause something to occur by legislating that it should occur' (1978, p. 597).

Testing to Raise Standards

It is remarkable that while it remains extremely difficult to formulate a set of prescriptive standards which will attract any kind of consensus, there are those who are quite certain that 'standards' are not being met. That many of these people believe that testing can play a direct part in rectifying that state of affairs or, what comes to the same thing, raising 'standards' (descriptive) is even more remarkable.

The idea that testing can raise standards, albeit narrowly conceived, is, of course, immensely attractive, but it is often accompanied by hyper-rationalization. As Gipps *et al.* note (p. 188) the stimulus (testing) is applied and the outcome (improved test performance) hoped for, but the process linking the two remains largely undiscussed. There is a reluctance to fill the black box.

This suggests that any proposal for raising standards through testing should be judged in terms of the plausibility and substantiability of the 'causal narrative' which connects testing and improved performance. If results do improve, we need to know how it has happened; and, then, whether it is the sort of instrumental intervention which is liable to produce only short-term gains while causing losses elsewhere, or whether it is the kind of enriching intervention in the instructional process which will show up in the end in improved test scores *on more searching tasks*, thus constituting a true raising of standards.

It is appropriate to consider national assessment programmes first. How can they be agents for raising standards? There is no suggestion that any of the three programmes were ever expected to raise standards, although some of those associated with them, and certain interested onlookers, might have cherished wishes in that direction. But interesting things have happened. The programmes have had side effects which, for the APU at least, will have to go down as unintended consequences even though, in its usual fashion, it is now behaving as if they were intended. We are talking about the *backwash* of test materials on school curricula and teaching practices. One of the APU's strong selling points in the beginning was that schools would experience no backwash (which was thought, in the conventional wisdom, to be strictly harmful in its effects). Pupils would try only samples of items corresponding to no coherent curricular unit, there would be no opportunity to prepare for them, and the materials would be whisked away, allowing no opportunity for them to circulate. Schools would be able to go on doing what they were doing before. Measurement would *not* change what is being measured, contrary to learned opinion.

It could be argued that such strenuous defensive activity on the part of the APU indicated a lack of confidence in its own materials — for what can be wrong with allowing good things to circulate? But it was the beginning, the APU had no idea how the materials would turn out, and anyway backwash was a bad thing and assurances must be offered. These days the APU is more relaxed. Oblivious of the past, the present professional head can enthuse about 'the "beneficial backwash" of the research' (Clegg, 1983). And there are no qualms about promulgating new orthodoxy. 'Good assessment' opines Clegg, 'is seen as indicative of clear teaching intention.' What does that mean? Borrowing the APU's assessment techniques will make teachers into good teachers? Get the assessment right and the rest will follow? Is he paving the way for assessment-led instruction (unlikely)? Who knows what Clegg meant? The fact is that it was always likely that APU materials would be seized upon. If the materials suggest curricular and instructional possibilities which are likely to constitute an improvement on what is happening at present, then of course they will be taken up. Gipps *et al.* (p. 189) discovered early on that local authority advisors who had seen the materials were 'delighted' with the APU mathematics and science tests, and positively wished them to affect the curriculum.

That the APU was able to produce superior materials is not to wondered at, given the funding and human resource input. The same can be said of NAEP. In fact, APU has been given the sort of support which used to be enjoyed by the big curriculum reform projects like Nuffield. This provokes the heretical thought that the APU is the nearest thing to a curriculum reform project in the United Kingdom, given that such projects have gone out of fashion. The APU Science teams have probably always seen themselves as being in the business of curriculum reform in the tradition of Nuffield and Science 5–13; almost from the beginning they were talking about the need to 'manage' backwash.

Black, Harlen and Orgee (1984, p. 17), members of the Science teams, are quite categorical. Far from the tests being opposed or rejected as an unwelcome or irrelevant intrusion, ideas from them are being taken up and considered for use in teaching and as indicators for possible lines of curriculum development.

Where NAEP is concerned, there has been less talk of backwash as such, positive or negative. In any case, NAEP has always been keen that its materials be used, and there is plently of evidence on this score (see, for instance, Sebring and Boruch, 1983). Whether such usage will lead to the sort of real rise in standards which could conceivably happen in the United Kingdom as a result of using tests to manipulate teaching practices, is not clear. The examples available suggest not. A statement such as 'the broad scope of the

National Assessment goals helped to guard against "insular thinking" and the tendency to emphasize lower-level, easy-to-measure objectives when setting district goals' (*NAEP Newsletter*, Winter 1983, p. 6) suggests at most that NAEP contact will help to stop standards falling rather than anything more positive. To set against that is a report by Atwater (1981) which claims that NAEP's method of evaluating writing can teach youngsters to write.

The fact is that the results are not yet in, or have not been collected, so the verdict must be withheld. Perhaps in the end, the continuing programmes, NAEP and APU, will be credited with genuine rises of standards in pockets, here and there, but more by the indirect routes discussed than by more direct methods, such as educators taking action to rectify deficiencies on the basis of national results alone — never a realistic causal narrative.

There is one national assessment programme not yet launched which aims for a direct raising of standards. The document, *A Proposal for Raising the Standards of Numeracy at the Primary Level in Trinidad and Tobago* (University of the West Indies, 1982) begins, 'The Ministry of Education has determined that the level of numeracy attained by the average primary school leaver does not constitute adequate preparation for functioning usefully in the rapidly changing society of Trinidad and Tobago'. It proceeds to set forth a plan for putting this right which depends crucially on one or more national assessments of numeracy. But it is not like the other national assessment programmes, for here the connecting rod between assessment and higher standards is a teacher training programme. The first national assesssment will aim to expose deficiencies, after which another national assessment will be used to check whether further remedies are necessary or whether, in the words of the proposal, an acceptable standard of mathematical achievement has been sustained. It is a national assessment model for the Third World. Notice, however, that all problems concerning the definition of standards and of numeracy and the veridicality of national assessments remain. But at least an effort has been made to fill the black box, in contrast to other programmes. McLean (1982, p. 94), writing of provincial assessment programs in Canada, and commenting on the absence of any plans to feed results back to schools, remarks that the implication seems to be that everyone will know what to do when they receive the monitoring results. They do not.

A school in the USA is never going to work deliberately to change its national assessment results. There would be no point. But it can work to change its state-wide assessment results, where that assessment is of all students in all schools, and is regarded, in the classic accountability formulation, as a measure of a school's capability to educate students. It can do so by teaching to the test, and if successful, can claim to have raised 'standards', thus lifting pressure off itself. An example in California raises in sharp relief this vexatious issue. Under a headline ' "Teaching to the test" credited with improvement in basic skills', the article (*San Diego Union*, 1982) describes how schools in San Diego County have registered sizeable score increases on the annual California Assessment Program (CAP) tests by teaching to the test. They did this by remodelling their curriculum to emphasize material tested by the CAP, and by schooling students to be test-wise. The most revealing quotation in the whole piece comes from a superintendent who defended his district's policy by arguing that the skills tested by CAP are 'skills which every school system believes are important anyway'. Here is the crux of the matter. Those who are persuaded by this superintendent will be inclined to reject a statement like 'lifting education standards must be more than raising test scores' (Green, 1983).

It is because the superintendent's defence has seemed to carry conviction that the opprobrium attached to teaching to the test has been relaxed in recent years. Fredericksen's (1979) anecdotal example of replacing the desks in gunnery school with guns and replacing pencil and paper tests with gunnery performance tests made an impression. That activity, however, was single-minded. In schools where there are so many claims on attention, it is not enough to decide that the skills are worth having; there is also the question of whether too much time is spent on having students acquire them, at the expense of other items on the curriculum not being tested. This has seemed to worry critics most. Madaus and McDonagh (1979) while allowing that the quickest way to introduce new curriculum material is to include it in an examination — not a bad thing, one would think — go on to state categorically that the principal negative effect on teaching is that inordinate amounts of time are often devoted to coaching for the certifying test, often at the expense of the uncertified subjects or of the broader aims of schooling, including vocational preparation. The statement is not substantiated; it is taken as a 'given' as we can judge from the fact that it is prefaced with the word 'historically'. Airasian and Madaus (1983) do the same. After carefully and soberly sifting through work relating testing to instruction, they launch, at the very end of their piece, and in a noticeably emotional tone ('corrupt', 'destroy', 'distort', 'devaluing'), into the same kind of diatribe which, if it were directed at a person, would have to be called character assassination.

Here is a problem already remarked on. So much of the discussion in this area is at the level of assertion without substantiation. The dangers are clear, but is that what happens? Examinations, it is said, have a 'narrowing effect on the curriculum' (despite their function as channels for new, and hopefully broadening material); they have a stultifying effect on students, and so on. No doubt we have all said this sort of thing, but where is the evidence? Perhaps examinations foster learning, or facilitate future learning; but has anyone taken the trouble to find out? (One of us remembers a few years ago reviewing a proposal to the old Social Science Research Council to do just this, and being surprised that no one had come up with it before. As far as we know, the proposal was not funded.)

The movement in the USA which goes under the name 'measurement-driven instruction' (in the United Kingdom 'assessment-led instruction', although it is hardly a movement there) represents an attempt to make respectable the notion of 'teaching to the test'. The prime mover, Jim Popham, argues that when educators are admonished not to 'teach to the test' it means that they should not 'teach to a particular set of test items'. To teach directly *toward the competency* (his italics) being measured by a test constitutes, he says, truly enlightened instruction (Popham, 1980, p. 533). Readers will have to judge whether there is much of a difference between Popham's position and that of the San Diego superintendent. Some will think that if Popham had added the rider 'but if preparing for the particular set of items, or items like them, causes students to acquire targeted skills' there would be no difference between the positions at all. It is true that elsewhere (Popham and Rankin, 1981) Popham provides an example of measurement-driven instruction in practice which attempts to fill the black box by providing a programme of support for instructors, but then the San Diego teachers also took steps to make their teaching more successful. We come back to the same point. We need to see the evidence concerning the efficacy, short-term and long-term, of measurement-driven instruction in Detroit (Popham and Rankin's test-bed) and elsewhere, for example, the so-called Network for Outcome Based Schools, for which extravagant claims have been made (Spady, 1982).

The idea that testing can raise standards (in skills that are testable) is either taken very seriously, or not seriously at all. There seems to be a lack of balance. Testing, or more broadly assessment, evidently produces so many effects that it would be foolish to rule out the possibility that it could actually be beneficial. So much depends on individual reaction to cases. We have mentioned some; here is another from Gipps *et al.* (p. 189). How might the introduction of testing result in improved test performance? By focusing attention on particular subject areas. It appears that some head teachers of primary schools in the United Kingdom insisted that reading be timetabled because the local authority had introduced a reading testing programme ostensibly (although they could not be sure) for monitoring purposes. Elsewhere the range of Edinburgh Reading tests has been chosen by some advisors precisely because these tests promote a wider view of reading. Madaus and McDonagh (*op. cit.*) have other examples of how tests or examinations have been used to manage curriculum change; indeed without them change could not have occurred. The belief that extrinsic motivation cannot possibly lead to consolidated learning is entirely in keeping with the notion, made fashionable a few years ago by Miller and Parlett (1974), that once an examination is over, the brain (or is it the mind?) 'dumps' whatever it has learned, just as if it were a computer. This must have come as bad news to all those who replied on professionals remembering something, at least, of what they had learned in order to pass examinations. Fortunately, they did.

Standards in an Individualistic Society

Lapointe and Koffler title their article 'Your standards or mine?' and promptly proceed to ignore the question, which is a valid and interesting one. Now that

Lapointe is running NAEP, which he has committed to a prescriptive position on standards, he will find it difficult to avoid the question. Perhaps he will deal with it as the College Board (part of the Educational Testing Service, as it happens) dealt with it, by trying to build a consensus impressive enough to nullify the question. The College Board claims to have secured a consensus from 'among hundreds of school and college educators, lay people concerned with education, and subject-matter specialists' for what it calls 'preferred patterns of preparation' for college in the 1980s and beyond. The 'patterns' fall into two broad categories: basic academic competencies, or skills a student should possess in order to succeed in college; and academic learning outcomes, or the specific subject-matter knowledge a student should have to begin college work (Hanford, 1982). They are 'standards' in all but name. But of course, they are College Board 'standards' despite claims of consensus, as Bollenbacher (1982, p. 9) was quick to point out. In her view, another test is on the way, and 'once again schools are likely to face another set of problems not of their own making'.

There are two points here. First, schools dare not avoid trying to meet 'standards' such as these on behalf of their students thus submitting to a form of coercion. What is also at stake is that if the 'standards' are other than hand-waving pieties, there is the strong likelihood that the schools (which means teachers, parents, children, the local community) will reject some of them, or, more likely, will disagree among themselves. An interesting little study carried out recently in the United Kingdom bears this out. When groups of parents, teachers, advisers, science educators and employers were asked, in relation to science questions given to 11-year-olds in APU surveys, what were the actual levels of performance, not only were there wide inter-group differences but also wide intra-group differences. Teachers, parents and employers could not agree among themselves, either on what children do know, or on what they should know (Black, Harlen and Orgee, 1984).

This study, of course, was done in an atmosphere where there was no press for consensus; indeed there was as much interest in exposing the lack of consensus. What, one wonders, would happen if Mondale's proposed national fund for excellence (*The Times Higher Education Supplement*, 20 May 1983, p. 6) was ever to get off the ground? The plan is for individual communities to determine their own standards of excellence, following which the United States government would fund them directly to implement their programmes. The press for consensus would be there, but it would struggle against individualistic tendencies which run deeper than surface disagreement on whether, for instance, children need to know chemical formulae. This is because people differ in their conceptions and understanding of what schools are like and what they should expect and strive to achieve for their children and those of others. The teacher with children is in a particularly poignant position. Moreover, these differences are heavily conditioned by social class, educational background, purposes, occupation, value system and concept of education. Finch and Scrimshaw (1980, p. 3) rightly point to the central role of discrepancies in values in the 'standards' debate, and to the confused ideological interface between the issues of standards, equality and social justice.

Raven's (1981) article illustrates very well how individualism collides with societal prescriptions. On asking parents whether educational provision should be tailored to the needs of individual pupils, the answer was emphatically that it should not. All children should be treated equally, otherwise children of the more powerful and articulate would get the 'best' deals. There was little recognition of the fact that different people define 'the best' in different ways. The next thing Raven discovered was that parents wanted children to develop qualities which were incompatible with those which other parents wanted their children to develop. Thus, some parents wanted their children to be independent and think for themselves, question authority and respect other people. Others wanted their children to learn dependence, to learn only what they were taught, not to ask questions, and to be strong, tough and able to get the better of others. These incompatible demands, taken in the context of an insistence on equality and lack of diversified treatment, lead schools (Raven thought) to teach towards the lowest common denominator in parental demand (of which teaching to a limited set of basic cognitive skills called literacy and numeracy may be the best example).

On the whole — APU's flirtation with moral and ethical development apart — national assessment programme planners have instinctively realized all this, which is why their products are so slight. Minimal literacy is at a high level, not-quite-minimal literacy is at a middling level, and so on.

We have struggled without success to understand what Wirtz and Lapointe meant when they wrote of an 'educational standards concept' and an 'educational standards' policy. We doubt that it means anything more than what has already been offered. Even well-meaning and disinterested commentators who talk about the need to foster 'quality' education seem only to have in mind going beyond minimum skills to the ways knowledge is used and concepts are applied (for example, Greene, 1983). The sort of bold alternative which would attempt to associate 'standards' with, say, a developmental view, in which the growth of meaning, understanding and intellectual processes are important, and the fostering of self-actualization and autonomy imperative, finds no mention. Standards, according to this paradigm, would be represented as complex descriptions of process and stage of development reached — a totally different formulation from a series of facility values on largely unconnected items. Of course, it too could founder on lack of consensus.

An American professor of education is quoted in *US News and World Report* (19 September 1983, p. 50) as saying that 'American education has bottomed out and is on the upswing', which suggests that boosterism has reached education. Husén (1983, p. 460) has 'dared to submit' that the new concern for excellence in the USA may be missing the point. Low standards, he says (presumably thinking of them defined in the usual prosaic fashion) are not the most serious problem with public schooling — either in the USA or elsewhere. Standards in terms of average performance can easily be raised by

227

making a system more selective. The real, and most serious problem ... well, we can all provide our own analysis; for Husén it is the emergence of a new educational underclass, encouraged by the promise of equality but defeated by the workings of meritocracy.

Husén is right; neurotic and panicky talk about 'standards', arguably a cyclical phenomenon which always reappears at times of economic and social crisis, does distract us away from the real and serious problems, and it may be meant to. Perhaps that is the greatest harm which 'standards' rhetoric — and, by extension, national assessment programmes — can do. From now on, any project which aims to survey what schools manage to do with students — let us drop the word 'standards', it is probably beyond redemption — ought to concern itself, as best it can, with the whole business of schooling and, above all, with teaching and learning. A study like that of Goodlad and his colleagues at UCLA (Sirotnik, 1983), based on observations in 1000 classrooms, is more informative than scores of national assessments.

National assessment programmes, whether or not they mean to, promote a view of 'standards' (that is to say, a view of what education is meant to be doing) which, in its emphasis on basic or minimal accomplishments of a severely selected kind, is narrowing and limiting, and definitely not conducive to the emergence of flexible and imaginative educational policies designed to cope with the future.

It is no good arguing that these programmes can safely be left to grind on, like many another social data-gathering exercise. The prospensity (understandable) of people to regard them as providing a true reading of a nation's educational health is too great. They ought to come clean, contribute to our understanding, or — failing that — be scrapped (as in Australia).

References

AIRASIAN, P.W. and MADAUS, G.F. (1983) 'Linking testing and instruction: Policy issues', *Journal of Educational Measurement*, 20, pp. 103–18.

APU (1980) *The APU — What it is — How it Works*, London, DES.

APU (1981) *Language Performance in Schools, Primary Survey Report No. 1*, London, HMSO.

ATWATER, J.D. (1981) *Better Testing, Better Writing*, Naugatuck, CN, Ford Foundation.

BLACK, P., HARLEN, W. and ORGEE, T. (1984) 'Standards of performance — expectations and reality', *APU Occasional Paper 3*.

BOLLENBACHER, J.F. (1982) Remarks in: *Educational Measurement: Issues and Practice*, 1, p. 9.

BURTON, N.B. (1978) 'Societal standards', *Journal of Educational Measurement*, 15, pp. 263–71.

CLEGG, A.G. (1983) 'Five lessons before Christmas', *APU Newsletter*, 4, p. 8.

DANCY, J. (1982) 'The APU and teachers', *APU Newsletter*, 1, p. 1.

DEPARTMENT OF EDUCATION AND SCIENCE (1983) *How Well Can 15 year olds Write?*, London, HMSO.

FARR, R. and OLSHAVSKY, J.E. (1980) 'Is minimum competency testing the appropriate solution to the SAT decline?' *Phi Delta Kappan*, April, pp. 528–30.

FEYERABEND, P. (1981) 'How to defend society against science', in HACKING, I. (Ed.) *Scientific Revolutions*, London, Cambridge University Press.

FINCH, A. and SCRIMSHAW, P. (Eds.) (1980) *Standards, Schooling and Education*, Sevenoaks, Hodder & Stoughton.

FREDERIKSEN, N. (1979) 'Some emerging trends in testing', in *Testing, Teaching and Learning*, Washington, National Institute of Education pp. 186–203.

GIPPS, C.V. and GOLDSTEIN, H. (1983) *Monitoring Children: An Evaluation of the Assessment of Performance Unit*, London, Heinemann.

GIPPS, C.V. et al. (1983) *Testing Children: Standardized Testing in Local Education Authorities and Schools*, London, Heinemann.

GREENE, M. (1983) Remarks in: *NAEP Newsletter*, winter, p. 7.

HANFORD, G.H. (1982) 'Tackling the crises in secondary schools', *New York Times*, 4 September, p. 21.

HANSARD (1982) 'Assessment of Performance Unit', *Briefing*, 345, pp. 13–14.

HER MAJESTY'S STATIONERY OFFICE (1977) *Attainments of the School Leaver*, London, HMSO.

HOWSON, G. (1978) 'Assessing the APU', Supplement to *Education*, 21 July, p. viii.

HUSÉN, T. (1983) 'Are standards in US schools really lagging behind those in other countries?', *Phi Delta Kappan*, March, pp. 455–61.

LAPOINTE, A.E. and KOFFLER, S.L. (1982) 'Your standards or mine?', *Educational Researcher*, December, pp. 4–11.

LINN, R.L. (1980) 'Issues of validity for criterion-referenced measures', *Applied Psychological Measurement*, 4, pp. 547–62.

MADAUS, G.F. and McDONAGH, J.T. (1979) 'Minimum competency testing; Unexamined assumptions and unexplored negative outcomes', *New Directions for Testing Measurement*, 3, pp. 1–14.

McLEAN, L.D. (1982) 'Educational assessment in the Canadian provinces', *Educational Analysis*, 4, pp. 79–96.

MESSICK, S. (1981) 'Constructs and their vicissitudes in educational and psychological measurement', *Psychological Bulletin*, 89, pp. 575–88.

MILLER, C.M.L. and PARLETT, M. (1974) *Up to the Mark*, London, Society for Research in Higher Education.

MURPHY, J.T. and COHEN, D.K. (1974) 'Accountability in education — the Michigan experience', *The Public Interest*, 36, pp. 53–81.

NAEP (1980) *Issues in the Analysis of Change of National Assessment Data*, Report No. 12-IP-57, Denver, Education Commission of the States.

NAEP (1982) *Standards and National Assessment*, Report No. AY-HS-50 Denver, Education Commission of the States.

NAEP (1983) *Newsletter*, winter.

POPHAM, W.J. (1980) 'Educational measurement for the improvement of instruction', *Phi Delta Kappan*, April, pp. 531–4.

POPHAM, W.J. and RANKIN, S.C. (1981) 'Minimum competency tests spur instructional improvement', *Phi Delta Kappan*, May, pp. 637–9.

POWER, C.N. and WOOD, R. (1984) 'National assessment: A review of programmes in Australia, United Kingdom and the United States', *Comparative Education Review*, 28, pp. 355–77.

POWER, C.N. et al. (1982) *National Assessment in Australia: An Evaluation of the Australian Studies in Student Performance Project*, EDRC Report No. 35, Canberra, Australian Government Printing Service.

RAVEN, J. (1981) 'The most important problem in education is to come to terms with values', *Oxford Review of Education*, 7, pp. 253–72.

ROSEN, H. (1982) *The Language Monitors*, Bedford Way Papers No. 11 University of London Institute of Education, an abridged version is available as Appendix 8 (iv) in Gipps et al., *op. cit.*

SAN DIEGO UNION (1982) 'County students improve CAP scores; "Teaching to the test" credited with improvement in basic skills', 2 December.

SEBRING, P.A. and BORUCH, R.F. (1983) 'How is national assessment of educational progress used?', *Educational Measurement Issues and Practices*, Spring, pp. 16–20.

SIROTNIK, K.A. (1983) 'What you see is what you get — consistency, persistency and mediocrity in classrooms', *Harvard Educational Review*, 53, pp. 16–31.

SPADY, W. (1982) 'Outcome-based instructional systems', *Evaluation Comment*, 6, pp. 10–11.

THE TIMES HIGHER EDUCATION SUPPLEMENT (1983) 20 May, pp. 1 and 6.

UNIVERSITY OF THE WEST INDIES (1982) *A Proposal for Raising the Standard of Numeracy at the Primary Level in Trinidad and Tobago*, St. Augustine, Trinidad, School of Education.

WIRTZ, W. and LAPOINTE, A.E. (1982) *Measuring the Quality of Education: A Report on Assessment Educational Progress*, Washington, D.C. Wirtz and Lapointe.

WISE, A.E. (1978) 'Minimum competency testing: Another case of hyperrationalization', *Phi Delta Kappan*, May, pp. 596–8.

WOOD, R. and GIPPS, C.V. (1982) 'An enquiry into the use of test results for accountability purposes' in MCCORMICK, R. (Ed.) *Calling Education to Account*, London, Heinemann/Open University.

WOOD, R. and POWER, C.N. (1984) 'Review of W. Wirtz and A.E. Lapointe. *Measuring the Quality of Education: A Report on Assessing Educational Progress*', *Journal of Educational Measurement*, 21, pp. 209–12.

VIII The Agenda For Educational Measurement

Comments

The first paper was written in 1982 and revised in early 1984. The second paper was begun in 1984 and completed in early 1986. Desmond Nuttall was kind enough to say of the first that it 'conducts and orchestrates the reconstruction of educational measurement that is long overdue' (Nuttall, 1986, p. 4). If I were to extend the musical metaphor, I would say that the second paper fills in some of the parts. It was certainly intended to take further the 'programme' for educational measurement set out in the first paper.

I would like to think that the distinction between educational and psychological measurement is acceptable and means something, and I write as someone who is active on both sides of the divide. I must confess — in the first paper — to contributing to the confusion when I urge that Sandra Scarr's proposals be assimilated into educational measurement. I am afraid my keenness to put daylight between educational and psychological measurement got the better of me. Now I would want — as I do in the Introduction — to categorize Scarr's proposals as educational assessment.

The second paper represents a considerable expansion of the theme of actualizing competence only touched on in the first paper. The power of Vygotsky's ideas is acknowledged. The references to competence in the first paper were vague and are superseded by the treatment in the second paper. Evidently, there is a need to work out suitable measurement routines and Power and I regard this as unfinished business.

The casting of competence strictly in developmental terms serves to emphasize the call for attention to individual growth and change which is a feature of Carver's 'edumetrics'. I would like to see more effort put into the measurement of learning and growth, whether within a competence paradigm or not. In that connection I would urge that greater attention be paid to the *metrics* of measurement, for what could be more fundamental to educational measurement? As far as I can see only Barbara Heyns has grappled with this subject in recent years (Heyns, 1980).

References

HEYNS, B. (1980) 'Models and measurement for the study of growth', in DREEBEN, R. and THOMAS, J.A. (Eds.) *The Analysis of Educational Productivity*, Vol. I. Cambridge, MA, Ballinger Publishing Co.

NUTTALL, D.L. (1986) 'Introduction' in NUTTALL, D.L. (Ed.) *Assessing Educational Achievement*, Lewes, Falmer Press.

Paper 21: The Agenda for Educational Measurement*

It is no longer necessary to plead for a distinction to be made between educational and psychological measurement but much remains to be done to elaborate and substantiate that distinction. To argue, as some of us have done, that educational measurement has for too long been under the sway of psychometrics is one thing, to establish what educational measurement is, or rather should be, is quite another.

The term itself tends to encourage people to equate 'measurement in education' with 'educational measurement'. What is needed is a striking word to signal a fresh enterprise. At one time I thought Carver's (1974) 'edumetrics' might do the job but it is an ugly word which does not seem to have stuck. What C.P. Scott is supposed to have said about television comes to mind: 'No good will come of this device. The word is half Greek and half Latin.'

Education has always been vulnerable to psychometric incursions and influence, although less so now than before. Lacking a distinctive and self-confident view about the purpose of testing in schools and about what kinds of tests were suitable and unsuitable, it has, rather like a client state, looked on helplessly as psychometric doctrines and practices have been installed and put to work. Which is not to say that there have not been, at all times, as in all client states, individuals in education ready and eager to embrace psychometric assumptions and beliefs about how children differ, and to suppress curiosity about the children themselves.[2] I should add that the classroom has been, for psychometricians, an excellent source of cheap available data.

But education and differential psychology do not have the same aims. Education is not, as far as I know, a permanent research endeavour, although in certain circumstances and at different times it can be made to yield research data (although not the sort that psychometricians took so freely). Educators, by and large, have to take children and students as they find them. This was the message which emerged from the 'Heredity and IQ' debate precipitated by

---

*Reprinted from *Assessing Educational Achievement*, NUTTALL, D.L. (Ed.) Falmer Press, 1986.[1]

Jensen (1969), an affair which symbolizes education's growing determination to fend off gratuitous psychometric thinking. At the end of it all even someone like Bereiter, in an article characterized by Jensen as 'an exceptionally intelligent and penetrating analysis', was obliged to state that, with respect to social and racial differences, knowledge of a possible genetic basis is relevant neither to the classroom teacher nor to the educational policy makers.[3]

Some History

That educational and psychological measurement have long been differentiated in *name* is not in doubt; as early as 1918 Ayres was able to write a *history* of educational measurement; there was Monroe's book in 1923 and the founding of the journal *Educational and Psychological Measurement* in 1941. But was educational measurement ever seen as anything other than the application of psychological measurement in an educational setting? The universal answer up to about 1950 would appear to have been 'no'. Nunnally (1975) revealed more than he knew when he wrote, 'Is there an important place for traditional measures of aptitude and achievement in modern education? In 1950 most persons who were prominent either in psychometric research or in education would immediately have answered 'yes' but now there is a lively controversy about the matter.'

It is possible Nunnally took too sanguine a view. Consider *Educational and Psychological Measurement*, admittedly a journal which in all respects has changed little over the years. If you read the inside front cover you will see that it is, as it always was, concerned first and foremost with studies of individual differences, that is to say, with psychometrics or psychological measurement. Other categories of paper are mentioned but you will search in vain for a definition or description of educational measurement, even one as partial as Carver's (1974) 'measurement of intra-individual differences'. In important respects, the psychometric hegemony persists, or do I read too much into the fact that Robert Thorndike's recent book (1982) about educational measurement is called *Applied Psychometrics*?

It could have been different. Levine (1976) draws a picture of 'professional test constructors' consistently overriding the requirement of classroom usefulness — 'test constructors wanted to construct tests with good measurement properties amenable to statistical analysis' — so fitting the educational foot to the psychometric shoe. There was an opportunity in the 1930s when Hawkes *et al.* (1936) pointed out that achievement could have been measured in absolute units, in relation to some absolute standard, or even in relation to some passing grade, but these same people managed to argue themselves out of this idea and the chance was lost.

Nunnally's choice of 1950 as a watershed year is significant because by then a group of American educators had already been working for two years on what turned out to be the *Taxonomy of Educational Objectives*, Vol. 1 (Bloom *et al.*, 1956). That ambitious and singular endeavour had little to say about measurement as such (although it did mention promising ideas like the Tab test, a primitive forerunner of the tailored test) but it was immensely successful — and subsequent denigration has done nothing to diminish this — in dramatizing (and often stimulating) a felt need among educators for an approach to measurement which would be reflective of and responsive to what is peculiar to education, in particular the cycle of planning, instruction, learning, achievement and measurement. The mistake Bloom and his colleagues made, as we can see with hindsight, was to formulate educational objectives in ad hoc and naive psychological language. That this formulation exposed a flank which critics, especially philosophers, savaged is of less concern than that the *Taxonomy* gave the impression that educational measurement was still concerned with psychological constructs, indeed more so than ever. The consequence was that lay people, who had hitherto talked about content or just material to be learned, having perhaps been weaned away from faculty psychology not so long before, now wedded themselves to a new orthodoxy whose categories they did not understand, naive though these were, and which, in the course of time, they came to reify.

But none of this held up the emergence of educational measurement. By the time criticism of the *Taxonomy* had become commonplace and its unfortunate side-effects had taken hold, a crucial event for educational measurement had long since taken place. This was the publication of Glaser's (1963) seminal paper in which he introduced the notions of criterion referencing and criterion-referenced testing (CRT) and differentiated them sharply from norm-referenced testing, emphasis on which, he thought, had been brought about by the preoccupation of test theory with aptitude and with selection and prediction problems. It is true, as Glaser acknowledged, that others had made this distinction previously[4] but it was Glaser's paper which caught the imagination. It can be said to mark the point at which educational measurement began to detach itself from classical psychometrics.

Since then there has been much embellishment, but little invention. Criterion-referenced testing remains the embodiment of educational measurement; notions like mastery testing (although not mastery learning) and minimum competency testing are only developed versions of the original conception, given a particular twist. There is an irony here. The original conception was borrowed from psychology, to some minds a rather dubious branch of psychology which education ought to have resisted.[5]

The odd thing is — and here is another irony — that a paradigm of learning which in the psychological context is not readily associated with a benign, caring disposition towards the individual is, when translated to the educational context, and by dint of a heavily emphasized contrast with norm-referenced testing, and the evils thereof, turned into an instrument of educational equity or even deliverance for the individual. The persistent tendency to disparage the norm-referenced test reached ludicrous proportions when two educators, English not American (Guy and Chambers, 1973 and 1974), wrote a bizarre article denouncing norm-referenced examinations as a violation of students' civil rights because they are made to show their ignorance. I wonder what they would say now as minimum competency tests, constructed on the most impeccable CRT principles, are being hauled regularly through the US courts by individuals who claim that their civil rights are being violated because the state is withholding learning certificates or diplomas granted as a result of these tests. Evidently there is a less benign aspect to CRT. The point is, of course, that the concept of referencing is ultimately irrelevant.[6] Powerful though it may be in mobilizing emotion, it is subordinate to that of function; that is to say, measures can be used for selection, screening or monitoring whatever the referencing assigned to them (Wood, 1976). We might object that referencing determines test construction policy which in turn rules out certain functions but the fact remains that CRT results can be put to purposes generally associated with norm-referenced testing. The effect is the same, as witness the example above.

Changing Functions of Measurement in Society

The Civil Rights legislation in the United States shook up the testing scene and it has never been the same since. Whereas psychological tests had been used for forty years without any obvious objection and apparently in the public interest, indeed the rationale for their use was that of promoting equal opportunity or advancement through talent rather than social connections (Resnick, 1981), the use of tests to sort people into predetermined categories now seemed distasteful, even obnoxious, and the whole testing system (or industry, as critics have always preferred to call it) a positive hindrance to the realization of equal opportunity in its now much broadened form. It had been noticed that equal opportunity to sit a test is not to be equated with equal opportunity for continuing education, not to mention other desiderata. The meritocratic principle no longer seemed sound or even admirable.

And the critics were right about the tests. They did have nothing to say about children themselves, only about where they stood in relation to each other on some fictional scale; nevertheless, position on this scale, however uninformative about what you could do, and could not do, was tremendously decisive in the matter of life chances. What was wanted now were forms of assessment which above all closed no doors but also drew attention to problems and strengths an individual might have (Gordon and Terrell, 1981). More generally, the search was on for approaches to measurement which would be reflective of and responsive to what is peculiar to education — learning and instruction and school life — and would also be in the best interests of individuals.

Educational measurement can be seen as an attempt to use measurement constructively in the service of individual children and students, to shift the emphasis away from between-individual differences to within-individual differences (Carver, 1974). But it is a matter of emphasis; clearly it would be humbug to suggest that we are no longer interested in individual differences or are not prepared to attend to them. One well-known American educator in the sixties seemed to be wishing away individual differences, or worse, thought he could remove them.[7]

Paying Attention to Where the Data Came From

Attempts to differentiate educational from psychological measurement have generally been made in terms of the function or purpose of measurement, and the consequences for the individual of the act of measurement. Further differentiation can, and ought, to be made in terms of the data the two kinds of measurement produce, and the methods of analysis which are appropriate for treating each. Evidently one major difference is that achievement data arise as a direct result of instruction and are therefore crucially affected by teaching and teachers. Any model for analyzing such data which neglects to incorporate some sort of teaching effect (never mind other effects which are responsible for variation, like interactions) is simply not credible, yet how often are models built expressly for treating psychological data, sometimes of a most specialized kind, taken over and offered as plausible descriptions of how achievement occurs? The experience with the Rasch model over the past decade (actually only one of his models and a rather thin psychological model at that) is instructive (see Goldstein, 1979, for fuller strictures). For the same reason, and because achievement data are 'dirty' compared to aptitude data, which plays havoc with given notions about dimensionality and traits, it is likely to be a waste of time applying the well-worn psychometric apparatus — reliability, validity, internal consistency, homogeneity, etc. But people go on doing it. No doubt the cause lies in the absence of theory to explain or elucidate achievement, which induces desperation and panic.[8] But it is not clear how enlightenment will come from applying inappropriate models to data.

An Extreme Proposal

A radical move would be to ignore psychology altogether and that is what McIntyre and Brown (1978) did. Until they came along no one was prepared to argue that educational achievement has nothing to do with psychology and, by extension, that educational measurement has nothing to do with psychometrics. This is such a bold forthright solution that one has to admire it, but it is also so provocative that it cannot be allowed to pass, especially as they go on to call for educational measurement to be abandoned.

Educational objectives, state McIntyre and Brown, have nothing to do with the psychology of thinking:

> When we talk about educational attainment, then we are concerned with whether or not intentions that various kinds of knowledge and ability should be mastered have been realized. Neither questions

about patterns of variation among people nor questions about processes of learning and thinking are relevant to such judgments, there is indeed no way in which psychology would seem to be logically relevant to such judgments.

They continue, 'Furthermore we would stress that it is on an understanding of the processes of thinking involved in these subjects that educational objectives depend, since the criteria which inform educational objectives are intrinsic to the subjects, not to the psychology of thinking' (p. 42).

Taking the last statement first, it presents no difficulty because it is tautologous, the consequence follows from the way educational objectives are defined. And does the definition have to be so heavily subject-bound? How would a cross-disciplinary ability like problem-solving be treated? Perhaps it would not be allowed as an objective. All the same, one knows what they are getting at. The application of Piaget's scheme to 'O' level science courses (for example, Shayer *et al.*, 1975) may have elucidated why students fail but they still failed, which means that educational objectives have not yet been realized. One cannot quarrel with this, given the terms of the argument, but, of course, it is precisely the uncurious character of this conceptualization of attainment which Shayer and others reacted against. The point about their work is that it can, and does, lead to improvement in the way mastery is ascertained, as well as to increased understanding of how a subject should be taught. Ascertainment of mastery is crucial to the McIntyre-Brown formulation. In the first quotation they are clearly right, logically at any rate, about variation being irrelevant, and this process I have dealt with. It is the first sentence from 'intentions' onwards which catches the eye. Allowing that 'knowledge' and 'abilities' must be classed as mental predicates, to use Gilbert Ryle's term, if not psychological constructs, the question arises, 'Can you check whether such predicates/constructs have been mastered without invoking psychological categories?'

This question would have appealed to Ryle. As a matter of fact, the McIntyre-Brown method of argument is distinctly reminiscent of the no-nonsense treatment of psychology meted out in chapter 2 of *The Concept of Mind* (Ryle, 1949). Compare the second quotation above with this from Ryle.

The competent critic of prose style, experimental technique or embroidery, must at least know how to write, experiment or sew. Whether or not he has also learned psychology matters about as much as whether he has learned any chemistry, neurology or economics.

Like Ryle, McIntyre and Brown want no truck with the 'ghost in the machine', preferring instead to deal with 'intentions'; tricky philosophical ground, one would have thought, on to which Ryle would not necessarily have been willing to follow them. Whose 'intentions' are we talking about? The teacher's, the student's, the parents'? If it is the teacher's, as appears to be the case, is it fair to tie a *student's* mastery to a *teacher's* intentions?

Ascertainment of mastery seems not to be thought particularly problematical; perhaps as Ryle would likely have done, McIntyre and Brown argue that knowledge and abilities can be observed directly, in the spirit of knowing *how* rather than knowing *what*. But judging whether a student knows the difference between a concept and a principle is not at all the same as judging whether a man knows how to shoot (to use one of Ryle's examples). This is true even if one uses the most direct means of ascertaining knowledge, which is presumably oral interrogation coupled with requests to demonstrate; it is patently true if one resorts to using paper-and-pencil tests to ascertain mastery. Evidently the test form interposes itself between knowledge or ability and judgment, and to the extent that it is an imperfect transducer of what the student knows or is able to do, so will the judgment be distorted. The multiple-choice item is particularly questionable in this respect. Robert Gagné (1970) has shown how shaky is the inference from response to mastery. Then there are the arguments concerning recall versus recognition (Brown, 1976) which can only be discussed in psychological terms but which affect judgments as to what is truly *known*: sometimes, too, you find an appeal to psychological reasoning to defend the use of a particular testing technique, for example, Keith Davidson's (1974) defence of the use of multiple choice for testing comprehension in 'O' level English language exams.

It may appear that what has been presented constitutes a more powerful argument against paper-and-pencil tests than against McIntyre and Brown and, indeed, they might retort that they are not interested in what are essentially artifacts of certain forms of testing. However, that would be to evade the point. What was said is true of oral questioning or of any mode of interrogative enquiry, that is to say, of any attempt to understand what is in the other person's head. You have only to read Margaret Donaldson's (1978) descriptions of the difficulties children experience in dealing with the language of questions and engaging in 'disembedded' thought to take the point. It may be possible to purge *content* of psychological contamination but it is hard to see how you can chase it out of educational measurement altogether when it persists in cropping up whenever a judgment about mastery has to be made.

I said that McIntyre and Brown were heard to call for the abandonment of educational measurement. How did this come about? It started with the question, 'Here are data from some tests (or items); what did they measure?' This, of course, is the classic psychometric method of proceeding. Finding no satisfactory answer to their question (and one cannot argue with them for their criticism of dimensionality is faultless), they conclude that there is no such thing as coherent measurement and therefore that quantification in education should be abandoned. I would like to suggest that by posing the question as they did, they were bound to arrive at that bleak conclusion. Ask the 'what' question before testing, as Gagné (1970) has shown,[9] and you have entirely different, and more hopeful, possibilities. What you must have, though, is the willingness to expend enough care on the *single item* to ensure, as far as possible, that unequivocal inferences from response to judgment of mastery can be made.

How do you do this? You build in controls which permit the ruling out of alternative inferences; distinctive and distortion-free measurement, he called it. Gagné's ideas for item writing deserve closer study.

If the 'what' question can be tackled, there remains the matter of aggregation, or 'how much'. Finding no answer to the 'what' question, McIntyre and Brown saw no point in asking the 'how much' question. It is pity Gagné did not deal with the matter of aggregation. For a recent opinion, there is Green (1981) who writes: 'Tests work by the weight of numbers ... of course, each item should be carefully designed and as good as possible, but no single item can ever do very much good or very much harm.'

I would not want to dispute this statement but I do wonder if test constructors are not too ready to fasten on to Green's first assertion and use it to justify their lack of attention to single items. Casual treatment of one item is casual treatment of all items. Gagné said you had to start with the single item and work up — there are no short cuts — but I fear such a severe injunction has often proved too much to take.

A Programme for Educational Measurement

Generally speaking, and thinking not of how things often are but rather of how they might or even ought to be, it can be said that, compared to psychological measurement, educational measurement:

1 deals with the individual's achievement relative to himself rather than to others;
2 seeks to test for competence rather than for intelligence;
3 takes place in relatively uncontrolled conditions and so does not produce 'well-behaved' data;
4 looks for 'best' rather than 'typical' performances;
5 is most effective when rules and regulations characteristic of standardized testing are relaxed;
6 embodies a constructive outlook on assessment where the aim is to help rather than sentence the individual.

Most of these themes, which are not exhaustive, have already been introduced. Consideration of theme 2 requires that McClelland's (1973) famous article be read or re-read, which would be a good thing to do anyway. Note, though, that it is being argued once again (Schmidt and Hunter, 1981) that tests of certain psychological constructs, notably verbal reasoning, are valid for testing suitability for a wide range of occupations, because the constructs are demonstrably or logically inherent in the expected performances. This is precisely the line of argument McClelland was challenging. The extension of the argument back into the schools — which would be a regression to where we were thirty years ago — has not yet been made explicitly, but that would be a straightforward matter since, of course, the argument is so much easier to sustain in the educational context.

Themes 4 and 5 are linked since it would appear that to implement 4 you would first need to implement 5. But that would not be possible if you were to try to observe to the letter the *Standards for Educational and Psychological Tests* (APA, 1974). This is what recommendation I2 (p. 65) has to say: 'The test administrator is responsible for establishing conditions, consistent with the principle of standardization, that enable each examinee to do his best.'

A commentary on the *Standards* (Brown, 1980, p. 34) explains why this recommendation is necessary: 'As testing is usually viewed as an evaluative situation by test takers, and as many people have evaluation apprehension, it is necessary to establish optimal testing conditions.' Note the euphemism for 'examination nerves'. Note also the blithe use of the word 'optimal'. Would we want to establish sub-optimal conditions? The issue at stake, of course, is 'How in group testing circumstances can you optimize testing conditions for everyone simultaneously?' In the commentary following I2, the *Standards* attempt to indicate how this might be done without ever convincing. Moreover, most of these suggestions are implementable only in a one-to-one testing situation. One attempt at relaxing typical conditions, which may even go beyond what the *Standards* had in mind, is a group test devised by the Educational Testing Service. The test is called PAYES, and ETS believes that

> it differs significantly from most standardized tests, particularly in the way supervisor and student interact. To begin with, the supervisor actually participates in the exam. No longer a combination timekeeper and proctor to prevent cheating, the supervisor reads each item to the student group — allowing time for low-verbal skill students to ask clarifying questions about individual items and to respond thoughtfully without fear of time running out . . . from all indications, people like it because it's designed to help people, not label them. (*ETS Developments*, 1979)

Note how theme 6 is touched on. It is necessary to pay attention to the way tests are administered but the greater threat to optimality may lie in the tests themselves, as Coffman (1979), among others, has warned. He, like others, draws the conclusion that only if students are given tests of appropriate difficulty will the problems of low motivation, test anxiety and withdrawal from the competition be minimized. The use of tailored testing and its variants is obvious but there is more to this than meets the eye. Tailored testing theory calls for examinees to be presented with items of 50 per cent difficulty *for them*, that is, they would be expected to get one out of every two items correct, once their level is found. But when I worked in this area a few years ago I was never convinced that such a policy would be optimal for the student *psychologically*. I believe we do not know enough about how motivation, task difficulty and immediate past experience work on each other.

The distinction underlying all of the foregoing discussion is that between *maximum* performance and *typical* performance. According to Brown (1980), maximum performance is to be identified with 'do your best' and typical performance with 'present an honest picture of yourself'. The first is associated with achievement and aptitude tests, the second with personality inventories, self-respect scales, etc. I wonder, however, if it is not typical rather than maximum performance which is wanted from tests of attainment, and particularly public examinations. If it were maximum performance we were after, we would not so readily deride the 'flash in the pan' performance. That phrase may serve as a sort of statistical judgment in the long run but the fact remains that the performance was produced. We are not even sure it was a maximum performance, just a lot better than expected. Conversely, consider those hackneyed phrases 'had an off day' and 'did not do himself justice'. Do these mean that the candidate failed to turn in a typical performance or that he failed to turn in a maximum performance? Note that both terms must be interpreted against the opportunities offered in the paper. There is a maximum performance beyond the ceiling. We have invented the terms 'over' and 'under' achiever to describe these kinds of performance. Is there such a thing as an 'overachiever'? Isn't he just an 'achiever'? It is time this wretched terminology was scrapped.[10]

I believe that the idea of maximum performance deserves more attention. Those interested in a fundamental treatment might look at the work of Andrew Sutton who is trying to popularize some Russian thinking on the subject (see, for instance, Sutton, 1979, also Sternberg, 1981). The core is Vygotsky's concept of the *zone of next development* which is the gap between the present level of development and the potential level of development. It indicates the level of task that a child is ready to undertake on the basis of what he can already do, *as long as he receives the best possible help from an adult* (my emphasis). The inappropriateness of standardized testing, and its administrative trappings, is obvious, since the actual content and manner of the help given will depend very much on the match between the needs of the child and the skills and styles of the teacher. Here, then we have the idea that the teacher/tester and student *collaborate* actively to produce a best performance — a sentiment expressed also by McClelland — instead of the tester and the agencies he serves conniving, through secrecy, at withholding of information and impersonal, unrealistic conduct, to produce typical performances, or worse. Here, too, is the valuable idea of achievement as *becoming* as well as being and experiencing (Harris, 1969).

Preaching into Practice

It is easy to say that educational measurement should be child-centred, rather more difficult to work out constructive proposals for doing so. Recent proposals from a Yale psychologist, Sandra Scarr, deserve consideration (Scarr, 1981).

They represent a considerable extension of what has hitherto been regarded as the province of educational measurement. That statement can be checked by reviewing the contents of *Educational Measurement* (Thorndike, 1971).

In Scarr's view, what is missing from discussions of what should be assessed in school is any reference to children's motivational and adjustment problems, whose expression she sees as decisive. This view derives from a developmental theory, or perhaps it is the other way round; there is no need to go into it here. Scarr maintains that we are assessing children's *functioning* in a school setting but only part of that functioning is cognitive. To capture what she is after she coins the term 'intellectual competence'. (The word is not used in the same way as McClelland but connections could be made.) Scarr calls for a 'new wave' of assessments and although she does not make that point explicitly, it is clear she believes that we should stop regarding motivational and adjustment problems as confined to children we label as 'slow learners', 'maladjusted', 'retarded' and so forth, but as inherent in all children. Is it asking too much of educational measurement to take on assessment in the round of 'normal' children? (It is certainly a long way from the impoverished view of achievement as the realization of behavioural objectives.) I do not think so, but much remains to be done in creating suitable assessment instruments (Wood, 1984b).

The British Measurement Scene

Much of this chapter has been concerned with the American experience because that is where the ideas have come from and the arguments have been fought. Differences in outlook and practices between the US and the UK are, of course, enormous. It is hard to imagine anyone in the States coming out, as McIntyre and Brown do (1978, p 49), with the statement that the con-ceptualizing of attainment is a philosophical task, although they do have the grace to add that 'there are nonetheless problems which the philosopher cannot solve on his own'. Actually, rather important problems, like how to put objectives in an order of priority or knowing what to do with teachers who adapt these objectives to their pupils as they go along.

In Britain, to talk of educational measurement is to talk of examinations. If Pidgeon and Yates (1969) were to rewrite or revise their book, I wager that they would begin it with the same sentence: 'Educational measurement is not accorded a generous measure of public esteem, largely because it tends to be identified with the complex system of public examinations which, in this country, regulate educational opportunity and vocational choice.' Moreover, their estimation of public esteem for educational measurement is probably still correct.

Actually public examinations are an interesting case because they con-stitute a subtle cross between educational and psychological measurement philosophies and practices. The tradition is psychometric — emphasis on individual differences, fiercely rigorous administration procedures defended in the name of fairness — but, increasingly, the practice, reflecting a changing outlook, is of the kind I have been claiming is characteristic of educational measurement — concern with content overriding statistical considerations, an acceptance of techniques of assessment, notably teacher assessment, which palpably cannot meet psychometric desiderata, however hard people try to make them.

That said, I cannot agree with those critics of psychological testing who were prepared to credit examinations with a 'lack of pretence to a scientific rationale' (Daniels and Houghton, 1972) and therefore could not be regarded as psychometric in character. The pretence has been and still is there — why else do the boards have research units? — and there is continuing uncertainty about whether examinations qualify as psychological tests.[11]

In that other department of British educational measurement — the school testing scene — functions associated historically with psychometrics, or at least not with educational measurement as I have expounded it, are quite evident. When we looked at testing practices in English and Welsh local authorities (Gipps and Wood, 1981; Wood and Gipps, 1982) we heard many protestations that testing and assessment are meant to be in the interests of children — otherwise why do it? — but practice seemed to indicate otherwise, that test results were used as often for record-keeping purposes and as political ammunition — the 'external management' function of tests — and, for providing, in the words of Gorden and Terrell (1981), 'an aid to pedagogical and/or rehabilitative intervention'. I might mention too the persistent belief, symptomatic of a regression to determinism, that administering verbal and non-verbal reasoning tests along with achievement tests is a good thing to do because it tells teachers (and managers) what to expect from children (under- and over-achievement again).

I would not wish to visit on Britain litigation of the kind and magnitude seen in the US. I would be inclined to agree with Lerner (1981) that it leads to rigidity and the stifling of reform, although it is significant that the reasons she offers for rejecting legislation[12] do not apply in Britain to anything like the same extent. It may be, however, that some test cases — on security or exposure, on cheating and generally on the theme of examinee's rights — might clear the air and help to clarify and determine what educational measurement should be, how it should be conducted and for whose benefit.[13] With Britain now a pluralist society in which the arguments concerning equal opportunity heard in the US apply well enough to be taken seriously, and where some legislation and institutions are already in place, American observers must wonder how British test givers are able to escape challenge, or else how a changed social context has not led to a noticeable shift in the predominant functions associated with assessment. The Dunning Report had the wholesome title *Assessment for All* (HMSO, 1977), which would seem to constitute an appropriate reaction but, as we know, it has long been a bone of contention whether the interests of the 'unexamined' are best served by being examined in the conventional way and the prominence Dunning gives to the guidance aspect of assessment, while welcome, is not enough to convince that some 'New Deal' is to be inaugurated.

Measurement and Instruction

Perhaps the most often expressed, and least regarded, platitude about educational measurement is that it is only of value when related to instruction. Test results, it is said, have at least as much to tell us about the teacher as the taught. It follows that teachers can learn something from test results. Allowing that the job of partitioning the variation into what is ascribable to the teacher and what is ascribable to the taught is about as difficult as you could imagine, I still find this model a refreshing counter to the prevailing view that information from test results is only about children, a view which must be responsible in part for the preoccupation with labelling and sentencing. Unfortunately it is this model which teachers resist most, with some justification, it must be said. Many teachers have evolved an elaborate defence mechanism to ward off tests and this seems to be true whether they are British (Gipps *et al.*, 1983), American (Salmon-Cox, 1981) or Irish (Kellaghan *et al.*, 1980). There is resentment at what is soen as surveillance, a conviction that tests give only 'part of the picture' and therefore can never be relied upon, overlaid with a belief, often demonstrable, that the tests and their instructional efforts do not match. Clearly, with this attitude towards tests, teachers are not going to take the rap from test results nor are they going to be prepared to learn from something which is seen as threatening. How do you persuade teachers to trust tests? I don't know, but I suspect the answer lies in coming to terms with the inevitably partial view of people's abilities which tests afford and in overcoming the rather natural inclination to blame tests because they do no more.

Notes

1 This revised version of the article that appeared in *Educational Analysis*, Vol. 4, No. 3, draws on material published elsewhere (Wood, 1982).
2 I have in mind Meredith's (1974) charge that 'generations of educational pscyhologists have been reared on a diet of psychometrics whose function is to demonstrate degrees of *ineducability*, to assign educational failure unequivocally to defects in the child, in his home, in his parents, and in his heredity, and *never* to failures of teaching, failures in school organization, failures in urban conditions, failures in commercial ethics, or failures in educational legislation'.
3 Bereiter (1970). In a later paper (Bereiter, 1980), he contended that it is the uncertainty introduced by genetic variation — making determinism manifestly unworkable — which is the most important contribution of genetic ideas to education.
4 Was Hamilton (1929) the first to do so?
5 Nunnally (1975) refers darkly to a 'philosophy of education spawned by the Skinnerian movement in operant learning'. Glaser was working on teaching

machines and programmed learning at the time he wrote the paper.

6   And the major distinction impossible to sustain. 'The problem of the standard is usually finessed in mastery learning studies through some sort of normative comparison' (Messick, 1981, p. 585).

7   Bloom, B.S. (1971).

8   Many of the points made by Levy (1973) with respect to testing and psychology apply with even more force to education.

9   'This is what I want to measure; how do I construct tests to do it?'

10   Wood (1983 and 1984a) makes a case for doing so.

11   It is instructive to decide if examinations fit the criteria for a psychological test suggested by a BPS Working Party (BPS, 1983). Although the Working Party themselves excluded examinations, in fact they fit the criteria rather well.

12   Educational policy *constitutionally* belongs to local educators who are informed about their communities' needs.

13   Bersoff (1981), again from an American perspective, writes that although legal interpretations of psychometric concepts can and do wreak havoc among test givers and test takers — not to mention test constructors — legal scrutiny has made everyone more sensitive to the pervasiveness of bias, has engendered more professional accountability and has accelerated the search for improved and alternative assessment techniques.

References

AMERICAN PSYCHOLOGICAL ASSOCIATION (1974) *Standards for Educational and Psychological Tests*, Washington, APA.

AYRES, L.P. (1918) 'History and present status of educational measurement', in WHIPPLE, G. (Ed.) *The Measurement of Educational Products: The 17th Year-book of the National Society for the Study for Education*, Part II, Bloomington, IL, Public School.

BEREITER, C. (1970) 'Genetics and educability', in HELLMUTH, J. (Ed.) *The Disadvantaged Child*, Vol. 3, New York, Brunner-Mazel.

BEREITER, C. (1980) 'The relevance of genetic ideas to education', in VAN DER KAMP *et al.* (Eds.) *Psychometrics for Educational Debates*, London, John Wiley and Sons Ltd.

BERSOFF, D.N. (1981) 'Testing and the law', *American Psychologist*, 36, pp. 1047–56.

BLOOM, B.S. (1971) 'Individual differences in school achievement: A vanishing point?' *Phi Delta Kappa Monograph*, Bloomington, IN.

BLOOM, B.S. *et al.*, (1956) *Taxonomy of Educational Objectives*, Vol. 1, New York, Longmans Green.

BRITISH PSYCHOLOGICAL SOCIETY (1983) *Bulletin*, 36, p. 192.

BROWN, F.A. (1980) *Guidelines for Test Use: A Commentary on the Standards for Educational and Psychological Tests*, Washington, NCME.

BROWN, J. (Ed.) (1976) *Recall and Recognition*, London, John Wiley and Son.

CARVER, R.C. (1974) 'Two dimensions of tests: Psychometric and edumetric', *American Psychologist*, 29, pp. 512–18.

COFFMAN, W.E. (1979) 'Classical test development solutions', *Iowa Testing Programs Occasional Papers*, 23.

DANIELS, J. and HOUGHTON, V. (1972) 'Jensen, Eysenck and the eclipse of the Galton paradigm', in RICHARDSON, K. and SPEARS, D. (Eds.) *Race, Culture and Intelligence*, Harmondsworth, Penguin.

DAVIDSON, K. (1974) 'Objective text', *The Use of English*, 26, pp. 12–18.

DONALDSON, M. (1978) *Children's Minds*, London, Fontana/Collins.

EDUCATIONAL TESTING SERVICE (1979) *ETS Developments*, 26, 1.

GAGNÉ, R. (1970) 'Instructional variables and learning outcomes', in WITTROCK, M.C. and WILEY, D.E. (Eds.) *The Evaluation of Instruction*, New York, Holt, Rinehart and Winston.

GIPPS, C.V. *et al.* (1983) *Testing Children*, London, Heinemann Educational.

GIPPS, C.V. and WOOD, R. (1981) 'The testing of reading in LEAs: The Bullock Report seven years on', *Educational Studies*, 7, pp. 133–43.

GLASER, R. (1963) 'Instructional technology and the measurement of learning outcomes: Some questions', *American Psychologist*, 18, pp. 519–21.

GOLDSTEIN, H. (1979) 'Consequences of using the Rasch model for educational assessment', *British Educational Research Journal*, 5, pp. 211–20.

GORDON, E.W. and TERRELL, M.D. (1981) 'The changed social context of testing', *American Psychologist*, 36, pp. 1167–71.

GREEN, B.F. (1981) 'A primer of testing', *American Psychologist*, 36, pp. 1001–11.

GUY, W. and CHAMBERS, P. (1973) 'Public examinations and pupils' rights', *Cambridge Journal of Education*, 3, pp. 83–9.

GUY, W. and CHAMBERS, P. (1974) 'Public examinations and pupils' rights revisited', *Cambridge Journal of Education*, 4, pp. 47–50.

HAMILTON, E.R. (1929) *The Art of Interrogation*, London, Kegan Paul.

HARRIS, C. (1969) 'Comments', in *Towards a Theory of Achievement Measurement*, proceedings of the Invitational Conference on Testing Problems, Princeton, NJ, Educational Testing Service.

HAWKES, H.E., LINDQUIST, E.F. and MANN, C.R. (1936) *The Construction and Use of Achievement Examinations*, Boston, MA, Houghton Mifflin.

HER MAJESTY'S STATIONERY OFFICE (1977) *Assessment for All, Report of the Committee to Review Assessment in the Third and Fourth Years of Secondary School in Scotland* (the Dunning Report), Edinburgh, HMSO.

JENSEN, A.R. (1969) 'How much can we boost IQ and scholastic achievement?', *Harvard Educational Review*, 39, pp. 1–123.

KELLAGHAN, T., MADAUS, G.F. and AIRASIAN, P.W. (1980) *The Effects of Standardized Testing*, Dublin, Educational Research Centre, St. Patrick's College and Chestnut Hill, MA., School of Education, Boston College.

LERNER, B. (1981) 'The minimum competency testing movement, social, scientific and legal implications', *American Psychologist*, 36, pp. 1057–66.

LEVINE, M. (1976) 'The academic achievement test: Its historical context and social functions', *American Psychologist*, 31, pp. 228–37.

LEVY, P. (1973) 'On the relation between test theory and psychology', in KLINE, P. (Ed.) *New Approaches in Psychological Measurement*, London, John Wiley and Son.

McCLELLAND, D.C. (1973) 'Testing for competence rather than for "intelligence"', *American Psychologist*, 28, pp. 1–14.

McINTYRE, D. and BROWN, S. (1978) 'The conceptualization of attainment', *British Educational Research Journal*, 4, 2, pp. 41–50.

MEREDITH, P. (1974) 'A century of regression', *Forum*, 16, pp. 36–9.

MESSICK, S. (1981), 'Constructs and their vicissitudes in educational and psychological measurement', *Psychological Bulletin*, 89, pp. 575–88.

MONROE, W.S. (1923) *An Introduction to the Theory of Educational Measurements*, Boston, MA, Houghton Mifflin.

NUNNALLY, J.C. (1975) 'Psychometric theory — 25 years ago and now', *Educational Researcher*, 4, pp. 7–21.

PIDGEON, D.A. and YATES, A. (1969) *An Introduction to Educational Measurement*, London, Routledge and Kegan Paul.

RESNICK, D.P. (1981) 'Testing in America: A supportive environment', *Phi Delta Kappan*, 62, pp. 625–8.

RYLE, G. (1949) *The Concept of Mind*, London, Hutchinson's University Library.

SALMON-COX, L. (1981) 'Teachers and standardized achievement tests: What's really happening', *Phi Delta Kappan*, 62, pp. 631–4.

SCARR, S. (1981) 'Testing *for* children: Assessment and the many determinants of intellectual competence', *American Psychologist*, 36, pp. 1159–66.

SCHMIDT, F.L. and HUNTER, J.E. (1981) 'Employment testing: Old theories and new research findings', *American Psychologist*, 36, pp. 1128–37.

SHAYER, M., KÜCHEMANN, D.E. and WYLAM, H. (1975) *Concepts in Secondary Mathematics and Science*, SSRC Project Report, London, Chelsea College.

STERNBERG, R.J. (1981) 'Cognitive-behavioural approaches to the training of intelligence in the retarded', *Journal of Special Education*, 15, pp. 165–83.

SUTTON, A. (1979) 'Measures and models in developmental psychology', in WOOD, R. (Ed.) *Rehabilitating Psychometrics: A Report on a Seminar Sponsored by the SSRC*, London, Social Science Research Council.

THORNDIKE, R.L. (Ed.) (1971) *Educational Measurement*, (2nd edn). Washington, American Council on Education.

THORNDIKE, R.L. (1982) *Applied Psychometrics*, Boston, MA, Houghton Mifflin Co.

WOOD, R. (1976) 'A critical note on Harvey's "Some thoughts on norm-referenced and criteria-referenced measures"', *Research in Education*, 14, pp. 69–72.

WOOD, R. (1982) 'Aptitude and achievement', *Caribbean Journal of Education*, 9, pp. 79–123.

WOOD, R. (1983) 'Quantifying underachievement', *Bulletin of the British Psychological Society*, 36, p. 415.

WOOD, R. (1984a) 'Doubts about "underachievement" particularly as operationalized by Yule, Lansdown and Urbanowicz', *British Journal of Clinical Psychology*, 23, pp. 231–2 and in this volume.

WOOD, R. (1984b) 'Assessment has too many meanings and the one we want isn't clear enough yet', *Educational Measurement: Issues and Practices*, 3, pp. 5–7.

WOOD, R. and GIPPS, C.V. (1982) 'An enquiry into the use of test results for accountability purposes', in MCCORMICK, R. *et al.*, (Eds.) *Calling Education to Account*, London, Heinemann Educational.

Paper 22: Aspects of the Competence-Performance Distinction: Educational, Psychological and Measurement Issues[*]

Introduction

This paper began as an investigation of the competence-performance distinction as it came to our attention in the literature, particularly the psychometric literature. Once embarked, it was apparent that competence was being used in two recognizably different ways. There was competence as enhanced performance[1,2] and competence as the deep structure responsible for the surface performance. The first is an atheoretical affair — whatever it was you were measuring, you are now doing it better — while the second has everything to do with theorizing. We now regard the distinction in this way: when we study competence we study what turns out to be an embryonic working model of the development of expertise; when we study performance we study the methodological problems common to all educational and psychological measurement wherein authentic expression of what a person is really able to do or really believes or really thinks is frustrated.

The Competence-Performance Distinction

Competence refers to what a person knows and can do under ideal circumstances, whereas performance refers to what is actually done under existing circumstances. Competence embraces the structure of knowledge and abilities, whereas performance subsumes as well the processes of accessing and utilizing those structures and a host of affective, motivational, attentional and stylistic factors that influence the ultimate responses. Thus, a student's competence might not be validly revealed in either classroom performance or test performance because of personal or circumstantial factors that affect behavior.[3]

[*]Reprinted from the *Journal of Curriculum Studies*, 1987, reproduced by permission.

The idea that there is something greater lying beyond performance is, of course, immensely attractive, speaking as it does of hidden resources, untapped potential and the like. Our view is that there is every reason not to take performance at face value. Here are two examples:

(i) A baby loses a rattle behind a cushion. Are we to suppose that the baby does not understand that the rattle still exists? Bryant has used this example to caution those who would ascribe incompetence too readily, or at all ('They are always meeting abilities that are not there').[4]

(ii) Changing the wording of an examination question can convert apparent incompetence to competence, or so it has been claimed.[5] It is possible that question wording and presentation together constitute the biggest single cause of competence being masked. All too often students do not understand what they are being asked to do.[6]

The competence-performance distinction was introduced into the study of cognitive development by Flavell and Wohlwill.[7] It was patterned on Chomsky's notion of competence as the knowledge and rules that are necessary to particular (linguistic) acts or performances. In Flavell and Wohlwill's formulation, a child's performance on a task has two determinants: (a) a possession of the structure embodied in the task (equivalent to competence); and (b) the operating rules which the child needs in order to process the information from the task and produce a result (performance). Generally, (a) and (b) jointly would be necessary for correct task solution. Incorrect task solution would not necessarily imply the total absence of (a); rather it could be that there is something defective in (b) which is preventing the expression of (a). The crucial idea, upon which later investigators have fastened, is that appropriate *elaborative procedures*[8] might be found to rectify or trigger off (b) so that (a) can be elicited or *actualized* providing, of course, it is there.

Elaborative procedures are prompts, hints, clarifications, requests for generalization, examples, helpful encouraging demeanour (of tester), anything which will work to bring out some performance we are prepared to believe the student to be capable of. There is a connection here with the ideas of the long dead Vygotsky. According to him, the *zone of next or proximal development* represents the gap between the present level of development and the potential level of development. It indicates the level of task that a child is ready to undertake on the basis of what s/he can already do, as long as s/he receives the best possible help from an adult. As with the elaborative procedures, here is the notion that the teacher/tester and student collaborate actively to produce a best performance, instead of a typical performance, or worse. For Vygotsky and later followers, the most serious limitation of conventional IQ measures (and we can extend this to achievement measures) has been that they test at lower rather than upper thresholds of performance. It was the strengths, not the defects of individuals which interested Vygotsky.[9] In that respect, his ideas are inspirational but their practical implications remain to be worked out.

Objections to Competence Theory

An obvious objection to Flavell and Wohlwill's formulation, and Chomsky's too, concerns how to get from performance to statements about the unobservable competence. What part does evidence based on performance (surface structure) play in evaluating the competence (deep-structure) theory? After all, in principle, any number of deep-structure theories could account for the same performance data. Piaget's theory, which is a structural theory of logical competence, has come under fire for this very reason.[11]

The difficulty of inferring competence from performance is made worse by an empirical fact — correlations across tasks ostensibly measuring the same competence or across the same task over time are often low. Inconsistency has been a problem for all structural competence theories. Piaget attempted to accommodate it through his notion of horizontal décalage. The difficulty here is that if too great an appeal is made to décalage, Piaget's account certainly lacks predictive validity, and perhaps much else besides.[12] (This in spite of Piaget's commitment to elaborative procedures; in that respect it is ironic that he should have been accused of regularly underestimating children's competence.) Flavell and Wohlwill try to take inconsistency into account by connecting competence and performance through a probabilistic model which allows for varying task difficulty and for what Brown and Desforges call 'the unpredictable and ill-defined relationship between competence and performance'.[13] Flavell now apparently thinks that evidence for stage-like development in the horizontal-structure, high-homogeneity meaning of the term is unconvincing.[14]

Biggs and Collis[15] are quite relaxed about inconsistency. There is nothing inconsistent, they argue, about saying that on a particular mathematics task, the student gave a response one day that looked like the sort of response that would be expected from a 'formal operational' student, and on another day gave a response that looked like a typical response from a middle concrete operational. This looks very close to saying that there is nothing inconsistent about inconsistency. What they mean, presumably, is that we ought not be surprised.

Our view is that the significance of inconsistency has been overlooked. Attention has been trained on how it threatens theory rather than on what it means, in developmental terms. Of course, it might mean only — taking a rather extreme environmentalist line — that there is no reason to expect a cognitive behaviour manifested in one context to share a common structure with behaviours elicited in other contexts. (Biggs and Collis come close to this position.) Leaving that aside in favour of retaining the possibility of structure, it might be that inconsistency arises because some of the tasks chosen to elicit competence, or the methods used in presenting the tasks and scoring the answers, do not belong together. This is always likely to occur and we take it seriously; in fact, we think it is amply demonstrated in much public examining. But the main reason for inconsistency, as we see it, is that the competences looked for have not yet cohered and may not do so for some years, if at all. Flavell asks when people are likeliest to show the least homogeneity in their thinking and supplies the answer that the likely period is 'between early infancy and whenever formal schooling or other systematic training ends — usually around the beginning of young adulthood'. He goes on to discuss the fact that during this period of seeming heterogeneity, people are constantly applying themselves to tasks and situations which they only partly understand; 'they are commonly somewhere in the middle game of one learning enterprise or another'.[16] This strikes us as a significant remark.

The purpose of elaborative procedures is both to elicit competence, in some context, if it can be elicited, and to explore the limits of generalization of claims about behaviour. 'How far are we willing', asks Rogoff, 'to generalize performance in a particular situation to a more general underlying ability? What conclusions can be drawn from successful performance on a syllogism problem? That the individual (a) will do well on the next syllogism? (b) will do well on other kinds of logic problems? (c) will be logical in many situations? or (d) is smart?'.[17] Rogoff's use of dramatically expanding universes reinforces the warnings against reckless generalization which is all too likely given widespread usage of the kind 'X scored highly on a logical reasoning test'.

Elaborative Procedures Versus Training

There are those who argue that assessing competence requires the development of training tasks to encourage the manifestation of latent competence in performance — successful training actualizes competence. Cross-cultural enquiries tend to take this line, for it is often the case that those being studied have never or rarely been in situations in which a certain latent competence was necessary for the accomplishment of some task.[18] Training is also a crucial feature in the learning potential assessment paradigms associated with the names of Budoff[19] and Feuerstein.[20] Budoff's paradigm involves training or practice outside of the actual testing situation (similar to coaching) while Feuerstein's Learning Potential Assessment Device (LPAD) aims to transform the test situation from a static snap-shot into a learning experience for the child — the child is taught while being tested.

There is a difficulty here. Ayers is undoubtedly right when he says that to learn what a child can do, the measurement procedure must ensure that the child is brought to the point of generalization of transfer through appropriate practice exercises.[21] Yet, for practical purposes, we have to agree with Dillon and Stevenson-Hicks that the training component is ill-suited for routine psychoeducational evaluation.[22] That said, there are types of training, before and after assessment, which we regard as important, if not essential. We see every reason why students should be trained beforehand in the etiquette of test-taking; on how to deal with certain test formats; on how to interpret questions; on how to use time to best advantage; on how to handle nerves and distractions; all of which are intended to counteract adverse situational circumstances and so help to actualize competence. This aspect of training is often looked down upon, as if it were unfair. The same is true of coaching, which is training or practice on the kinds of tasks those doing the coaching expect students to encounter. Our position would be that coaching only becomes unacceptable when it produces performance without competence. Critics may have jumped to the conclusion that this invariably is the case but it need not be. Training after the event is nothing but teaching in the light of what the assessment, and particularly the elaborative procedures, have revealed. This teaching is a natural sequel to a school assessment which has been conducted along the lines we shall recommend later.

Inferring Competence from Performance

A useful way of looking at what is involved in inferring competence from performance, which applies even to single items, is through this table.[23]

Table 1: Error types in relating performance to competence

	Success on Task	Failure on Task
Child has underlying competence (in sufficient degree)	Performance correlated with competence	False negative error. Failure due to factor other than lack of competence
Child has not underlying competence (in sufficient degree)	False positive error. Success due to factor other than competence	Performance correlated with competence

A false negative error involves concluding that the child or student is without competence when in fact s/he has competence. A false positive error, on the other hand, involves assuming the child has competence when s/he has not. In assessing performance on tests of underlying competence, it must be established that there is only one source of failure — a lack of competence; and only one route to success — that deriving from the appropriate competence.[24]

Taking the competence-performance distinction seriously implies a belief that false negatives will occur more often than false positives, and will also be more damaging to the victim. But false positives need attention, too, and good elaborative procedures will detect and remove both.

An example of a false positive which cannot be cleared up without elaborative procedures occurs when students manage to give the 'correct' answer, but on interrogation reveal that their understanding is superficial, that behind it they have been employing idiosyncratic theories or notions which are seriously at variance with adequate structures or formal theories in the field; what have been called 'alternative frameworks'.[25]

Where false negatives are concerned, there has to be much discounting of plausible rival sources of poor performance, such as inattention, anxiety, low motivation, fatigue, adverse testing conditions, misunderstanding — all the situational variables we have already pointed to and more. Obviously, such an investigation cannot be truly exhaustive. Where decisions have to be taken, there must be a discretionary limit on the deployment of elaborative procedures. There would be no danger of that limit being reached at present. It is, of course, tempting to explain away all performance shortfalls by reference to adverse situation factors on the assumption that the competence must be there.[26] While that is going too far, the benefit of the doubt must go to the person being tested. 'One lesson to be learned from this kind of analysis is how risky it is to conclude that some ability definitely does not exist in children'.[27]

Evidently it will be difficult to ascribe competence, or lack of it, or locate genuine false positives and negatives, if there is no theory of competence in play and the investigator engages in a fishing expedition to extract regularities from the data (the common fate of psychometricians). A false positive may not be that at all but rather a sign that the competence of real interest, C, is embodied in the performance which is adjudged a false positive, conditional on competence C^1.

Hints

Hints are a rather special kind of elaborative procedure. It is axiomatic that a hint can be useful only to those in possession of sufficient competence to make sense of it. It follows that to give someone a hint is not to instruct the person, and hints that fail to satisfy that dictum are not hints at all. The fundamental problem with the use of hints hinges on the relationship between the hints and the competence which is being assessed.[28] The point is not whether a hint is an instruction but whether the nature and sequence of the hints is informed by a description of the competence we seek to actualize, or by an hypothesis about the obstruction we imagine the hint will remove. It is not enough to replace the risk of false negative errors with the risk of false positive errors, which you might do if hints are simply ad hoc instructions and demonstrations; rather, the hints must be generated from the theory. So some a priori theory and structure are needed after all. The routine generation of hints which will satisfy the criteria placed on them is not likely to be a straightforward affair. This is clear from an analysis of the only examination paper known to us which included hints in explicit form[29] and the almost non-existent psychological literature on hints.[30] Studies using hints are bound to remain ad hoc in character until relevant conceptual work is done.[31]

The Nature of Competence

The ability to use knowledge, product and process skills and, as a result, act effectively to achieve a purpose.

The possession and development of sufficient skills, knowledge, appropriate attitudes and experience for successful performance in life roles.

These and other definitions of competence in reports on education and training suggest that competence is the product of some education, training or other experience, rather than being an inborn or natural characteristic. Job competence, it is argued, involves the application of knowledge and skills, and is exhibited through purposeful and real, rather than simulated activity.[32] There are connotations of wholeness and maturity in which the parts necessary to function effectively have been integrated to the point of habituation.

Evidently job competence is not something which can be realized at school, and could not be even if the disjunction between school and work were to disappear. There is not the time — thus the inconsistencies of behaviour. These we were inclined to attribute to skills which had not yet solidified. However, we are bound to ask whether, somewhere on the agenda of what schooling is for, there appears the development of competence (for use beyond school). A study of the conventional output measures of schooling — tests and examinations — suggests that it does not. These measures merely give an impression of the surface structure of performance based on an estimate of 'how many' of the skills, techniques and pieces of knowledge prescribed by a curriculum (which might be called 'competencies') can be reproduced at a given point in time. They rarely provide insights into 'how well' the deep structure (which in the end will be the realization of competence), is developing. Tallying successes on a sample of measures of specific 'competencies' is very far from providing a clear-cut transformational rule enabling one to get from surface structure (performance) to deep structure (competence).

As Messick and others have pointed out, education entails not just the accretion of knowledge, but the constant structuring and restructuring of knowledge and cognitive skills. Successful adaptation to the circumstances encountered as one develops is more often accomplished through the coordination of abilities and appropriate knowledge, affect and behaviour patterns than through the capacity to utilize a single ability or reproduce a piece of information on demand. 'Competence' then must be distinguished from the 'competencies' assessed in contemporary testing programmes. It rests on an integrated deep structure ('understanding'), on the general ability to coordinate appropriate internal cognitive, affective and other resources necessary for successful adaptation.[33] A successful conceptualization of competence would show how specific competencies are integrated at a higher level, and also accommodate changing patterns of salience among these skills and abilities at different ages and in different contexts.

In designing curricula and teaching strategies we have to ask 'What develops?' and having got an answer, 'What should we measure?'. The operationalist is fixated on performance — whatever we can measure is what develops. Competence as a developmental construct is subordinated to method. A construct-oriented approach would begin instead with the attempts currently being made by cognitive and developmental psychologists to conceptualize the acquisition of integrated knowledge and ability structures in developmental terms. Developed competence is to be conceived of and assessed as a continuous variable reflecting various degrees of integration of knowledge and skill, of understanding and proficiency which has relevance for individuals and their education across ages and settings.

It is a matter of regret that mental testing has been characterized by a separation between psychometrics on the one hand and cognitive and developmental psychology on the other. As a result, the focus in measurement has been on the performance in the competence-performance distinction, with performance conceived in static, atomistic terms without variation of context and judged against arbitrary standards.

Whether Curtis and Glaser are right [34] that we are nearing a threshold in the transition from education based on a theory of human differences to one which focuses on the development of educated and competent people, remains to be seen. If this threshold is to be bridged in the field of educational measurement, competence, conceived in developmental terms and at a superordinate level, must be put back into the competence-performance distinction.

Development of Competence

Research evidence points unmistakably to significant age-related differences in performance on cognitive tasks — vocabulary, numerical reasoning, general knowledge, general problem solving and so forth. It also indicates that variation increases steadily throughout the years of childhood and adolescence.[35] The development of competence seems to be contingent on the simultaneous development of general cognitive abilities through learning and transfer from a variety of developmental contexts (school, home etc.) and of special knowledge structures, generally through systematic instruction. It is fostered by extending the domains to which particular procedures are applied through lateral transfer of a given kind of generalization or replacement of domain-specific formulations by more broadly applicable formulations at the same level of analysis.[36]

In cognitive psychology, there has been a shift from the consideration of general cognitive abilities to the study of the structure of domain-specific knowledge.

Current studies of high levels of competence ... appear to support the recommendation that a significant focus for understanding expertise is investigation of the characteristics and influence of organized, hierar- chical knowledge structures that are acquired over years of learning and experience.[37]

Work in this field has concentrated on producing accounts of the knowledge structures and problem-solving processes of 'experts' and 'novices'. Studies of problem-solving in knowledge-filled domains (like chess, geometry, physics, and political science) have revealed significant differences in the knowledge bases of individuals at the extremes of 'competent-incompetent' continua.

Experts tend more than novices to anticipate information to be presented, to keep track of information being presented, to hold more main-point information in short-term memory; to recall more com- plicated events and elaborative detail; to devote more effort to analyzing abstracted representation of a problem rather than analyz- ing the specifics of the problem; to be more flexible in the use of their knowledge in problem representation and solution.[38]

Given that domain-relevant knowledge also plays an important facilitative role in the acquisition of information in a subject, it may be that low levels of competence in an area have more to do with inadequacies in the knowledge base than with limitations in either the architecture of cognitive systems or information processing abilities.

Another potentially useful source of information pertinent to the develop- ment of competence comes from studies of 'children's science'. Researchers are attempting to uncover the ways in which rudimentary knowledge structures might act as 'alternative frameworks' to those accepted within mainstream sciences.[39] These frameworks or 'intuitive schemas' are in some instances vague, poorly articulated and unstable versions of the structures held by those 'competent' in an area — in which case, performance on tasks in the area is likely to be inconsistent. In other instances, 'alternative frameworks' may be based on strongly-held beliefs and misconceptions which produce common patterns of error and are hard to dislodge.[40]

From a long-term developmental perspective only the broad contours of competence in knowledge-filled domains are known. It seems that the knowledge structures of students initially in a subject are likely to be varied, to be incomplete and to incorporate a number of misconceptions. As instruction proceeds, new information is likely to be assimilated within existing structures, the structures themselves modified, new structures of concepts and relation- ships among them built up, and relevant general abilities mobilized (hopefully facilitating transfer). Ausubel has argued that the dynamic cognitive structure which develops through instruction and experience is what moderates mean- ingful learning and retention. Given developmentally sensitive programmes and systematic instruction, individuals' cognitive structures in a domain can be expected to become more stable, ordered and complete.[41]

Ultimately, in the case of the expert, a structure of knowledge and abilities is built up over the years of learning practice and application which enables us to infer competence from consistent, correct task performance. In most cases, however, individuals have not studied long enough or been taught in a way which would lead to structures deep or stable enough for us to expect the type of consistent performance which enables any supportable inference about competence to be made. A consideration of how most people stand on school subjects a year or two after they have been 'taken' will show how swiftly the foundations of competence crumble away.

Measurement and Assessment in the Light of the Competence-Performance Distinction

We have comments to make on two issues, which correspond to the two views of competence noted in the Introduction.

1   The extent to which current procedures take the competence-performance distinction into account, or what attempts, if any, are made to enhance performance.
2   The extent to which current procedures might be measuring something which resembles competence, as we conceptualize it.

Finally, we ask which psychometric model is most suitable for treating the development of competence and find that generalizability theory combined with Guttman's facet theory is preferred on all counts.

Competence regarded pragmatically is defined operationally as the level of performance obtained under elaborative procedures beyond the performance level obtained under standard conditions. Given that formal external examining is done under standard conditions without amelioration we can expect to find performance and not enhanced performance. And that, by and large, is the way it is where external assessments, notably public examinations, are concerned. For internal or school assessments, amelioration is possible and so the probability of obtaining enhanced performance is, in principle, greater.

For what concerns us here, the shortcomings of external assessment can be summarized thus:

(i)   Little or nothing is offered in the way of clarification at the outset, or at any other time; indeed clarification would probably be considered unfair, since it might benefit some candidates more than others. Controlling for individual differences in willingness to seek clarification is obviously impossible, as is controlling for capacity to profit, except that clarification is like a hint — only those with the competence sufficiently highly developed can expect to benefit from it.

(ii) Offering deliberate clarification within a test in the form of hints is, to the best of our knowledge, rare.

(iii) Whatever the formula governing item selection, not all candidates can be tested to the limit, or anywhere near. This is a consequence of group testing. Even for those poorer candidates whose threshold appears to be identifiable by the test, it is unclear whether they have been given the opportunity to show what they can do. Nor, importantly, have they been given the opportunity to show that whatever they can do is interpretable in terms of some coherent view of how achievement occurs or fails to occur; or what we would call a model of competence.

(iv) Following on from the last, there is a curious notion that tests and examinations should produce a 'typical' performance.[42] This is a direct consequence of psychometric orthodoxy, of the continued allegiance to a 'snapshot' model of testing whereby a person is caught at a particular point of time and in a particular pose.

So, the method of administration and the general approach to test construction do nothing to actualize competence. But that is not all. The assessment techniques get in the way too.

Multiple-Choice Testing

Multiple-choice items are liable to induce false positives and perhaps also false negatives. Positives happen because of guessing (blind) and guessing (informed) through the elimination of alternatives or even using the format of the item, what is known in the trade as test-wiseness. With the latter, it is necessary to distinguish between situations where using cues in distractors is tantamount to using hints (and studies indicate that profitable use of partial information is correlated with ability) and situations where the correct answer is obtained without the competence being present. The best example of this is the correct answering of multiple-choice items set on a comprehension passage without reading the passage.

How can multiple-choice items produce false negatives? Banesh Hoffman's famous charge was that multiple-choice questions favour the second-rate mind and punish the first rate.[43] The charge has never been satisfactorily answered. The best evidence we have is a 1969 paper, incredibly enough.[44] If that paper was even half right, the possibility of false negatives and positives is strong.

Conspicuously missing has been any analysis of why multiple-choice tests are suitable for ascertaining competence development. (Multiple choice for ascertaining 'competencies' we know about.) What we have had instead are futile construct validation attempts, a good example being the failure to verify empirically the Bloom Taxonomy categories. Too little attention has been given to the consequences of what happens when task presentation and context are

259

varied. The effect that changing the format or the distractors can have on responses is well-known.[45,46]

As things stand, multiple-choice is too likely to shape the competences being tested and in unknown ways. Moreover, there is still the measurement problem of deciding what can be inferred confidently from a response to a single item. Robert Gagné drew attention to the problem but generally it has been overlooked.[47] Perhaps the advice that only aggregations count, has encouraged complacency.[48] Aggregation contributes to reliability but may do nothing for validity.

Open-ended Questions

It is not difficult to spot where the problems lie with questions for which the response has to be supplied:

(i)   Marking bias (handwriting, style, personal idiosyncracies); all can lead to false negatives.

(ii) Questions too vague or too awkwardly phrased to elicit sought-for answers and of course to allow expression of competence — false negatives again.

(iii) Bluffing the examiner — writing down statements and arguments without understanding them; false positive, this time.

When it comes to rectifying these problems, there is, on the face of it, not a great deal which can be done. As long as people are going to grade other people's work, idiosyncratic judgments will occur. Bluffing the examiners is perhaps not all that common — most will see through it — but there is cause to worry how well students understand the arguments which they trot out — and their consequences. How many are using 'alternative frameworks'? It takes elaborative procedures to reveal fragile and insecure understanding. To say that elaborative procedures start with clearer questions is not a platitude; in public examinations clearer questions are all we have in lieu of one on one interaction with candidates. (But interviews afterwards are a useful research tool.)

It has been said that examination questions 'act as directives to produce certain performances'.[49] The implication is that the relationship between questions and answers is under fairly tight control — apply the stimulus and you will get the reaction anticipated. It is a view of examining difficult to sustain. If questions are providing information and the act of answering is crystallizing what was previously only dimly understood, then there can be no guarantee that the answer to a single question, without follow-up, impinges at all on what the questioner had in mind.

School Assessment

School assessment appears to offer the opportunity to flush out what students know and can do. Compared with external examinations the conditions are much more favourable for establishing limits of performance and exploring extent of generalization. The possibilities for actualizing competence would seem to be good.

The work horse for school assessment has been the rating scale, sometimes behaviourally anchored, sometimes not. There are doubts whether it has got teachers any closer to competence than the suspect techniques just dealt with. Here are the end points (a and e) of a five-point rating scale.

(a) Very neat and skilful with his hands. Attracted by any task involving mechanical intricacies. Good craftsman and sensible in handling and using apparatus.

(e) Very clumsy and hamfisted in using tools and instruments. No interest in practical toys or hobbies.[50]

This was an early example of a behavioural rating or grade-related scale offered to teachers, and refinements have been made since. Yet the impression remains that, for purposes of capturing states of competence, descriptions like these are not nearly comprehensive enough, nor are they written in language which calls up recognizable and significant competence states, much less pins them down. What is particularly lacking is any indication of the limits of generalization or extrapolation which may be permissibly read into these behavioural descriptions. To go back to Rogoff's example, where is generalization outwards into succeedingly larger universes of inference supposed to stop? Are these judgments guaranteed for any reasonable application within school? Do they apply outside of school? How were they reached, and just what authority do they have?

It is a truism that an assessment can say as much about the assessor as the assessee. Vygotsky knew this — 'investigations of intellectual capacity . . . necessarily test the experimenter as well as the subject' — but saw in it only the necessity of training teachers in how to interact with children to bring out the best in them.[51] This is not the kind of training teachers will receive from the school examination boards in advance of the introduction in the UK of the new GCSE examinations. More likely it will be training in how to use five-point rating scales. The boards could not be expected to be interested in a method where standardization of teachers' prompts and of elaborative procedures generally is so obviously problematical. Yet by placing the emphasis on the training of teachers rather than on, say, the purchasing of better tests, on developing the teacher as the instrument rather than the task, the Vygotskian perspective asserts the primacy of the teacher as connoisseur in the assessment process,[52] which is presumably what the introduction of school assessment was meant to acknowledge.

Assessment has always been recognized as a part of teaching even if this has been conveniently ignored when it suited. It is time to worry when assessment is carried out by poor teachers. If the purpose of teaching is to help people to learn, assessment has something to offer there too, even if it is only a source of extrinsic motivation. Regrettably, the ways in which assessment can help teachers teach have never been properly laid out, and this as much as anything accounts for the resistance expressed in the conventional wisdom that time spent on assessment is time not spent on teaching.

Defects in Current Assessment Methodology

It seems to us that emphasis on assessing competence, in the way we have outlined it, ought at the very least to be as useful to teachers as present methods of assessment, which are so firmly trained on fragments of achievement. No wonder that teachers feel dissatisfied and frustrated with assessment, their own included, as they try to discern some pattern and regularity in the spotty, inconsistent performances turned in by their students. Putting the emphasis on competence would at least have the virtue of explaining why these spotty, inconsistent performances might occur.

The paradigm on which much of present testing and examining is based goes straight back to Binet, eighty years ago. We still mimic the way he constructed tests, although we have added embellishments like behavioural objectives and criterion-referenced testing.

What Binet did was to think of tasks which would reveal intelligent behaviour and then sample from these as widely as possible in the time available for testing. His sampling was not conducted according to any rule, like random or stratified random sampling; it was guided by his own sense of fitness — what he thought ought to go in. Later commentators[53] have complained of Binet that, despite his greatness as a psychological theorist, he did not support his practical test-making activities by a coherent theoretical justification of his choice of sampling 'points' or items. The complaint that achievement testing is pragmatic, arbitrary and quite devoid of theoretical underpinnings can still be levelled today. At any rate, the result is the same — an assortment of tasks, a scattershot across the syllabus. The consequences are inevitable. The responses students give are just as disarticulated, reflecting, or so it appears, haphazard learning experiences which have not as yet, and may never be, related and coordinated in order to acquire the higher order cognitive operations and structures which are the cornerstones of competence.

There have been attempts to formalize Binet's sampling approach, chiefly the notion of domain sampling and the associated concept of domain mastery, and Guttman's facet theory. With domain sampling, the formalization lies in the more rigorous definition of the domain or universe of content and the use of rules for sampling, like random or stratified random sampling. With facet theory the idea is to treat achievement as multidimensional and to locate those facets which contribute to that achievement. A domain of items is then created by permuting systematically and perhaps even exhaustively the facets so as to form, through their combination, single items from whose aggregate sampling can take place, again according to rules.[54]

There is no reason to believe that the domain mastery model is any more theoretically grounded than Binet's original way of doing things. While we might have trusted Binet, with his pedagogical acumen, to come up with a set of tasks which might just make collective educational and psychological sense, replacing the seat of his pants with a mechanical item selection procedure is pointless if there has been no theoretical input concerning what the items might be measuring. All that is served is a spurious claim to statistical sophistication and orderliness. The domain mastery paradigm is the embodiment of the 'How many' approach to assessment: take a selection of 'teachable' bits of disposable knowledge, produce a set of scores and pronounce on mastery. But mastery of what exactly? It has been the mistake of well-meaning revisionists to try and wring meaning out of these scores and their constituent parts by, for instance, attempting to report grades in criterion-referenced terms. These efforts have come to grief[55] and were bound to do so either because the tests had not been constructed in such a way as to permit criterion-referencing, or because the skills constituting the criteria had not yet gelled enough to permit consistent expression across task and so allow coherent descriptions of performance within grades. To find out 'How well' rather than 'How many' requires a quite different approach to test construction.

Guttman's facet theory is much more interesting — and promising. Its most attractive feature is the way it formalizes directly what is required in the exploration of any competence — the systematic variation of task method, exercise format, method of response, point of application, visual cues (where relevant), and so forth. Being an expert implies being able to cope with all (or most) variations, or facet combinations; being a novice means being unable to cope with most variations (no transfer). Item difficulty and cognitive processing requirements can be thought of as varying according to how facets are combined.[56]

The object of measurement procedures should be to determine the extent of competence (cf. Rogoff). This is true whether it is students unable to add numbers presented in columnar form when they can add them in rows, or machine operators unable to operate a piece of equipment once it is rotated 30°.[57]

Facet theory provides a framework for studying competence. The psychometric model known as generalizability theory uses the same structure to derive estimates of the variability attributable to each condition of measurement (facet).[58] As a result, it is possible to quantify the influences which bear on the development of competence.

Concluding Remarks

Success with a problem now seems to depend more on the way the task is presented and on children's understanding of what they have to do than was formerly realized. Pupil progress is therefore seen to be sensitive to teachers' choices of content and task. Systematic exploration of variation in performance with alteration in task and social context would inform teachers in ways which might promote pupil learning and enjoyment.[59]

As this passage shows, thinking about the determinants of achievement is undergoing a change. One result is that it is now necessary to ask what counts as achievement. The introduction of the competence-performance distinction has drawn attention to the importance of context in assessment. Soon it may be possible to drop the distinction. What should not be dropped is the construct 'competence'.

We have argued that the focus in curriculum design should be on developing competence, and not on sampling from domains of what is, all too often for students, thoroughly disposable school knowledge. The job for educational measurement is to estimate the extent of competence. This leads us to press for more extensive use of elaborative procedures in school-based assessment (especially the use of interview about instances, vivas, oral assessments on the part of teachers with the appropriate subject and assessment expertise) and, where possible, in public examinations (through the use of hints, coaching etc.). We are also concerned that the commonly used assessment techniques and paradigms are ill-suited to this new enterprise.

Competence itself plainly needs a lot more unpacking and in this connection we would point to the efforts being made within school subjects by developmentally sensitive connoisseurs — to the types of questions asked by Brumby[60] and Carr[61] in science public examinations and to the techniques used to probe the knowledge structures and cognitive strategies of children, novices and experts. What seems to be needed now is a drawing together of emerging ideas and methodologies relating to the development and assessment of competence in knowledge-filled domains, into models capable of guiding the design of curricula, teaching and assessment programmes. The best bet at the moment appears to be a combination of expert-novice analysis, faceted design and generalizability theory.

Notes

1 DILLON, R.F. (1979) 'Improving validity by testing for competence', *Educational and Psychological Measurement*, 39, pp. 363–71.
2 DILLON, R.F. and STEVENSON-HICKS, R. (1983) 'Competence vs. performance and recent approaches to cognitive assessment', *Psychology in the Schools*, 20, pp. 142–5.

3   MESSICK, S. (1984) 'The psychology of educational measurement', *Journal of Educational Measurement*, 21, pp. 215–38.
4   BRYANT, P.E. (1978) 'Miscellaneous book reviews', *Quarterly Journal of Experimental Psychology*, 30, p. 766.
5   JOHNSTONE, A. and CASSELS, J. (1978) 'What's in a word?' *New Science*, pp. 432–33.
6   EGGLESTON, S.J. (1983) *Learning Mathematics: How the work of APU can help Teachers*, London Assessment of Performance Unit, Department of Education and Science.
7   FLAVELL, J. H. and WOHLWILL, J.F. (1969) 'Formal and functional aspects of cognitive development', in ELKIND, D. and FLAVELL, J.A. (Eds.), *Studies in Cognitive Development: Essays in Honour of Jean Piaget*, Oxford, Oxford University Press.
8   DILLON, R.F. and STEVENSON-HICKS, R. *op cit*, pp. 142–5.
9   VYGOTSKY, L. (1979) 'The genesis of higher mental functions', in WERTSCH, J.V. (Ed.), *The Concepts of Activity in Soviet Psychology*, Armonk, NY, Sharpe, Inc., p. 149.
10 BROWN, A.L. and FERRARA, R.A. (1982) 'Diagnosing zones of proximal development', in WERTSCH, J.V. (Ed.) *Culture, Communication and Cognition: Vygotskian Perspectives*, New York, Academic Press.
11 KEATING, D.P. (1980) 'Thinking processes in adolescence', in ADELSON, J. (Ed.) *Handbook of Adolescent Psychology*, New York, Wiley.
12 BROWN, G. and DESFORGES, C. (1979) *Piaget's Theory: A Psychological Critique*, London Routledge and Kegan Paul, p. 102.
13 *Ibid*, p. 132.
14 Cited by FRESE, M. and STEWART, J. (1984) 'Skill learning as a concept in life-span developmental psychology: An action theoretic analysis', *Human Development*, 27, pp. 145–62.
15 BIGGS, J.B. and COLLIS, K.F. (1982) *Evaluating the Quality of Learning: The SOLO Taxonomy (Structure of the Observed Learning Outcome)*, New York, Academic Press Inc., p. 22.
16 FLAVELL, J.H. (1982) 'Structures, stages and sequences in cognitive development', in COLLINS (Ed.) *The Concept of Development*, The Minnesota symposia on child psychology, Vol. 15, Lawrence Erlbaum Associates, p. 13.
17 ROGOFF, B. (1981) 'Schooling and the development of cognitive skills', in TRIANDIS, H. and HERON, A. (Eds.), *Handbook of Cross Cultural Psychology*, Boston, MA, Allyn and Bacon.
18 BRISLIN, D. (1983) 'Cross-cultural research in psychology', *Annual Review of Psychology*, pp. 363–400.
19 BUDOFF, M. (1974) *Learning Potential and Educability Among the Mentally Rretarded*, final report Project No. 312312. Research Institute for Educational Problems, Cambridge Mental Health Association.
20 FEUERSTEIN, R. (1980) *Instrumental Enrichment*, Baltimore, MD, University Park Press.
21 AYERS, J.D. (1971) 'Assessing cognitive development via measures of optimal performance', in GREEN, D.R., FORD, M.P. and FLAMER, G.B. (Eds) *Measurement and Piaget*, New York, McGraw-Hill.
22 DILLON, R.F. and STEVENSON-HICKS, R. (1983) *op cit.*, pp. 142–5.
23 BROWN, G. and DESFORGES, C. (1982) *op cit.*, p. 120.
24 *Ibid.*
25 DRIVER, R. (1982) 'Children's learning in science', *Educational Analysis*, 4, pp. 69–79.
26 GREENO, J.G. and RILEY, M.S. (1984) 'Conceptual competence and children's counting', *Cognitive Psychology*, 16, pp. 94–143.
27 BRYANT, P.E. (1974) *Perception and Understanding in Young Children*, London. Methuen, p. 54.

28 BROWN, G. and DESFORGES, C. (1982), *op cit.*, p. 132.
29 ORMELL, C. (1983) 'Marking the passing of an exam.', *Times Higher Educational Supplement* 12 August.
30 DANNER, F.W. and DAY, M.C. (1977) 'Eliciting formal operations', *Child Development*, 48, pp. 1600–6.
31 BROWN, G. and DESFORGES, C. (1982), *op cit.*, p. 132.
32 MANSFIELD, R. and MATHEWS, D. (1985) *Job Competence: A Description for Use in Vocational Education and Training*, Blagdon, Further Education Staff College.
33 WATERS, E. and SROUFE, L.A. (1983) 'Social competence as a developmental construct', *Developmental Review*, 3, pp. 79–97.
34 CURTIS, M. and GLASER, R. (1981) 'Changing concepts of intelligence', in BERLINER, D.C. (Ed.) *Review of Research in Education*, Vol. 19, Washington, DC, American Educational Research Association.
35 KEATING, D.P. (1980), *op cit.*
36 LABORATORY OF COMPARATIVE HUMAN COGNITION. (1982) 'Culture and intelligence', in STEINBERG, R.J. (Ed.), *Handbook of Human Intelligence*, New York, Cambridge University Press, p. 707.
37 CHI, M., GLASER, R. and ROES, E. (1984) 'Expertise in problem solving', in STERNBERG, R.J. (Ed.), *Advances in the Psychology in Human Intelligence*. Hillsdale, NJ, Erlbaum.
38 MESSICK, S. (1984) *op cit.*
39 DRIVER, R. (1982) *op cit.*
40 POWER, C. (1984) 'Tinker, tailor, soldier, spy — implications of science education research for teachers', *Science Education*. pp. 179–93.
41 AUSUBEL, D.P. (1963) *The Psychology of Meaningful Verbal Learning*, New York, Grune & Stratton.
42 BROWN, F. (1980) *Commentary on AERA Standards for Educational and Psychological Tests*, Washington, DC, National Council for Measurement in Education.
43 HOFFMANN, B. (1962) *The Tyranny of Testing*, New York, Crowell-Collier.
44 ALKER, H.A., CARLSON, J.A. and HERMANN, M.G. (1969) 'Multiple-choice questions and student characteristics', *Journal of Educational Psychology*, pp. 231–43.
45 LINN, R.L. (1980) 'Issues of validity for criterion-referenced measures', *Applied Psychological Measurement*, pp. 547–62.
46 FREDERIKSEN, N. (1984) 'The real test bias: Influences of testing on teaching and learning', *American Psychologist*, 60, pp. 193–202.
47 GAGNE, R. (1970) 'Instructional variables and learning outcomes', in WITTROCK, M.L. and WILEY, D.E. (Eds.) *The Evaluation of Instruction: Issues and Problems*, New York, Holt, Rinehart & Winston, Inc.
48 GREEN, B.F. (1981) 'A primer of testing', *American Psychologist*, 36, pp. 1001–11.
49 THYNE, J.M. (1974) *The Principles of Examining*, London, University of London Press.
50 DUFFEY, J. (1972) 'The assessment of progress in science', *School Science Review*, 54 p. 186.
51 VYGOTSKY, L. (1962) *Thought and Language* Cambridge, MA, MIT Press, p. 37.
52 JOHNSON, P.H. (1984) 'A Vygotskian perspective on assessment in reading', (paper presented at the annual meeting of the American Educational Research Association, New Orleans, April).
53 DONALDSON, M. (1963) *A Study of Children's Thinking*. London, Tavistock Publications Ltd.
54 For example, PELED, Z. (1984) 'The multidimensional structure of verbal comprehension test items', *Educational and Psychological Measurement*, 44, pp. 67–84.
55 KEMPA, R.F. and ODINGA, J.L. (1984) 'Criterion-referenced interpretation of examination grades', *Educational Research*, 26, pp. 56–54.

56 HAERTEL, E. (1985) 'Construct validity and criterion-referenced testing', *Review of Educational Research*, 55, pp. 23–46.
57 ZIGLER, E. and SEITZ, V. (1982) 'Social policy and intelligence', in STERNBERG, R.J. (Ed.) *Handbook of Human Intelligence* New York, Cambridge University Press.
58 CRONBACH, L.J., GLESER, G.C., NANDA, H. and RAJARATNAM, H. (1972) *The Dependability of Behavioral Measurements* New York, Wiley.
59 BRITISH PSYCHOLOGICAL SOCIETY (1986) 'Achievement in the primary school: Evidence to the Education Science and Arts Committee of the House of Commons', *Bulletin of the British Psychological Society*, 39, p. 123.
60 BRUMBY, M. (1981) 'The use of problem solving in meaningful learning in biology', *Research in Science Education*, 11, pp. 103–10.
61 CARR, M. (1984) 'Model confusion in chemistry', *Research in Science Education*, 14, pp. 97–103.

Index

ability 24, 238–9
  achievement and 181
  multiple choice guessing and 67–9, 71
  separate measurement 91–3
ability grouping 121, 122–3, 143–6
absolute halo effects 31
academic achievement, tests for 169
academic performance, association with
  occupational performance 209
achievement 158
  as mastery of content 157
  assessment 10
  compared with aptitude 204–5
  effects of teaching 237
  measurement 234
  prediction 127–8
  present levels 212, 214, 219
  sex differences 38
  skewed distribution 11
  social class and 141
achievement tests 115, 181–7
  compared with aptitude tests 200,
    201–2
  internal consistency 100
  physics 85–7
adjustment, children 243
administration, Verbal Test D 171
affective constructs 17, 18, 22–3
affective objectives, syllabuses 157, 158,
  161
age standardization, test scores 171–2
Ahlawat, K.S. 89
Airasian, P.W. 10, 224
Aitkin, M. 197
Akeroyd, F.M. 45, 46, 116
Alexander, H.W. 34
Alker, H.A. 52

Allen, A. 24
alternative frameworks 253, 257, 260
American Psychological Association 132,
  241
analysis of variance models 28
Anastasi, A. 6, 203, 208–9
anchoring, item bank calibration 85–8
Ancoff, W.H. 166
Anderson, J. 83
Anderson, L.W. 96
Anderson, R.C. 77, 116, 182, 183
application 24
aptitude 190, 237
  definitions 203–4
  measurement 234
aptitude testing, educational equality
  and 200–10
Army Alpha test 120
assessment 6–8
  by teachers see teacher assessment
  competence-performance distinction
    and 258–63
  current methodology 262–3
  graded 146
  meanings of 2–3
Assessment of Performance Unit 3, 103,
  139, 190–1, 211, 212–14, 217, 218,
  219, 220, 221–2, 223, 226, 227
Assessment of Performance Unit.
  Language Performance in Schools 213
assessment-led instruction 224–5
attainment, conceptualization 243
attitudes, assessment 10
Australian Council for Educational
  Research 216, 217
Australian Studies in Student
  Performance 191, 211, 212, 216–17,